RISKY BUSINESS

RISKY BUSINESS

Unlocking Unconscious Biases in Decisions

Anna Withers and Mark Withers

Foreword by Andrew Haines, OBE
CEO, Civil Aviation Authority

First published in 2016 by Libri Publishing

Copyright © Mightywaters Consulting Ltd 2016 – all rights reserved

ISBN: 978-1-909818-79-8

A CIP catalogue record for this book is available from The British Library

Book and cover design by Carnegie Book Production

Printed in the UK by Short Run Press

Mightywaters, Hidden R-I-S-K, the Hidden R-I-S-K graphic arrangement, and the circular character graphic arrangement are trademarks of Mightywaters Consulting Ltd.

Libri Publishing
Brunel House
Volunteer Way
Faringdon
Oxfordshire
SN7 7YR

Tel: +44 (0)845 873 3837

www.libripublishing.co.uk

We dedicate this book to our two wonderful daughters –
Mireille and Amelia – and to Bryan and Dorothy Withers.
Without your encouragement, patience and wisdom this book
would never have been written.

"Unconscious bias influences all our decision making, and it is an extremely important area for us all to understand how we, and our teams and organisations, can make better decisions. Anna and Mark's book draws on the extensive body of research in this field and makes it practical and memorable, giving us the keys of awareness and understanding to unlock this very human challenge."

Peter Cheese, CEO, Chartered Institute of Personnel and Development

"I commend this book to anyone who makes decisions and especially to those in leadership, risk management and governance roles in organisations. I hope you enjoy and get as much out of this book as I have."

Andrew Haines, OBE, CEO, Civil Aviation Authority

"The framework is clear and memorable and the numerous examples are relevant and entertaining. Risk professionals are still learning how to influence decision making behaviours inside organisations and this provides some practical approaches to implement."

John Gill, Chief Risk Officer, Standard Life UK & Europe

"At the heart of transformational change sits a tangle of individual decisions – that are anything but rational – that can determine the change outcome. So any change leader looking to deliver more effectively needs to understand the mindsets, motivations and biases that determine the acceptance and behavioural responses of those affected by the changes.

"The Hidden R-I-S-K™ framework makes the unconscious conscious by bringing into vivid relief the kinds of biases and distortions that can derail effective decision making during times of change. Eminently readable and richly illustrated with examples galore, this book will help decision makers develop a deeper understanding of how people see and experience change, take action to mitigate the hidden risk of decisions and increase their own effectiveness as leaders."

Dr. Linda Holbeche, Visiting Professor, Cass Business School and Author

"After more than 30 years in financial services, although the businesses I have worked for have been very successful overall, I have seen too many mistakes. Poor judgement has destroyed billions of pounds of value that could have made us even more successful. *Risky Business* explains how talented, intelligent, rational people can make such costly errors. Original, engaging and well researched, this new framework for simplifying complex psychological constructs is a must read for any decision maker or risk manager."

Chris Gillies, Chairman, Sterling ISA Managers Ltd. – a Zurich Insurance Group company

"As a financial trader I am constantly seeking to gain an edge over other market participants. However, information is now cheap and universally distributed. Mark and Anna's timely book has helped me become more aware of some common thinking errors that have undoubtedly hindered my historical trading performance. The genius is in their distillation of tomes of research into eight memorable characters that personify the biases and errors in our decision making. I believe that, going forward, this will help provide me with a much-needed edge in my trading and I highly commend it to others."

Andrew Davisson, financial trader and owner of Upward Capital

"A powerful and accessible way to make our unconscious thinking conscious."

Dr Paul Cozens, Partner, Mathys & Squire LLP

"This book is a gem. Fascinating, relevant, practical and persuasive. It really is a must read for our times."

Jerry Arnott, recently Director of Civil Service Learning

Contents

Illustrations

Foreword by Andrew Haines, OBE

CEO, Civil Aviation Authority

My career has been spent in industries where poor or sub-optimal decisions have a significant impact on operational performance and, at their worst, can lead to fatalities. What has become apparent to me over the years is that at the point of decision we encounter many blind spots in our thinking. Academics call these blind spots 'unconscious biases' and they are at work in all of us. Understanding and addressing these unconscious biases in our decisions is key to making better decisions and it is why this book is so important. It gets to grips with the unconscious forces in decisions with an impact that few other books have succeeded in having.

My own interest in this area has arisen from both personal experience and professional practice. At a personal level I passionately believe that self-awareness is a critical first step to self-improvement. Understanding our own patterns of thinking, behaviour and predilections offers an essential key to unlocking our understanding of why we do what we do and how we change our thinking and behaviour in the interests of better outcomes. When we can see our patterns, this process of reflection and learning is more straightforward. It isn't so easy when we are trying to understand and mitigate unconscious forces in play.

This is why I have found this book so helpful. It challenged me at a personal level and helped me to think about my own unconscious biases.

At a professional level, I lead the UK's aviation regulator. Our regulatory role is all about risk management. Regulators only exist because successive governments have identified potential risks to the public – resulting from failures in safety or security standards, financial collapse of companies or the abuse of a monopoly position in the absence of competitive markets. In all these areas and more there is a perceived and actual risk, and the holy grail for a regulator is to identify risk patterns and make timely and proportionate interventions that effectively mitigate those risks.

What is clear is that the human dimension of risk management is significant. Mechanical and technical failures do occur, of course, but often it is decisions made by individuals that heighten risk. We are all prone to unconscious biases in our decisions and we all have a different risk appetite. One thing I have observed in my own family is that my wife and two, grown-up, children have a different risk appetite to me. The simple act of crossing the road will result in me being across and well advanced on my journey whilst the rest of the family is still waiting for a gap in the traffic – every time! – because my perception of risk is different to theirs. At one stage, this was a source of frustration and even hurt. I felt it was an indication of a lack of trust in me that they didn't share my risk appetite. Now it is more a source of amusement.

Of course, the subject of risk appetites and risk appetite statements is often on the agenda for an organisation these days. But the extent to which this is determined by the prevailing and unconscious risk appetite of individuals is not as ubiquitous a topic. In my current role, one of the trends I observe is a high percentage of fatal accidents in general or private aviation in which the pilot was apparently employed in a high-risk role, such as entrepreneur, or else participated in high-adrenalin, high-risk pursuits. This might seem obvious, given the costs and inherent risks in aviation, but many aviators of course fly safely for many years without incident. I have not done any robust statistical analysis but my observations are that the correlation is quite startling. Depending on your unconscious risk bias, the same risk appetite that can encourage you to pursue an activity can also cause you to underestimate the risk.

Understanding the unconscious biases in decisions isn't just relevant for life-threatening situations. Unconscious biases can distort a whole range of decisions from the relatively straightforward to the highly complex. What is highly valuable is a way to recognise and understand these unconscious forces and the tools to take action to mitigate them. This book gives both the framework and the tools to help us achieve this.

From a professional perspective, I have also seen the importance of good governance as a mechanism to check the unconscious forces in decision making. Effective governance is an important counterbalance to unconscious biases. Good governance speaks to the way boards, sub-committees, executive teams and specific governance groups work. In all these groups, checks and balances are needed so that robust challenge and enquiry occur around key decisions and that individuals aren't left to pursue their own agendas without accountability. This means that genuinely independent voices, along with multiple and diverse voices, are important ingredients in ensuring any unconscious biases are surfaced and addressed.

Left unchecked, unconscious biases can quickly find their way into the DNA of an organisation and become embedded in the culture. During my career, I have come across situations in which overwhelming evidence was discounted in favour of a decision that others considered to be right. To use a familiar metaphor, the burning platform was ablaze yet people were oblivious to the sight of the flames and the smell of the smoke. This has been particularly true in situations where decision makers had a personal stake invested in a particular course of action and where decision makers were more cautious by nature.

I am delighted that this book addresses these areas too. It explores the environment within which better decisions can occur and explores the conditions that will encourage people to speak up without fear. The book also addresses the issue of how to create mutual accountability around decisions, especially in the context of decision making and governance groups.

You may recall the 2010 volcanic eruptions of Eyjafjallajökull in Iceland that led to the largest air-traffic shutdown in the UK and other northern European countries since 1945. At the time, the impact of this volcanic ash on air transport was huge. Within a matter of weeks two main schools of thought emerged. The first saw this incident as a one-off event, a black swan or aberration unlikely to be repeated and the second as something for which others were to blame. Yet there are important lessons that fallout of that incident and taking the time to understand, learn and then embed these lessons will enable governments, airlines and regulators to respond better when a future unexpected natural event occurs.

Daniel Kahneman, the Nobel Prize winner for economics, and his co-researcher Amos Tversky helped us to understand that we are not rational beings. Kahneman has more recently helped us to understand that most of our decision making occurs in what he calls 'System 1' mode. We think fast and we decide fast. It reflects the fast-moving world we live in and echoes the need for speed. The problem with this is that when we decide fast, we open up more space for unconscious biases to influence our thinking. Speed of decision makes us more dynamic and agile but it doesn't encourage deeper reflection and learning. Our aim is surely to achieve *and* rather than *or* – to be dynamic and agile *and* to reflect on and learn from what we do.

A final observation from my professional life is that there is an increasing appreciation of the impact of 'mind talk' – the background conversations we all have running in our heads. These underlying conversations often obscure reality. These conversations in our heads tell us stories about people we meet that may or may not be true; they convince us that there is no point in doing something because 'X' might happen; they persuade us that 'Z' might work because it did in the past; they create fear of the unknown. There is much falsification that goes on in our heads and unless we are honest with ourselves about this, we risk limiting the future to the patterns we observe in the past.

Mind talk is the material our unconscious biases work with. As these forces are unconscious, we find it difficult to make sense of them all. As these forces are unconscious, we don't observe patterns in our thinking and subsequent behaviour. I recently heard a talk by the highly respected lawyer Baroness Helena Kennedy. She discussed the difficulties in establishing truth within the legal system and our ability to convince ourselves that something is true when it isn't. She quoted the cognitive psychologist Jean Piaget who apparently claimed for many years to have recall of an incident that happened when he was 18 months old, only to be told in his 60s by the woman who had been his nanny that she had made the story up. Piaget is not alone in this. Our recall can be flawed and the boundary between what is true and what we are utterly convinced is true is often blurred.

Knowing this is an important step to better decision making and to understanding the role of the unconscious in our decisions. The good news is that there are ways to mitigate our unconscious biases and this book offers a range of practical tools that can be used. This is why this book has the power to be so useful. It's practical and the Hidden R-I-S-K™ framework and tools are readily applicable. Moreover, the authors have taken time to paint rich pictures everyone can work with. They have created eight characters that have depth and instant recognisability – characters that we can meaningfully identify with and make use of when reflecting on the decisions we have made and the decisions we are in the process of making.

None of us makes flawless decisions. We can probably all make better decisions. For those of us in leadership positions where our decisions can impact the lives of many and the success of our organisation, getting better at decision making is a must do. Knowing that there are clusters of unconscious thinking errors we are all prone to gives us a language and a window to become more self-aware as individuals and in decision-making groups.

The book is an easy and enjoyable read, and the style very approachable. This isn't a genre of book I would normally read but I read this one with interest, quickly and I learnt a lot.

Why should you spend time reading this book? For me it boils down to three things:

First, none of us can ignore the vast amount of research out there that points to unconscious biases in our decisions. We simply aren't as good at making decisions as we think we are.

Second, we should value the understanding of hidden risks in our decisions and this book helps us to make the unconscious conscious in an engaging and memorable way.

Third, without wanting to sound melodramatic, it might just save your life. It will certainly save you the high cost of making poor decisions.

I commend this book to anyone who makes decisions and especially to those in leadership, risk management and governance roles in organisations. I hope you enjoy and get as much out of this book as I have.

Preface

I have spent the whole of my career working in the field of human relations and organisational development. Outside of work I have held leadership roles in a volunteer capacity in a wide range of organisations and groups – housing associations, NGOs, professional institutes, youth groups, churches and community groups. During these 30-plus years I have observed people (including myself) in all capacities – whether organisational leaders or humble workers – making preventable mistakes.

We have made wrong assumptions about people; we have defended situations that ought to be changed; we have been far too optimistic about the time and costs required to do something; we have told people what they want to hear, not what's really going on; we have been seduced by appearance rather than substance; we have made our minds up and then selected the evidence to justify the decision already made; we have relied too much on the past to deal with the problems of the present; and we have failed to see options and possibilities beyond the field of practice we have been trained in. The list could go on, but I'm sure you will have encountered similar preventable mistakes.

So I started to get curious about how we make the choices we make. I am particularly fascinated by how we seem to repeat mistakes – why we get locked into habitual patterns of thinking. As a consultant and coach, I have been fortunate to have worked with individuals and teams across a wide range of organisations. I would like to be able to say that one sector or group has been far better at decision making than another, but I can't. We may think we are great decision makers, but we all make preventable mistakes.

My curiosity has led me to explore the worlds of cognitive psychology and the new fields of practice – behavioural economics and neuroscience. What I discovered was that cognitive psychologists have built up a robust body of research over a long period of time that casts a light on the unconscious thinking errors that skew our choices. We know this stuff and yet we haven't been able to embed this evidence-based research into the actual decision-making processes we use. We haven't been able to make the unconscious conscious.

This is the gap that *Risky Business* has been written to bridge. I have written this book with my wife and fellow director Anna Withers. Anna was on a journey parallel to mine. The first half of her early career was spent in investment banking and then she retrained as a psychologist, working as a director in Mightywaters Consulting and as a family therapist. She too became absorbed in the process of decision making – whether in financial markets, relationships or in organisations.

We have therefore invested much time over the past few years researching the field of decision making and are delighted to offer you the fruits of our labour. This book will help you to cast a light on the unconscious forces that influence your choices and, through understanding these forces, will help you to re-think the way you decide. It is a book that will help you personally and one that will help groups of decision makers to address the hidden risks in choices and make better decisions.

Mark Withers

Introduction

Police said the bomb was hidden in the back of a dark blue tipper truck parked in Bishopsgate, in the heart of the City of London. It was a homemade device containing about a ton of fertiliser. Police had received the agreed coded warnings and were still evacuating the area when the bomb went off at 10.25am on Saturday 24th April 1993. Press speculation afterwards suggested that the attack was timed to coincide with a visit of over 1,000 international politicians, officials and bankers attending the annual meeting of the European Bank for Reconstruction and Development (EBRD). I was one of them and what happened that morning was to have a profound impact on my life.

My memories of the incident itself are fragmented. I remember crouching behind a wall together with hundreds of others and protecting my head with my arms. I remember hearing an almighty bang and looking up and seeing a cloud of debris falling with thousands of papers slowly descending in the wind. I recall the ashen face of the managing director of the large Japanese fund-management company for which I was working at the time. He had sheltered with me behind the wall, and kept apologising to me over and over again: "Anna, I am so very sorry that I asked you to come with me on a Saturday morning to represent our company at the conference. To put you in harm's way like that is unforgiveable on my part. I mean you are expecting and this can seriously harm your unborn child!" I reassured him that I was feeling fine, which was, of course, absolutely true. Physically, I was unharmed and there was never any question about the explosion having any negative impact on my pregnancy as our little girl was born healthy only a few months later.

Yet something fundamental within me had shifted. When I crouched down trying to protect myself from the falling debris, I made a split-second decision, a decision that as far as I was concerned was cast in stone. "We are moving abroad. London has become a war zone," I blurted out when I walked through the door later that afternoon. My husband Mark tried to calm me down and suggested that we might want to think this over more carefully. However, I was adamant and, as the weeks progressed, it became clear that nothing was going to shift my perception that danger was lurking around every corner.

Up until then London had held a special place in my heart. I had arrived in London 13 years earlier from Germany as a student and it was the place where Mark and I had studied together, fallen in love and married. It is where we made our home in the leafy suburb of Highgate, pursued exciting careers and had a great community of friends. In short, we had a good and successful life in London. Yet with one big bang, all my perceptions of London changed and shortly afterwards an opportunity presented itself for us to live and work in Budapest, Hungary. So we upped sticks without, on my part, giving it a second thought.

Was I right to make this decision? What would you have done in the circumstances? What I can guarantee is that your brain will already be processing this information and will have started to form an opinion. At the time, my decision to abandon our life in London felt entirely rational. Today, with greater understanding of the processes that shape the way we make decisions, I know that my decision back then was anything but rational. I used the information taken from one event to extrapolate into the future. I wrote a script about what life working in the City of London would be like and an alternative script of how life in another place would be and I was prepared to defend this decision in the face of compelling evidence that suggested an alternative scenario.

We have come to learn that, in its normal state, the mind forms intuitive feelings and opinions about almost everything that comes its way. We also know that we are quick to jump to conclusions because we put too much weight on the information that is right in front of us and fail to take into account information currently outside our view. This pulls us into the trap of believing that "all I see is all that's there".[1]

Psychologists would call the decision I made behind that wall a 'flight response'. When we see something or someone that feels dangerous, survival instincts kick in and we launch into action before we have even started to evaluate the situation in detail. These responses are hard wired into us. After all, deciding quickly who or what was coming up the path or hiding behind a bush would often have been a life-or-death decision for our ancestors. Our brains are constructed to facilitate quick decision making. And so our fundamental way of looking at and encountering the world is driven by this hard-wired pattern of making decisions on the basis of what 'feels right' without us even realising it.

As it happened, London never became the war zone I imagined and, as a result of this bomb, the City of London became one of the safest places in the world to work. Ironically, shortly after we arrived in Hungary, a bomb exploded in Budapest's Castle District not too far from where we lived!

Everyone can be misled when it comes to their choices. In their excellent book, *Decisive,* Chip and Dan Heath conclude that humanity does not have an impressive track record when it comes to decision making.[2] They point to statistics showing 44 percent of lawyers not recommending a career in law to students; 40 percent of senior-level hires leaving within 18 months of appointment; 83 percent of mergers and acquisitions failing to create any value for stakeholders; and 88 percent of New Year's resolutions being broken (this statistic may be understated)! Our gut guides many of our decisions, but our gut is often wrong. Yet we all want to make good decisions.

Much of my professional life has been about helping people make better decisions. At the start of my career in the area of investment banking, I advised large institutional investors on investment decisions affecting the wealth of millions of people through their retirement funds. Later, when I retrained as a psychologist and family therapist, I counselled people who were making often heart-breaking decisions around their personal and family life. Today, I am a director of a management consultancy which advises executives on decisions impacting organisational effectiveness that can affect many of their employees.

Throughout this long and varied career, I have probably seen all the mistakes presented in this book, but I have also gained three fundamental insights:

1. Nobody makes bad choices out of choice. We all want our choices to contribute to our happiness and not to take away from it; and/or we want our choices to be beneficial to the wellbeing of those people we care about; and/or promote the issues we are concerned about.

This insight rang especially true when I served as a trustee for a local not-for-profit organisation whose aim was to help vulnerable and disengaged young people put their lives back together. Many of these youngsters came to us in a bad way. Drug and alcohol addictions, law breaking, teenage pregnancy and inability to secure and hold a job were some of the issues we encountered. In all these situations I do not believe that these young people set out to make bad choices. They made bad choices often because what they did 'felt right' at the time. Their gut guided their decisions, but their gut was often wrong. Talking to those young people often reminded me of the lines in the song by the Animals – "But I'm just a soul whose intentions are good: Oh Lord! Please don't let me be misunderstood".

Those kids were souls whose intentions were good: they just wanted to be happy and make those people they cared about happy too. Yet in the pursuit of that happiness they made poor choices that not only damaged them, but had a negative impact on their families and the wider community. These decisions, made in the moment, failed to take the wider picture and the implications of their choices into account. That was why the organisation employed ex-convicts and ex-addicts to reach out to young people, so that they could get other perspectives and hopefully avoid falling into the same pitfalls as their friends. The key to this work was to encourage young adults to ask questions of themselves and their friends before they made their decisions.

2. Bad choices often occur when we stop asking questions. As a therapist, counsellor or coach, I have learnt that it is always one's job to ask questions. These are often questions your clients are unable or unwilling to ask themselves. Questions can be dangerous. If honestly answered, questions might throw up information that can point to some inconvenient truth – truths we would rather not look at because of what we might discover. The answers might have painful implications that challenge our status quo, affecting how we view ourselves and questioning our worldview.

As human beings we are terribly good at building 'systems' which prevent us from asking questions. This holds true in the context of small systems like a couple or a family where it sometimes takes an outsider to ask questions about 'the elephant in the room'. In the counselling room I encountered many a situation in which just about everything was discussed except the most important thing. For some people, the real issue was sex, whilst for others it was money or relationships with people outside the family or behaviours within the family. Whatever the real issue, it was avoided and questions were not asked.

This is also true of much larger groups and organisations – even institutions set up as places of academic inquiry with the express purpose of posing questions and stimulating debate. In 2008, at the peak of the global financial crisis, Queen Elizabeth II visited the London School of Economics (LSE) – our old university. During a briefing by academics on the turmoil in the international markets and subsequent meltdown in public finances she posed a simple, but incisive question:

"Why did nobody see this coming?"

Prof Luis Garicano, Director of research at the LSE's management department, is reported to have told the Queen: "At every stage, someone was relying on somebody else and everyone thought they were doing the right thing".[3] In other words, no-one asked the right questions.

Much has been written since about the causes of the financial crisis. In the UK the British Academy convened a group of leading academics, economics journalists, politicians, past and present civil servants, and other practitioners for a roundtable discussion to address the question posed by the Queen. Tim Besley, a professor at the LSE and a member of the Bank of England's monetary policy committee, and Professor Peter Hennessy, a political historian, wrote a letter summarising the views raised through this discussion. They wrote:

> There were many warnings about imbalances in financial markets and in the global economy... But the difficulty was seeing the risk to the system as a whole rather than to any specific financial instrument or loan... Risk calculations were most often confined to slices of financial activity, using some of the best mathematical minds in our country and abroad. But they frequently lost sight of the bigger picture... It is difficult to recall a greater example of wishful thinking combined with hubris.[4]

The Queen had certainly scratched at a very powerful itch. It is a great example of where questioning the prevailing worldview might have led us to a better outcome.

Albert Einstein is usually attributed with the insight that we cannot solve our problems with the same thinking we used when we created them. Often we try to change something within the system rather than change the way we view a problem or deal with a problem. Many in corporate life will have come across sales teams selling work that cannot possibly be delivered profitably, overconfident forecasts and the all-too-frequent cost overruns in projects. These examples are just tips of the iceberg. Whilst senior managers do not set out with the intention of making suboptimal decisions – because no-one makes bad choices out of choice – errors slip in "under the radar" and we seem to return to the same issues time after time. Instead of questioning and seeking to understand the underlying issues, executives fall back on knee-jerk responses that simply reinforce patterns of thinking and behaviour. This leads me to my third insight.

3. *The quality of what we do depends on the thinking we do first.*
To improve the quality of our decisions we first have to improve our thinking. Thinking and questioning certainly characterised our time at the LSE during the early 1980s. The LSE attracts students from all over the world, which makes it an incredibly diverse and intellectually stimulating place. Everyone had an opinion and these were freely expressed and debated whether in the cafeteria or bar. However, during our lectures on economics, a fundamental assumption about human behaviour was made: that humans are rational beings and make rational decisions. At the time, this underlying assumption didn't ring true and there was certainly a disconnect between the teaching of economic models and our understanding of economic reality. But at the time, we had no language or evidence to help us see things differently.

Whilst these discussions were raging in London, two cognitive psychologists from the Hebrew University of Jerusalem were asking some great questions and thinking differently about this issue. They had already started ground-breaking research that was to challenge the fundamental assumptions in economics about rational decision making. Their research shook the foundations of economic thinking and culminated in the award of the 2001 Nobel

Prize for Economics to one of these researchers – a psychologist, Professor Daniel Kahneman. (Kahneman's fellow researcher Amos Tversky sadly died prematurely which meant that he could not receive this highest of accolades.)

Tversky and Kahneman's findings have made economics a richer and more complete science and their research has spawned a whole new branch of economics – behavioural economics. What this means is that we now have an opportunity to incorporate this evidence on decision making into our own thinking so that we can tune in to the unconscious processes that are at work in our decisions, rather than being guided solely by our gut – by what 'feels right'.

Making best use of this ground-breaking research and integrating it into our decision making is what this book is all about. It is about becoming more intentional so that we match our choices more closely with the outcomes we want. Until Kahneman and Tversky's assault on our assumption that people are rational beings, very little was known about how humans made decisions. That has now changed. We now have a substantial body of research from the fields of psychology, behavioural economics and neuroscience that helps us to understand the mental processes behind decision making.

Just as we can be misled by optical illusions, this research has exposed how we can easily fall prey to distortions in our perception of situations. Researchers have identified over 100 of these distortions in decision making, which they call *thinking errors* or *unconscious cognitive biases* and which operate outside our conscious awareness. That is why slip-ups happen and why, however smart or indefatigable or charismatic a person may be, he or she will still fall prey to these unconscious distortions. Knowing about them is the first step towards improving the quality of our thinking before taking action. Integrating this knowledge into our decision-making processes is the second step to help us mitigate these thinking errors and reduce the risks associated with our choices.

However, there is a problem that needs to be overcome. This compelling research hasn't been translated into tools and methods we can easily use. It is near impossible to keep over 100 thinking errors in mind and we don't have a language to discuss thinking errors in a constructive and generative way. Often we also lack the right organisational environment in which people feel safe to speak out, ask questions and take mutual accountability for decisions made. As a consequence, we haven't yet had the opportunity to use fully this research to inform our choices and mitigate these thinking errors. It is here that this book can make a powerful contribution.

Risky Business bridges this gap between knowing about thinking errors in decision making and actually integrating them into our choices. We introduce a ground-breaking framework that will help you recognise the thinking errors that distort your choices and drive a more robust process for decision making. As a result, you will be better able to identify the unconscious processes at work and take actions to create new patterns of thinking that will help you make better choices.

Anna Withers

Why Choose this Book?

"Ninety-nine percent of who you are is invisible and untouchable."

R. Buckminster Fuller

We would like to be able to say that this book will solve all your decision-making problems and usher in a lifetime of contentment and great wisdom. As this is unlikely, our goal is rather more modest. Through understanding the unconscious processes at work in our decisions, we aim to help you to get better at making good decisions and better able to help your family, friends and work colleagues in their choices – after all, it's easier to see the mistakes others make than our own!

Our focus is on more significant decisions, decisions that should take more than a few minutes (or seconds) to make. Whilst our focus is primarily on the world of work, the principles in this book have application to decisions made in all areas of life. The aim of this book is to explore the ninety-nine percent of ourselves that is invisible and untouchable so that we are able to make the unconscious more visible.

Over the past decade there has been much debate about the place of intuitive decisions. Intuition will always play a role in our decisions and our purpose is not to dismiss or suppress it, but rather to embrace and understand it. We can do this by trying to appreciate the contexts that best suit intuitive decisions, which are generally environments where there is quick, unambiguous feedback and high predictability. Examples of these environments are video games and chess. Indeed, much has been made of the role intuition plays for chess grand masters – so if you are a great chess player, trust your gut. However, if you are an executive making significant strategic choices, a manager making recruitment or promotion decisions, or someone with major life decisions to make, we would say that you should use your intuition as one source of information and then intentionally evaluate it – which includes bringing in other perspectives.

The evidence that points to fundamental thinking errors, drawn from the fields of psychology, behavioural economics and neuroscience, is in the public domain. It provides us with many pointers to improve our capacity to make good decisions and mitigate the risks of our choices. Yet our work in the area of decision making has bumped up against four significant challenges:

1. It is too much to expect people to remember and work with over 100 cognitive biases or thinking errors
2. The language used to describe these cognitive biases is academic and not easily memorable to non-specialists
3. We don't really use this body of knowledge about unconscious biases to inform our actual decisions
4. The environment in which decisions are made does not always encourage honest enquiry into why we are making the decisions we make.

The origins of this book were in direct response to these four challenges. In researching this book we have been able to develop a ground-breaking framework to help us get to grips with the hidden risks that will be present in our decisions. We have clustered thinking errors under four areas: **R**elationships, self-**I**nterest, **S**hortcuts, and **K**nowledge and experience (R-I-S-K).

Across these four areas of R-I-S-K, we have been able to embody the essence of thinking errors in eight characters. Examining decisions through the lens of each of these characters brings into focus our own thinking errors and the thinking errors of others. Through understanding the habit loop, we are able to identify the triggers that bring these characters into play in our choices and take actions to break habitual patterns of thinking. Finally, we offer ways to equip you so that you can create the right environment and underlying processes to scrutinise key decisions more effectively.

Throughout the book we will point to key research findings from the fields of psychology, behavioural economics and neuroscience. We also offer real-life illustrations that cast a light on different thinking errors. We hope this book will appeal to anyone faced with a difficult decision, but particularly to busy professionals who want to gain a rapid insight into better decision making and to those who wish to go deeper into this emerging field.

Book Structure

We have tried to make this book an easy and interesting read. The book does tell a story and the chapters are set out to unpack this story. However, we are mindful that reading a book cover to cover isn't always possible and isn't the way everyone likes to read books. If this is the case for you, we hope the following guidance will help steer you to the places you want to explore.

Part 1 sets out how academic research has helped us to understand the work of thinking errors in decision making and sets out a high level view of our ground-breaking Hidden R-I-S-K™ framework. In Part 1 we explain why thinking errors can be clustered around the four areas of **R**elationships, self-**I**nterest, **S**hortcuts and **K**nowledge (R-I-S-K).

Part 2 explores the Hidden R-I-S-K™ framework in detail. We explain the habit loop and introduce each of our eight characters, showing how understanding the work of each character can help you mitigate thinking errors and support better decision making. The chapter on each character stands alone and you can tackle them in whatever order you choose. Be mindful that to understand the Hidden R-I-S-K™ framework fully you will need to come to know each of the characters.

Part 3 focuses on the practical application of the Hidden R-I-S-K™ framework as a tool for a human due diligence around key decisions. We explain how the framework can be used itself as a tool for self-reflection; for coaching; for decision-making groups and specialists such as auditors, risk managers, programme leaders and consultants. We also set out critical cultural factors that will enable organisations to create the right environment for more honest conversations and collective accountability.

As our primary goal in writing this book is to help you make better decisions, there is a strong practical bent. Throughout the book we will challenge you directly with questions aimed at encouraging you to reflect on your own experiences and the ways you make decisions.

In reading this book, our hope is that you will acquire a practical and memorable framework you can apply to decisions big and small, and in all kinds of situations. We particularly hope that it will equip leaders and decision makers across all sectors with an accessible framework to conduct a human due diligence on all key decisions; and that as a result, better outcomes will be achieved for all.

PART 1

What You See Isn't Always What You Get

"We don't yet see things clearly. We're squinting in a fog, peering through a mist. But it won't be long before the weather clears and the sun shines bright!"

1 Corinthians 13:12 (The Message)

The Illusion of Certainty

"In this world nothing can be said to be certain other than death and taxes."

Benjamin Franklin

As a child, one of the performers I always looked forward to seeing on British television was Ray Alan, who was always accompanied by his friends – Lord Charles or Tich and Quackers. I was always mesmerised by his shows because Ray Alan had a particular gift that I spectacularly failed to emulate. You see, Ray Alan was a ventriloquist and he was able to breathe life into his dummies, giving them distinct personalities.

The skill of the ventriloquist to create the illusion of engagement with a dummy was perhaps best seen in the USA when, in 1993, the ventriloquist Shari Lewis and her dummy Lamb Chop appeared before Congress to testify in favour of protections for children's television. Lamb Chop was actually granted permission to speak and by all accounts made a pretty good job of testifying. (Arguably, Lamb Chop wasn't the first or last dummy to speak before Congress.)

The beauty of good ventriloquism is that we know intellectually that the words spoken by the dummies are the words of the ventriloquist, but our senses distort the information to create the amusing illusion of a dummy with personality and often with a cheeky attitude. The brain plays tricks on us.[5] We know this and the world of magic and illusion has made a living from it for as long as humans have been around.

Take a look at the drawing below by the Swiss artist Sandro Del-Prete.[6]

What do you see?

Figure 1: *D'Amour des Dauphins*, © **Sandro Del-Prete /** **sandrodelprete.com**

The answer to this question will almost certainly depend on your age. When adults are shown this picture, they tend to see a couple in a passionate embrace. If elementary school children are shown this picture, they marvel at nine cute little dolphins! (Look closely: they really are there.) In most cases, adults are completely oblivious to the dolphins in the picture whereas young children, unless they have been exposed to age-inappropriate images, never see the couple.

This clever piece of art masterfully demonstrates that we do not experience a situation with an empty slate. The different meanings children and adults attributed to the same picture reveal that perception is a creative act and what is already in our mind will determine how we judge a situation and ultimately determine the actions we take.

To improve our decision making, we need to have a better understanding of what is already in our mind. For the discerning decision makers, the billion dollar question is: *how do I know what is already in my mind?*

Thanks to over three decades of research in the areas of cognitive psychology and neuroscience, we now have a pretty good understanding of what is in our mind. Scientists working in these fields have meticulously explored the vast, unconscious, automated processes that run under the hood of our conscious awareness and they have come to some startling discoveries.

One of these discoveries is that, objectively speaking, a person is not a single entity of a single mind. In all of us there are several unconscious automated processes at work which compete with each other for our attention and are responsible for interference with our perceptions of situations. This discovery has been eloquently explained by the Nobel Prize winner Daniel Kahneman in his bestseller *Thinking Fast and Slow*. In this book Kahneman explains the workings of these automated processes in terms of two distinctive systems of thought – which he calls System 1 and System 2.[7]

System 1 thinking is fast, reflexive, intuitive and automatically programmed to help us assess a situation quickly. System 2 thinking is slow, rational, considered and deliberate. We use System 2 thinking to analyse and reason logically. The interplay between these two systems is complicated by the fact that we prefer System 1 thinking to System 2 thinking. This is fundamentally because System 2 thinking requires more effort on our part. Although the slower System 2 thinking can sometimes override our intuition, this is less likely because at heart it requires extra effort and we are naturally lazy. Kahneman also made another alarming observation. He found that we don't particularly differentiate between the time we spend on smaller, relatively unimportant decisions and those decisions that have significant consequences. This discovery has important implications for decision makers.

Whether consciously or unconsciously, many of our decisions happen at the emotional, intuitive level. Let us stress here that there is nothing innately wrong with intuition (which is often guided by shortcuts and rules of thumb). There are times when we must make fast decisions in which intuition plays an important role. A good example of this happened on 15th January 2009 when US Airways Flight 1549 proved that a miracle could happen.[8]

Three minutes after Flight 1549 took off from LaGuardia airport in New York City, a flock of Canada geese collided with the engines. Jet engines can cope with small birds but a flock of geese each weighing around ten pounds (4.5kg) was just too big a hit and both engines shut down. The flight recording captured Captain Chesley Sullenberger informing air traffic control: "Hit birds. We've lost thrust in both engines. We're turning back towards LaGuardia."

With 150 people on board, landing short of the airport would have resulted in a major disaster for passengers and people on the ground alike. While air traffic control gave Captain Sullenberger a number of landing options, he needed to evaluate this information and make his own decision – and quickly. The amount of time Sullenberger had between the flock of geese shutting down both engines and the plane crashing was around three minutes. There was no time for him to read through the emergency procedures handbook or take extensive consultations. The situation required fast thinking. He decided that he could not get the plane back to LaGuardia safely and chose to risk a landing on the river Hudson instead.

Much has been written about the heroics of this story, particularly as it has a happy ending. One of the System 1 approaches used by Sullenberger was a simple rule of thumb – to fix his gaze on the airport control tower and observe whether the tower rose or descended in his windshield: if it rose the plane wouldn't reach it; if it descended the plane would overfly it. In this instance, fast thinking was required and the right call was made.

Those writing about this incident note that the decision-making process was no fluke nor was it a purely spontaneous choice.[9] The apparently intuitive choice made by Sullenberger was the result of considerable personal training – often in uncertain conditions on the flight simulator – combined with a well-trained crew who were clear about their accountabilities and a pilot who was able to step back under stress, consider and eliminate options rapidly and execute his choice effectively.

This kind of decision taps deep into our human history, back to when early humans didn't have time to weigh up whether to stand or run. In these situations, we simply needed to make a call and hope it was the right one.

Where reliance on System 1 thinking bumps into limitations is when we add two other factors that we now know. First, we live in an increasingly complex and uncertain world and many decisions we need to make aren't clear-cut or framed within a narrow range of options. Second, research over the past few decades has identified well in excess of 100 ways our choices are distorted through unconscious processes at work – *thinking errors* or *cognitive biases* – that interfere with our perceptions of situations.[10] These thinking errors are systematic (routine, regular, repeating) and interfere with what we might consider as optimal, rational, reasonable thought and behaviour. What this means is that we are not as considered in our decision making as we think we are and are often prone to thinking errors because System 2 is not activated.

There are a number of reasons for this that extend beyond simple laziness on our part. In the introduction, we pointed to the lack of an accessible language or terminology to discuss thinking errors in a constructive and generative way. We also pointed to the lack of the right organisational environment in which people feel safe to speak out, ask questions and take mutual accountability for decisions made. As a result, we also haven't learnt the habits of effective decision making.

We know that creating new habits is not an easy task. We need some incentive to make the change and we then need 'easy to use' tools along with the encouragement and support of others to help us make the changes we seek. This book speaks to each of these areas and will be an invaluable aid in breaking old patterns of thinking.

An important first step is to become aware of these unconscious forces at work in our choices and to accept that we all fall prey to *thinking errors*. Returning to the Sandro Del-Prete picture of the lovers and the dolphins, the thinking error you are likely to have fallen prey to is known as *the 'salience effect'*. 'Salience' refers to a prominent feature, a standout attribute, a particularity or something that catches your eye. The salience effect means that these 'stand out' features receive much more of our attention than they actually deserve and usually at the expense of noticing other features. In this case, what caught the eye was age-group specific because invariably children and adults are interested in different things.

There are lots of examples of the salience effect manifesting itself in everyday life. Brands often focus on stand-out features, so the salience of a brand such as BMW, Nike or Apple immediately triggers associations with the attributes of quality, design and innovation. The most successful brands create huge loyalty even when alternative products may offer as good as, if not better, performance. Other common everyday examples we come across include the relationship between font size and price. A lower sales price in a smaller font put next to the regular price in a larger font is proven to result in greater interest than when the sale price is shown in a relatively large font.[11] We are all also familiar with the positioning of confectionary and other goods near cashiers in stores and cafes. If you ever wonder why this is so, research into the salience effect has shown that (in this case, bottled water) sales were boosted when the product was positioned close to the cashier.[12]

The salience effect is just one example of over 100 thinking errors. Although we cannot dismiss or easily eradicate these thinking errors we can, through our awareness of them, build self-regulating and group-regulating processes to surface, quantify and address them. This knowledge and understanding has huge implications for business.

Part of the value to business is to gain competitive advantage through exploiting fast thinking, even taking advantage of thinking errors by using targeted advertising to build quality brands or by engaging in what experts call "choice architecture" – arranging products in a particular fashion that catches our attention or simply moving bottled water closer to the cashier. Those in marketing and sales have long understood intuitively the psychology behind their work. Recent studies now offer the evidence to back up the practices they have developed through trial and error over the years. With the research available now, they can be even more intentional in the presentation of the goods and services they offer. In the UK, central government is leading in this field due largely to two American Professors – Richard Thaler and Cass Sunstein.

In 2008 Thaler and Sunstein published their bestseller *Nudge*. The book looked at how choices are presented to people and how that presentation will affect their decisions. With reference to many fascinating examples, Thaler and Sunstein concluded that "small and apparently insignificant details can have a major impact on people's behaviour." Some ways of presenting the choices may give a gentler 'nudge' than others and we may think some settings are neutral only because we are used to them. But with their book, Thaler and Sunstein highlighted that whoever is presenting the choices will inevitably bias decisions in one direction or another.

Thaler and Sunstein were interested in changing public policy by nudging people towards healthier, safer and more prosperous lives. Following the success of *Nudge*, Thaler and Sunstein were called upon as advisors to governments at the highest level. Sunstein was appointed Director of Information and Regulatory Affairs under President Obama and Thaler became advisor to the UK Behavioural Insight Team, which reports through the Cabinet Office.

Since their involvement with government, many examples of the successful implementation of nudge-influenced public policy initiatives can be seen. A good example is the use of phrases implying reciprocity in the literature advocating organ donation, along the lines of "if you needed an organ transplant, would you have one?" This approach has resulted in substantial increases in the number of people prepared to offer organs for transplant. Another example is the automatic enrolment of people into pension schemes. This approach guarantees very high levels of uptake – some investment firms report in excess of 90 percent – as people dislike opting out. These principles can also be applied to some fundamental questions such as "how do you get people to pay their taxes?" and "how do you get people to wear car seat belts?" For the first question, a nudge approach is to state how many other people are already paying their tax. This plays to people's desire to 'do what others are doing' and has resulted in increased payment rates without resorting to more draconian measures. Addressing the second question has most powerfully been addressed by a UK organisation – the Sussex Safer Roads Partnership. Instead of the usual 'shock and awe' approach showing lots of statistics and gruesome accident scenes, the 90-second video simply portrays a man driving whilst wearing a seat belt formed by the arms of his daughter and partner. It's a very powerful image and a real tearjerker.[13]

Nudge-type public policies are now gaining increasing acceptance amongst policy makers. As Oliver Letwin (a UK Minister) remarked: "As the Minister responsible for government policy, I have seen how some of these insights can be applied in practice to help generate policy that's smarter, simpler and is highly cost effective."[14]

Whatever the benefits of *Nudge* – and there are undoubtedly many – this book is not about how we can leverage the thinking errors that behavioural scientists worked so hard to identify. What it is about is giving you a deeper understanding of those thinking errors so that, with increasing awareness, we can make better decisions and break established patterns of thinking.

Throughout the book we will offer examples from corporate and public life that illustrate thinking errors at work. Without wanting to indulge in too large a spoonful of schadenfreude, the three examples below give us an opportunity to reflect on some notorious misjudgements in corporate life where there was an apparent high level of certainty and ask ourselves "what is going on?"

The following real-life examples illustrate how key decision makers can fall prey to thinking errors. They also show the consequences of thinking errors and their impact not just on the decision maker but on many other people too.

When Swissair Went Bust

Under a mountain of debt amounting to 17 billion Swiss Francs ($13 billion), the collapse of Swissair in 2002 shook a nation. Swissair was the national carrier of Switzerland and revered by many as a national treasure. It had been once so financially stable that it was known as the 'Flying Bank'. Founded in 1931, Swissair epitomised high-class international air travel. In the late 1990s, under the leadership of its CEO Philippe Bruggisser, Swissair embarked on an aggressive and costly borrowing and acquisition strategy. The company pursued that strategy even when it was clear that the strategy was failing and the company was overextending itself.

Bruggisser was very close to McKinsey, the consultants who helped shape this strategy. This close association was a focus of attention during two public inquiries and was seen as a major contributing factor to the bankruptcy. By all accounts Bruggisser and his board had succumbed to a number of common thinking errors:

- *Emotional tagging:* The close association with McKinsey became an emotional investment that stopped Bruggisser and his board from asking searching questions about the strategy and the consequences of its implementation. We explore this thinking error later in Chapter 9 but the result was a defensive response where the preservation of the relationship became more important than the success of the strategy. This same dynamic is often seen in family systems and teams where the proverbial *elephant in the room* is never discussed through fear of endangering relationships.
- *Loss aversion:* In the case of Swissair, the CEO and board held onto the strategy because they were frightened to cut their losses. Two justifications often used by decision makers to defend their original decisions are "it will come good in the end" and "it is a long-term investment". We explore this thinking error further in Chapter 9.
- *Groupthink*: In this case, nobody was prepared to say "the emperor has no clothes" and point out that the strategy had failed. This desire within a group of decision makers to reach a consensus and sing from the same hymn sheet is often a source of thinking errors. We explore this thinking error further in Chapter 11.

Bernard Madoff and the Security and Exchange Commission

The prize for the biggest fraud of all times goes to Bernie Madoff who ran a Ponzi scheme[15] for well over two decades, defrauding wealthy investors out of a staggering $50 billion. The inquiry into this scandal pointed the finger at the Securities and Exchange Commission (SEC). The inquiry stated that the SEC had overlooked "more than ample evidence" including numerous credible and detailed complaints. Despite these red flags, the SEC never even took the necessary, but basic, steps to determine whether Madoff was operating a Ponzi scheme. This was not because of collusion or foul play, but simply because the key decision makers could not believe that someone with such impeccable credentials as Bernie Madoff (who had even served as the Chairman of the National Association of Security Dealers, a self-regulatory securities industry organisation) could be involved in an illegal operation. He was simply too credible!

In this instance, the SEC decision makers fell prey to a thinking error known as the *'champion bias',* which is our tendency to judge a person's work or performance on the basis of their past reputation, rather than on the basis of the evidence in front of our eyes. We explore the champion bias in more detail in Chapter 9.

Decca

One of the worst judgement calls ever made in music history is the Decca record label's rejection of the Beatles. The executives who made that decision maintained at the time that guitar groups were on their way out. To put icing on the cake with a cherry on top, Decca also gave feedback to the Beatles that they had "no future in show business".

Much has been written on the circumstances surrounding that decision, but one of the overriding factors appears to be that the executives did not want to sign a group from working-class Liverpool. Instead they signed a London group, Brian Poole and the Tremeloes, which also auditioned with the Beatles on the same day. Decca's Dick Rowe, one of the most important producers and record executives in the United Kingdom in the 1950s and early '60s, famously advised the Beatles' manager to stay local too – "You have a good record business down there [in Liverpool] Mr Epstein. Why don't you go back to that?"[16] The rest, as they say, is history.

The thinking error the Decca executives succumbed to when they turned down the Beatles was the *in-group bias*. This is the tendency for people to give preferential treatment to others they perceive to be members of their own group. In this case, the executives preferred a southern middle-class group to a northern working-class group. We explore this thinking error in more detail in Chapter 4.

These three examples are salutary lessons that cannot be easily ignored. None of these highly qualified professionals set out to make those judgement calls – after all, no-one makes bad decisions out of choice. These examples show that we are all prone to thinking errors, that these thinking errors are situational and that not attending to them can have a significant impact. So, does this emerging knowledge about thinking errors and unconscious biases mean that we cannot trust our brains?

The good news is that we are not helpless in the face of these deceptions of our own mind. Unless faced with a genuine fight-or-flight decision, we can choose to override System 1 thinking by consciously activating System 2. Research tells us that awareness is the key to mitigating thinking errors and increased awareness gives us a chance to break patterns of thinking and behaviour.

One of the great findings of neuroscience in the last 50 years is that our brains build our learning *and* our learning in turn builds our brains. Plasticity, or neuroplasticity, describes how experiences reorganise neural pathways in the brain. Long-lasting functional changes in the brain occur when we learn new things. We *can* learn how to recognise thinking errors and we can in turn learn new habits to mitigate human risk in our choices.

Does that sound too hopeful? As they say, the proof of the pudding is in the eating; and in this case, the pudding is that we are not prisoners of the deceptions of our own minds.

Coming back to the Sandro Del-Prete picture, I wonder whether you will ever look at this picture in quite the same way as you did when you first came across it.

In all likelihood the answer to that is a resounding "no". Thanks to the plasticity of your brain, your brain has already built neural networks that will alert you to the salience effect – the very thinking error that had misled you in the past. Should you be shown this picture or a similar picture in the future, you will be not only looking at the salient features of the picture, but you will be looking more closely at the parts of the picture which do not immediately catch your attention. You will be consciously activating System 2 in order to override any earlier judgements you made about the content of the picture. In other words, you have now developed a strategy that will help you avoid falling for the same error again.

This is the focus of our book as we endeavour to provide you with a thinking strategy to recognise and identify the most common thinking errors in yourself and others so that you can ask those insightful questions which will help you make better decisions in the future and break the patterns of thinking.

2

The RISK in Our Decisions

"The fishermen know that the sea is dangerous and the storms terrible, but they have never found these dangers sufficient reason for remaining ashore."

Vincent van Gogh

In Chapter 1 we noted that what is already in our mind will determine how we judge a situation and how we judge a situation will ultimately determine the actions we take. We also noted that whilst certainty exists in some areas of our lives – such as, with deference to Benjamin Franklin, death and taxation – much of the time, our decisions are loaded with degrees of uncertainty. Making sense of what we know to be reality and uncovering the things we don't yet know is a critical area for decision makers, especially when it comes to significant decisions.

What Do We Know and What Don't We Know?

You may be familiar with the Johari Window (see Figure 2).[17] Devised by American psychologists Joseph Luft and Harry Ingham in 1955 (Jo and Hari), the Johari Window is used to support the development of effective relationships through helping us to think about what information is open, transparent and known to all parties involved in a conversation or decision, and what isn't. Luft and Ingham found that effective interactions took place when all parties to a conversation or decision dealt with the same information – this they call the "open area". They also discovered in their work that some information is "known to me" but undisclosed. This represents the façade we often put up and this information remains hidden. They also highlighted that some information is "known to others" but *not* known to me. This is our blind spot. Some other information lies deep in our subconscious and is *unknown*.

The Johari Window is used to encourage higher levels of disclosure so that the open area is as large as we can make it.

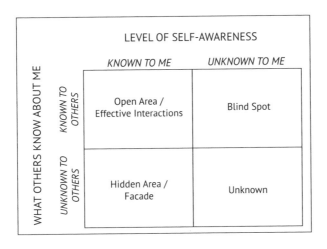

Figure 2: The Johari Window

Whilst often used in personal coaching and with teams, the Johari Window is a very useful lens through which we can understand decisions and choices. Let's look at an example of a decision in the open area, in an industry where the stakes are high and where there is a threat to mortality.

With a massive following in over 200 countries, *Deadliest Catch* is a hugely successful reality TV series shown on the Discovery Channel. The show portrays the real-life events aboard fishing vessels in the icy Bering Sea during the Alaskan king crab fishing season. The show emphasises the dangers to the fishermen who work under extremely hazardous conditions. In the midst of some of the coldest and stormiest waters on earth, even a minor problem may become complex with the nearest port often hundreds of miles away. The crews are seen ducking heavy crab pots swinging into position, manoeuvring hundreds of pounds of crab across a deck strewn with hazards and leaning over the rails to position pots for launch or retrieval as gale-force winds and high waves constantly lash the deck.

Anybody watching *Deadliest Catch* cannot fail to be impressed by the courage and the fortitude of these weather-hardened men who endure long absences from home in order to earn their living in such an inhospitable environment. But few viewers of the show will be fully aware of the true extent of the dangers the Alaskan crab fishermen face. By any measure, commercial fishing is one of the most hazardous occupations. According to the US Coast Guard, 1,903 commercial fishing vessels sank between 1992 and 2007, which resulted in 507 fatalities. However, the death and injury rates associated with ordinary commercial fishing pale into insignificance compared to the hazards involved in Alaskan crab fishing. The death rate during the main crab season averages nearly one fisherman per week, while the injury rates for crews are well over 90 percent due to severe weather conditions, like frigid gales, rogue waves and ice formations on and around the boat, and the danger of working with such heavy machinery on a constantly rolling boat deck.

So why would anyone in their right mind choose to work on an Alaskan crab fishing boat? Alaskan crab fishermen accept the risk of death and injury in order to gain handsome pay outs. A deckhand can make $100,000 for just a couple of months of work. Sig Hansen, the captain of the *Northwestern* and one of the most experienced captains of the series, explains the fisherman's relationship with risk as follows:

> If they're afraid of taking a risk, they'll never succeed, number one. Most fishermen are the biggest risk takers on planet Earth. Number two, they're all entrepreneurs; they're always looking for the bigger, better, badder boat, pot, fishing ground, crew, you name it. They're always trying to make it better.

For most of us, those risks would be unacceptable and this is one of the main reasons why *Deadliest Catch* makes such compelling viewing. Yet we often forget that all human endeavours involve risk because when we make choices we always face a trade-off between the potential of losing something of value (a downward risk) against the potential to gain something of value (an upward risk).

This risk trade-off lies at the heart of every choice to varying degrees. What we observe in *Deadliest Catch* is that there are many known risks. Captain Hansen has done this job for a long time. For many it is a family business and even the crews are generally experienced. These people are conscious of where the critical risks are and how to mitigate them.

This is true of other occupations where the risk of serious danger to life and limb is high such as in energy, mining, construction and emergency services, to name but a few. In these situations much time and investment is made in quantifying risks and putting in place mitigating actions, whether health and safety processes, protective clothing or creating the right team environment to alert people to danger. There are also other circumstances where some or all of the risks in choices are known. Risk governance groups, risk registers and mathematical modelling all play their part in surfacing, quantifying and addressing known risks.

These examples fall into the 'open area' of the Johari Window. This is a productive space where we can hold effective interactions because we are dealing with a shared understanding of what is known. Our challenge remains one of working in those areas that remain unknown: to oneself, to others or both.

From the work of cognitive psychologists discussed here, two critical insights emerge that spotlight the limitations of working exclusively in the open area. First, that unless we are engaged in highly dangerous activities where the likelihood of the downward risk occurring is high, that risk trade-off is something we do not consciously consider. In Johari Window terms, the open space could be quite small and we don't see our blind spot, or the hidden area or the unknown. Second, that the human dimension of risk is largely represented in the 100-plus unconscious thinking errors that steer our choices and these, because they emerge at the unconscious level, are below the surface and thus far less obvious to us. As a result, unconscious biases are often left unconsidered in our decisions.

What this means is that even in situations where there are many knowns and a large open area, we still need to be intentional and attentive to unconscious forces at work. Where we need to make decisions in situations of high uncertainty and many unknowns, this attentiveness to the unconscious becomes even more important.

If we return to *Deadliest Catch,* the ability to mitigate risk is possible even for the hugely hazardous king crab fishing operation in the icy Bering Sea. Despite the popular perception that many accidents in that industry are caused by the violence and unpredictability of nature, the reality is that many of these fatal accidents are actually preventable and are often the result of poor decision making, human error in equipment maintenance and/or inadequate training.

Sig Hansen, the captain of the *Northwestern*, also has some compelling insights when it comes to 'in the moment' decisions. Speaking from years of experience, he talks about how he prevented his boat from capsizing:

> The first thing was fear and panic, and the next thing was just what you learn through time. And that was: *"Assess the situation."* Those words echoed in my brain. So, rather than

panic and scream and yell, I just stopped for a second. I just forced myself to become calm, think through it, and then guide the boat and the people on board and do what we needed to do.[18]

It is this process of correctly assessing the situation that has kept Hansen alive for so long, and this is why he still sails the mighty waters of the Bering Sea when others found a watery grave.

No-one makes a bad decision out of choice. The Johari Window can help to remind us that we have a blind spot where self-awareness is low. When we encounter the unfamiliar it is important to step back and assess the situation. If time permits, we should slow down and assess the situation with others.

What we are doing here is giving System 2 thinking a chance. The quality of what we do depends on the thinking we do first and we are able to improve our thinking *only* by stepping back and assessing what bits of information should be given a greater weighting in our decision than others. Ideally, we would like to come quickly to a clear view of our options; however, as explored in Chapter 1, our view of reality can easily be obscured by the deceptions of our own mind. The 100-plus thinking errors that work at the subconscious level present real obstacles to better decision making. When we are called upon to assess a situation, we need an early 'in the moment' warning system to alert us to the fact that we are about to fall prey to such dangerous deceptions.

Our focus in this book is about enlarging the open area in the Johari Window through understanding more fully and intentionally the unconscious forces at work in the other three quadrants. This is what professionals working in the area of risk management call 'people risk' and the Institute of Risk Management (one of the leading professional bodies for risk management in the UK) states that "people risk is a major component – some would say **the** major component – of risk management, irrespective of organisational type and industry sector."[19]

A Greater Understanding of the Human Dimension of Risk

If risk is defined as the "the effect of uncertainty on objectives"[20] then a key part of understanding uncertainty is the impact of thinking errors on our choices. We know that risk is inherent in all our choices and that the level of risk depends on circumstances. We also know that scientists have identified over 100 different types of thinking error that can impact our choices. The evidence is there to help us understand and mitigate human risk in decision making.

The problem is that we simply cannot remember 100-plus thinking errors. So, our first challenge has been to determine whether it is possible to cluster thinking errors into a memorable framework.

In their book, *Think Again*, Sydney Finkelstein, Jo Whitehead and Andrew Campbell have sought to develop exactly such a model of risk assessment.[21] This research by Finkelstein, Whitehead and Campbell was a catalyst in helping us to cluster thinking errors. We are deeply indebted to this research. We have been able to develop and elaborate their work through capturing a greater number of thinking errors and, in clustering around the acronym 'R-I-S-K', we have created a more memorable way to locate these thinking errors.

A Hidden R-I-S-K™ Framework

The acronym 'R-I-S-K' takes us a significant step further as it clusters thinking errors around the most common sources of error.[22] The acronym is not only easier to remember, but also accurately describes the impact of thinking errors on our environment. We should never forget that in themselves the thinking errors are not 'bad' choices, but they certainly can have significant downsides. As risk is inherent in our choices, being aware of these downsides is the first step to breaking patterns of thinking in decision making.

Clustering thinking errors around the acronym R-I-S-K helps us to undertake a form of cognitive due diligence for important decisions. This gives us deeper insights that can help to mitigate the downward and maximise the upward consequences of our choices.

We acknowledge that 'risk' isn't a particularly sexy word for many and can come across as somewhat negative. You may even be already making unconscious associations with the word. 'Risk' is a word often used in conjunction with other words like 'averse', 'registers', 'management' or 'prevention'. The risk in our choices is, nevertheless, a reality. What is important to appreciate is that risk in itself is neither good nor bad. Risk is just there. Let's look at the four clusters of R-I-S-K more closely.

3

How Relationships Influence Our Decisions

"Attachment is the great fabricator of illusions; reality can be attained only by someone who is detached."

Simone Weil

R = Relationship-driven Thinking Errors

Forging relationship is our first survival strategy when we come into the world. A baby will bond with its principal caregiver. This strong relationship assures that the baby will get food, security, shelter, care and affection in order to survive in what is, for the new-born child, a hostile environment.

Throughout our lives we replicate this drive to forge relationships as a strategy to gain what we need from others. These attachments can be the social bonds forged with family, significant others and friends. They can also be relationships we form with communities and colleagues, with animals, with organisations, with places and with more conceptual things such as brands, icons, logos, symbols, ideas and even the status quo.

Most of us are aware of the positive benefits a strong relationship can bring. In the jungle of life, having a close relationship with someone who can help us navigate through the potential pitfalls can be hugely beneficial. We are less aware that strong relationships create unconscious attachments that can lead to sub-optimal choices. Many psychologists believe that when the brain creates a memory of a person, an experience or an action, it also attaches an associated emotion with it. The term given by psychologists to this is *emotional tagging*. What this means in practice is that when we are faced by choices, we recall past situations that seem similar and access the emotions that are tagged with them.

What we have discovered is that there are two manifestations of thinking error linked to relationships, which occur:

1. Where past relationships are a reference point for current choices; in other words, when we make our choices through the lens of past relationships
2. When we defend the attachments and relationships that we have forged – often to a point that defies the evidence.

We set out below examples of how these inappropriate attachments expressed through relationships can have a detrimental impact on our choices.

Relationships with People

In Chapter 1, we noted that the relationship between the Swissair CEO and the consultants McKinsey led to the continued pursuit of a failing strategy in the face of compelling evidence. Another high-profile example of a relationship leading to a series of poor decisions is that of Paul Wolfowitz's March 2005 appointment as President of the World Bank.[23]

During contract negotiations, Wolfowitz disclosed that he was in a romantic relationship with Shaha Ali Riza who was a senior communications officer on the World Bank staff. Continuing this relationship after taking up his post would be a violation of World Bank rules on conflicts of interest. The matter was referred to the Bank's Ethics Committee who ruled that Wolfowitz was to comply with Bank rules and have no direct or indirect supervision over Riza or, indeed, any professional contact. Wolfowitz did not accept this decision and over the following months made a number of interventions on Riza's behalf that clearly furthered the interests of his girlfriend, including insisting on significant salary increases and promotion guarantees linked to her transfer to an external service organisation. After a series of investigations, Wolfowitz resigned as World Bank President in June 2007.

This is a clear example of how personal attachments can influence decisions. This level of clarity is not always to be found. Deeper, unconscious forces can also shape how we respond to others. For example, our experience of past relationships can trigger associations we are barely aware of. Psychologists use the term 'transference' to help explain why it can sometimes seem as if people are re-enacting a drama from the past rather than seeing the current situation for what it is in the present. What happens is similar to the experience of 'flashback', where a person or situation stirs up emotions and perceptions from a previous experience. This leads us to associate the present with the past, even though there is unlikely to be any connection at all. This use of old relationships as a reference point for new relationships can easily result in skewed thinking – in positive or negative ways.

The subconscious impact of transference was once brought home to me very powerfully when, for no obvious reason, I found myself taking an immediate dislike to a new colleague. Reflecting on my reactions with my husband, I discovered that my colleague reminded me of a teacher I'd had at school with whom I'd had a poor relationship. I had inadvertently transferred my latent anger and frustration from that past relationship onto this innocent colleague. Once I was able to understand what was happening,

I was able to put in place strategies to take this person at face value.[24]

The subconscious impact of past relationships plays a crucial role when we have to make up our mind quickly, such as in recruitment situations. It often happens that something about the job applicant creates a favourable or a negative impression on the interviewer and this first impression might colour how the interviewer then views the candidate's suitability for the job. The interviewer might, for example, find the applicant's manner, accent and appearance pleasing, or might discover that he or she attended the same school. In the highly popular TV show *The Apprentice*, this dynamic can be observed in real time as Lord Sugar often selects the candidate who comes from a working-class background similar to his own, instead of the candidate who according to him "has been born with a silver spoon in his mouth".

Our Attachment to Animals

In 1911, Captain Scott and Captain Amundsen set off from their respective base camps on the Antarctic coast, each trying to reach the South Pole first. Amundsen reached the South Pole on 15th December 1911, walking into the history books, and then returned safely to 'civilisation' within three months. Scott and his four companions arrived at the South Pole 33 days later on 17th January 1912 and faced an agonising struggle to get back to base camp. None of them ever made it back.

Why Amundsen's team completed the return journey with comparative ease and Scott's party died has been the source of much discussion ever since. All commentators agree that the choice of transportation was a key differentiator between the two teams. Scott always planned to man-haul using harnesses attached to sledges. This was exhausting work, but he believed it was nobler and less cruel than using animals. Scott loved dogs and did not want to use them because it meant having to slaughter them if they weakened or became difficult to handle: "One cannot calmly contemplate the murder of animals which possess such intelligence and individuality, which have frequently such endearing qualities and which very possibly one has learnt to regard as friends and companions".[25]

Amundsen did not have such a sentimental attachment to dogs. He had used man-hauling sledges in the Arctic and did not want to repeat this experience, so he took dogs bought in Greenland that had been trained specially for this task. Dogs that weakened or became disobedient were indeed killed or set free. The dogs were part of the Norwegian's meal plan too and at Butcher's Camp, about half way to the Pole, enough dogs were killed to feed the hungry men and the remaining dogs. Amundsen and his men did not particularly enjoy their dog-meat meals. However, by not letting any attachment to the dogs get in the way of the necessity to eat high-protein food, Team Amundsen was able to live to tell the tale.

Scott and his men would not contemplate eating dogs because they saw the dogs as trusted friends and companions. They chose, however, to eat their ponies. The ponies taken as pack animals were consumed early on in the journey, as they quickly succumbed to the arctic conditions at the South Pole.

Relationships with Objects and Organisations

People can form strong bonds with the strangest of things. Consider office moves or desk moves, or any move that destabilises a routine to which we have become accustomed. On the whole we find them tough, don't we?

We live near Oxford in the UK and, if you have visited the area from the south, you will almost certainly have passed Didcot power station. Didcot power station lies on flat land and can therefore be seen from a considerable distance away. You couldn't describe the power station as beautiful. Many would say it is an eyesore and a blot on a very picturesque landscape. Or at least that seemed to be the situation until a decision was made to demolish three of its six cooling towers. Once the demolition was announced, it was astonishing to read the sentimental articles written about these features. Phrases such as 'iconic', 'the Stonehenge of the industrial age' and 'symbols of our industrial heritage' started to dominate social-media sites. People recalled how the cooling towers were an important milestone that marked their journeys to visit family, friends or go on holiday. Attachments had clearly been made and many were surprised at how emotional they felt about the demise of these utilitarian buildings.

Another well-publicised example comes from the business world and occurred when Lee Kun Hee became chairman of the South Korean corporate, Samsung, in 1987. At that time, Samsung was a very profitable memory chip and electronics business. In 1995, having grown the business considerably, Hee announced that Samsung would enter the automotive market and become a carmaker. Samsung had no experience of this market but, despite much opposition from within South Korea, Hee pressed ahead with his plans. In his book *Why Smart Executives Fail*, Sydney Finkelstein concluded: "In the face of so many drawbacks, it would have taken a miracle for the car business to work".[26]

So why did Hee pursue this strategy in the face of so much opposition? There are many possible reasons but it is highly likely that it was simply because Lee Kun Hee loved cars. He was a car enthusiast who had always dreamt of building them one day. He realised his dream in 1998 when the first cars rolled off the production line. That year, Samsung motors sold fewer than 50,000 cars and posted a net loss of 156 billion Won. In early 1999, Samsung motors went into receivership and was sold to Renault in 2000 for one tenth of Samsung's investment.[27]

In 1988, Marks & Spencer (M&S), a successful UK clothing, furnishings and food retailer, acquired Brooks Brothers, a US retail chain, for $750 million. Derek Raynor, chairman of M&S, led the acquisition. Raynor was a highly experienced retailer and wanted to secure a foothold in the US market. The acquisition was a flop and M&S sold Brooks Brothers for just $225 million three years later. This venture into the US market is estimated to have cost M&S over $1 billion, so what went wrong?

M&S were no novices when it came to the North American market, already having a track record of failure. Judi Bevan, in her book *The Rise and Fall of Marks & Spencer*, noted that the M&S format just didn't work in this market.[28] If we lay alongside this experience of failure the additional knowledge that the M&S acquisition team estimated Brooks Brothers to be worth only $450 million, a more fundamental question emerges: why did M&S bother to pursue this acquisition in the first place?

The answer is almost certainly that Raynor loved the Brooks Brothers product, which sat well with his age, his style and also his attachment to the idea of 'quality'. Raynor was an M&S man through and through. He had already worked at M&S for thirty years when he took over as chairman. His career had flourished under the mentoring of the previous chairman, Marcus Sieff, and he was steeped in the M&S that valued quality of product and quality of supplier. Brooks Brothers had a strong reputation for quality and this, combined with Raynor's attachment to the product, meant that despite six acquisition options being put to him he was convinced not only that Brooks was a good fit with M&S but that the acquisition couldn't fail.

As the authors of *Think Again* put it: "This would have made it almost impossible for him to appreciate the extent to which he was being influenced by emotional attachments of which he was only partly conscious, and difficult for him to see why Brooks Brothers was worth only half of what he paid".[29]

Relationships with Icons, Brands and Symbols

Marketers have long understood our emotional attachment to the concept of a brand. Strong brands connect deeply with us at an emotional level. The launch day of the iPhone 6 in 2014 saw long queues outside Apple stores despite the product being largely a 'catch up' with leading Android smart phones such as those made by Samsung. We have heard heated debates between Apple and open-source enthusiasts. The Cola wars are notorious and footwear with the right logo on the side is a highly valued commodity.

In the 1980s, Wang were leaders in the world of word processing. This is a world far removed from that of today's word processors, but at the time it was a leading technology. Then the personal computer (PC) came along and founder An Wang needed to consider how to respond. The Wang word processor was successful and seeking to improve it was certainly an option. He may also have considered the PC a high-end product that posed no substantive threat to his mainstream word processor. He also thought that the PC was one of the stupidest ideas he had come across!

When IBM launched their PC into the market, Wang had to rethink his strategy. He decided to develop a PC product but also faced the choice of whether to copy IBM or develop an alternative operating program. He opted for the latter. There may have been sound analytical reasons for this decision and there was almost certainly a gut feel derived from his knowledge of the markets. However, the most likely reason was Wang's utter dislike for IBM.[30] Here, the relationship he had with the idea of IBM played out at the emotional, unconscious level and the consequences were that Wang ceased to be a player in this new world of personal computing.

Our lives are relationship rich and it's easy to understand why. Our ability to form and sustain deep and often complex relationships marks us out as human beings. Relationships can be a source of joy; they shape our identity; they inspire love, affection, commitment and sacrifice. As we have seen, they also hold a subtle power that can entrap us without our realising it and lead to distortions in the choices we make.

Adam Smith, one of the founding fathers of economics, once wrote: "How selfish soever man may be supposed, there are evidently some principles in his nature, which interest him in the fortunes of others, and render their happiness necessary to him, though he derives nothing from it, except the pleasure of seeing it."[31] Adam Smith also shone a huge spotlight on self-interest as a critical force driving economies and it is this side of human nature that we discuss in the next chapter.

4

How Self-Interest Influences Our Decisions

"We have always known that heedless self-interest was bad morals; we now know that it is bad economics."

Franklin D. Roosevelt

I – Interest-driven Thinking Errors

If forging relationship is our first survival strategy then, as Adam Smith noted, self-interest follows on closely as our second. We seek to influence others and win them over to our point of view. We put ourselves into situations and places where we can prosper. There is no question that self-interest can be a dynamic and positive force for good in our world. Nevertheless, 'what's in it for me', 'dog eat dog' and 'survival of the fittest' are phrases that also speak to our core interests. Boardroom battles and office politics are all manifestations of self-interest – who is in the ascendant, whose star is waning, who gets to exercise power, who allocates resources – and it is misdirected self-interest that forms our second cluster of thinking errors.

The impact of misdirected self-interest[32] is pervasive and affects the choices of the most thoughtful and upstanding people. It can creep into our choices even when we are actively trying to prevent it from doing so. This is because it is difficult for us to be self-aware about the personal interests in play when making our choices. We have already noted that all decision-making operates to a large extent below the level of consciousness. As such, we unconsciously filter out self-interest from our conscious mind. We are unaware of what is going on and this makes it particularly difficult for us to guard against the impact of self-interest in our choices. We need the help of others to see our blind spot. This is particularly true when there are high levels of uncertainty surrounding our choices. Here decision makers can easily persuade themselves that they are making a rational decision when they aren't.

Self-interest-driven thinking errors are the result of two different ways of looking after 'Number One':

- When we manipulate situations to our own advantage through displaying overconfidence and over-optimism concerning the outcome of the situation
- When we take a passive role by adopting a subservient stance in relation to those who have power over us.

Here are some examples of how the unconscious effects of self-interest have a detrimental impact on our choices.

Overconfidence and Over Optimism

In summer 1944, the Allies needed to achieve a decisive breakthrough to take advantage of German disarray following their defeat in northern France. Field Marshall Montgomery proposed a single thrust into the Netherlands along a 64-mile corridor. The aim was to capture three strategic bridges over the river Rhine at Grave, Nijmegen and Arnhem. The offensive was to involve an armoured corps on the ground and three airborne divisions.

If you have ever watched the film *A Bridge Too Far* or are a student of military history, you will know that the offensive didn't turn out as intended. It was a bold, high-risk plan when viewed in the most favourable of lights. When new intelligence arrived just two days before the planned offensive suggesting that two SS panzer divisions were being refitted in the Arnhem area, the risk of failure increased further. Despite the warnings, the offensive was launched and resulted in what the historian Max Hastings called "a rotten plan, poorly executed".[33]

This operation raises questions about the commanding officers who decided to proceed in the face of compelling data pointing to the opposite course of action. In *On the Psychology of Military Incompetence*, Professor Norman Dixon suggests that a key driver was self-interest.[34] Montgomery had a point to prove with General Eisenhower who had removed him from the Allied ground command. Had the plan been successful, Montgomery would have re-established his position amongst the Allied command and could have possibly become the man who 'ended the war by Christmas'. Lieutenant General 'Boy' Browning, a First World War veteran, was keen to command troops in action before the war ended. He was a driving force in creating British airborne capability and saw this offensive as his big opportunity to prove his concept in practice and lead the biggest airborne assault in history.

Cheating Just a Little Bit!

An experiment conducted by Dan Ariely and reported in his wonderful book *Predictably Irrational* suggests that most of us will bend the rules to serve our personal interests. Ariely gave students a test containing 50 multiple-choice questions. The first group transferred their answers to a separate scoring sheet and handed the completed sheet to the moderator. They were given ten cents for every correct answer and the average score was 32.6 out of 50. A second group had the same test and incentive but were also given opportunities to cheat – an example being that the correct answers were indicated on the scoring sheet so that students could change the answer put in their workbook if it was incorrect. This led to a significantly higher average score of 36 out of 50 – but interestingly not 50 out of 50.

What Ariely found was that we will cheat when we think we will get away with it *and* that most of us cheat a little bit.[35]

The Darker side of Self-interest

There are occasions when thinking errors can take us firmly into the illegal. The collapse of Enron in 2001 is a very visible example of a high-profile corporate failure that stemmed from excessive self-interest and corrosive decision making. The outrage surrounding the Enron scandal wasn't just provoked by Enron executives having set up a network of offshore companies whose aim was to amplify Enron's profitability; nor was it because these executives became extremely rich and influential on the back of the misreporting of profits (at the expense of shareholders, employees and other stakeholders). Whilst these actions were awful in their own right, the greatest outrage was that a small group of people inside and outside the organisation (including the auditors, Arthur Andersen) knew what was happening and convinced themselves that they could get away with it. Even when Enron executives knew the game was up, they kept talking up the share price whilst quietly selling their own personal stock.

In August 2014, the UK retail giant Tesco announced that the UK business had overstated half-year profitability by £250 million. We still need to see how this story will unfold but it is a cautionary tale that no organisation is too big, and no person too powerful, to fall prey to the dark side of self-interest.

Who Pays the Piper Calls the Tune

Max Bazerman of Harvard Business School has researched over many years the psychology of conflicts of interest, including the role of self-interest in decision making. One experiment involved external auditors – professionals who are supposed to offer objective and unbiased views in the service of shareholders. These auditors were asked to audit the accounts of a fictional company to assess whether it had been compliant with generally accepted accounting principles. Half the auditors were told they were employed by the firm's management and the other half were told they were employed by the management of a different firm who wanted to do business with the company being audited. Using the same data you would have expected truly impartial auditors to draw broadly similar conclusions. Not so. The research showed that the first group notionally employed by the company's management were 30 percent more likely to find the business was compliant than the second group acting for a different firm.

Bazerman concluded that auditors were unlikely to offer an objective assessment when their interest is to choose one interpretation of the data over another: after all, client managers may be more disposed to retain an auditor that delivered a favourable report. This conclusion was further underlined when we consider the conditions of this experiment. First, the auditors were explicitly asked to give an impartial view. Second, this was a hypothetical relationship in which no actual gain was involved. Bazerman wrote that: "one can only imagine the degree of distortion that must exist in a long-standing relationship involving millions of dollars in ongoing revenues".[36]

Auditors are not the only profession whose opinions can be distorted by self-interest. In *Think Again*, Finkelstein and colleagues[37] note that "a large number of studies conducted by independent medical researchers, but financed by the pharmaceutical industry, report results that are favourable to the financial sponsors". They go on to quote a study of clinical trials on breast cancer treatments sponsored by pharmaceutical companies that found these treatments significantly more effective than research that was independently financed; and another study of clinical trials that showed 84 percent success in company-sponsored research, but only 54 percent success in independent trials. There are other similar correlations between who finances research and the research outcomes. The same is true of marketing promotions and Finkelstein and colleagues also reference research, again amongst medical practitioners in the US, that confirms that marketing promotions do indeed affect prescribing practices.

Is this intentional manipulation? Maybe it is sometimes, but the Ariely research mentioned above would suggest that there are also unconscious forces at work, driven by self-interest, that lead us to favour those who can help us prosper.

When Win–win Remains Illusive

Sometimes our blind spot is so well guarded that we convince ourselves that we are being rational, reasonable and responsible and it is the other person who is irrational and self-interested.

There is a well-known study in our world of change management that asked managers why other people resisted change. A number of reasons were suggested including self-interest, conservatism, bloody-mindedness, fear and irrationality. When asked to consider occasions when they themselves had resisted change, the overwhelming response was that they had thought deeply about the proposals and didn't think they were right.

In 1986, the leaders of the two superpowers of that time, the USA and the Soviet Union, met in Reykjavik, Iceland.[38] The talks collapsed without any agreement (although eventually the 1987 Intermediate-Range Nuclear Forces Treaty did emerge from the rubble of this summit). When quizzed about the collapse of these talks, both leaders – Ronald Reagan and Mikhail Gorbachev – claimed that the other side had been rigid and obstructionist. Both claimed to have come to the table with far-reaching proposals on arms control and both claimed that the other side came empty handed.

Can both have been correct in their assessments? The reality is that both sides could have indeed believed that they were prepared to be flexible whilst the other side wasn't; and they could also have believed that their own intentions were honourable whilst others' were not.

Academic and researcher George Loewenstein conducted a controlled experiment in which participants were invited to take on the role of either a plaintiff or defendant in a mock legal case based on a real example. (Note that this was a mock legal case: none of the participants had any actual real interest or gain in the outcome.)

The case involved the plaintiff suing the defendant for compensation resulting from a car accident and each party was offered an incentive if they could reach an out-of-court settlement. Before negotiating, they were also asked to make an estimate of what the actual judge had awarded the plaintiff.

What is interesting about this experiment is how quickly people took on the roles allocated to them: those playing the role of plaintiff estimated an average of over $14,000 more in compensation than those playing the role of defendants. When asked what a fair reward would be, those playing the role of plaintiff estimated nearly $20,000 more than those playing the role of defendant. What this shows is that even when there is no actual benefit to be gained, self-interest kicks in. Even when asked to give an unbiased, private estimate of compensation, the interests associated with each of the two roles dominated.

Self-interest is a powerful force at play in our choices and a force we can't easily see in ourselves. The authors of *Think Again* make a telling observation: "The evidence from our experience and from other researchers suggests that decision-makers are far more affected by self-interest than they claim and realise. It is this lack of awareness of the effects of self-interest that makes it particularly important to diagnose, because an unconscious influence is much harder for the decision maker to guard against."[39]

Self-interest is a potent unconscious force at work in us. When we consider self-interest in the light of the findings of Daniel Kahneman – that we tend to use System 1 thinking to make many of our decisions – we can see how a powerful cocktail starts to blend with the ingredients of self-interest and our third cluster of thinking errors: shortcuts also known as heuristics.

5

How Thinking Shortcuts Influence Our Decisions

"Too often... we enjoy the comfort of opinion without the comfort of thought..."

John F. Kennedy

S – Shortcuts that Lead to Thinking Errors

We have already noted our deeply embedded fight-or-flight response to situations of danger. These decisions require us to make fast decisions and hope for the best. Simple, straightforward decisions processed in System 1 work well with shortcuts (or 'heuristics'), as do emergency situations. Where shortcuts have their limitations and even dangers is when we apply the same principles to more complex decisions.

Psychologists have also long understood that humans use cognitive shortcuts to expedite decision making. These shortcuts give more weight to information which is more recent and therefore more easily retrievable. As a result, we are often lazy thinkers who put more value on speed than on quality of decision.

Shortcut-driven thinking errors are the result of two different ways of processing information quickly:

- Zooming in on the information that elicits an emotional response from us and, as a result, rating this information as more significant
- Selecting information in order to confirm an already predetermined decision.

In Chapter 1 we discussed how salience plays an important role in understanding what is already in our minds. Remember the Sandro Del-Prete vase? Salience is where our brain spotlights stand-out information and dims the rest. Here are some examples of how thinking errors are driven by the use of shortcuts in decision making.

What Stands Out Gets Noticed

Häagen-Dazs launched two types of chocolate ice cream – Original Chocolate and 'Five' Milk Chocolate (named 'Five' because it is made from five ingredients). Just to be clear, the ingredients in 'Five' Milk Chocolate are:

1. Skim milk
2. Cream
3. Sugar
4. Egg yolks
5. Cocoa processed with alkali.

And just to be even clearer the ingredients of the Original Chocolate ice cream are:

1. Cream
2. Skim milk

3. Sugar
4. Egg yolks
5. Cocoa processed with alkali.

The new 'Five' ice cream is supposed to be inspired by Michael Pollan's[40] 'rule': don't eat foods with more than five ingredients. The marketing blurb puts it this way: "All-natural ice cream crafted with only five ingredients for incredibly pure, balanced flavour... and surprisingly less fat!" But the Original already had only five ingredients! 'Five' does have less fat, but not because it's made from five ingredients. It has less fat because it uses more skim milk and less cream.

Another example of salience is close to our hearts. We live in Great Britain and, although Anna is German, we just love talking about the weather. Most Brits do. This is no coincidence and researchers[41] have identified salience as the reason why: "people residing in continental and temperate climates expressed significantly more weather salience than those living in dry climates". There it is. In Britain we get a greater variety of weather and we notice it more. As a result, we tune into weather information frequently and generally use the weather as a conversation opener when we are feeling a little awkward.

A more serious issue concerns sub-Saharan Africa, which has the highest prevalence of HIV/AIDS in the world. Despite this, surveys measuring attitudes to AIDS across these African countries consistently report that people do not attach great importance to the issue. Given the impact HIV/AIDS has on families and communities, this appears strange – it ought to be salient in people's mind. What research[42] has found is that, despite the impact of AIDS, many people are too poor to consider the disease important. Instead, issues such as poverty, hunger and unemployment figure far higher in their minds.

Research[43] published in 2014 examined the drivers of households commissioning a home energy audit. The research found that energy costs and energy usage were salient features. In other words, the more people were aware of energy scarcity (and associated rising costs) the more they were likely to focus on their own energy usage and commission an energy audit. Linked to salience, they also found that people focus disproportionately on attributes such as concentration of benefits and greater dispersal of cost. The research also found another thinking error in play – *prospective memory* – which suggests that whilst people may intend to take beneficial actions, they put them off and then forget to take them. This latter point can partly be explained by people's unwillingness (possibly laziness) to self-educate on the benefits of energy improvement as they consider it to be too time consuming.

We Focus on Things that Interest Us

Another example of the impact of salience is found in how we form political opinions.[44] A study of political attitudes in the US found that, irrespective of party affiliation, if someone was interested in a particular issue they were more likely to gather information from a broad research base in order to form an opinion. Where they weren't interested in an issue they formed their opinions based on the cues offered by their preferred political party. For many of us, this suggests that we are likely to allow ourselves to be influenced by those we trust in order to short circuit our own research into an issue.

A good case study from the business world is presented in *Think Again*. It focuses on the decision by Steve Russell (a former chief executive officer of 'Boots the Chemist') to pursue a strategy of diversification into health care.[45] When Russell took the helm of Boots, he needed to identify new opportunities to grow the business. Russell had formed a view over 10 years previously that Boots should diversify into health care. When he became CEO, he was determined to make it happen.

Amongst Boots' senior management and external shareholders there was mixed opinion about this strategy. Although there was a gap in the market, opinion was divided on whether the venture was worth pursuing. Russell believed his job was to push on and he wasn't interested in alternatives. Unfortunately for Russell and for Boots, the strategy did not succeed. Execution problems were identified, such as having sufficient know how to offer health-care services, along with the challenges of working in a low-margin market. What drove this strategy was Russell's vision, the thing that interested him – for Boots to become a 'health-care provider to the nation'.

Confirming What I Have Already Decided

As far back as the 1950s, psychologists discovered a trait they called *cognitive dissonance*. This highlights our tendency to seek evidence to confirm a decision we have already made or something we believe to be true. The dissonance happens when we are presented with two incompatible pieces of information: our brain seeks to eliminate the dissonance either through changing what we believe or have decided, or (and this is more likely) reinterpreting the information so that it sits more comfortably with our existing beliefs or decisions.

When Random Information Guides Our Thinking

If we were to suggest to you that a random number could influence your thinking or impact a negotiation you were involved in, you might be rather dubious. Those researching our approach to decision making have made some interesting discoveries that may surprise you. What they have found is that we tend to make assessments by using an initial value and then adjust this initial value to make our decision. Researchers have also found that, in the main, we don't adjust enough.

This effect, known as *anchoring* and *adjustment heuristics*, has been researched in a variety of ways. Here are some examples.

People were shown a bottle of wine and were asked what they would be prepared to pay for it. Before they gave an answer they were asked to take out a ping-pong ball from a bag. The first bag contained ping-pong balls all with the number 15 written on them. For this group, the prices people were prepared to pay were adjusted around the £15 mark. For a second group of people, the ping-pong balls had the number 50 written on them. For this group the prices people were prepared to pay were significantly higher.

Daniel Kahneman and Amos Tversky conducted ground-breaking research into anchoring.[46] In one experiment they asked participants to estimate the number of African countries in the United Nations. Before people gave their answer they spun a numbered 'wheel of fortune'. Participants saw and heard the number the wheel stopped at. They discovered that the number the wheel stopped at significantly influenced the answer given. Participants whose wheel stopped at 10 estimated, on average, twenty-five countries. Participants whose wheel stopped at 65 estimated, on average, forty-five countries.

In other examples people were asked to estimate the population of South East Asia or the distance to Mars. Before they gave an answer they were asked to write down their social security number. Their answers were influenced by the social security number they had written down. Similar effects have been observed in negotiations about price with the first figure mentioned by either party acting as an anchor for subsequent discussions.[47]

In all experiments, there wasn't a replication of the random number. Some adjustments were made. Nevertheless, the findings (that a completely un-related number can influence the answer we give to a question we have been asked) are both clear and puzzling. We know that the brain anchors information but we still don't know why. What this also means is that although we may think we have taken into account the effects of anchoring by adjusting our answer, the research suggests that we don't adjust enough. We remain selective in the information we pay attention to.

When We Only Have a Plan A

In 1942, Admiral Yamamoto Isoroku had already commanded the Japanese Imperial Fleet for three years. He was a radical thinker and was the brains behind Japan's attack on Pearl Harbour. His next strategy was to draw the US fleet into combat before they had fully recovered from the Pearl Harbour attack and, arguably, before they were strong enough to win such a naval battle. Eventually Yamamoto identified the tiny island of Midway (an important US flying-boat base) as the bait to lure the US fleet into combat.

There were flaws in this strategy and Naval General Staff proposed an alternative strategy. Yamamoto wasn't at all happy at being rebuffed and launched his own political offensive in order to win through. As the authors of *Think Again* recall, "one of the most fascinating parts of the ensuing month was the 'war games' held on board the battleship Yamamoto. When the officer of the red team (American forces) chose tactics that exposed the weakness in the battle plan, the umpire, Yamamoto's chief of staff, ruled against them".[48] This dismissal of legitimate tactics that the US could use to thwart Yamamoto's plan was repeated time after time, including in the case of a scenario that mirrored the actual battle plan later executed by the US. As a result, Yamamoto chose not to adjust his original plan in any substantive way.

Admiral Yamamoto was extremely experienced. He had been a successful naval commander during an earlier war with Russian and Chinese navies. He also fell back on a common military error, which was to fight the current battle with the successful tactics of a former one. His Midway battle plan was informed by past experience (see also the final cluster of thinking errors below) but the dominant thinking errors in play were those of anchoring (only seeing the possibilities of Plan A and none other) and confirmation bias (only accepting information that confirmed the original decision).

In the Battle of Midway example, we noted how knowledge and past experience could also influence our choices. We turn now to our fourth cluster of thinking errors which explores knowledge and experience thinking errors in more detail.

6

How Our Knowledge and Experience Influence Our Decisions

"The greatest obstacle to discovering the shape of the earth, the continents and the ocean was not ignorance but the illusion of knowledge."

Daniel J. Boorstin, *The Discoverers*

K – Knowledge and Experience as a Driver of Thinking Errors

We put a value on expertise. Many of you reading this book will be experts in one field or another. The authors are experts. We study and work hard to become experts and even harder to remain at the leading edge of thinking in our field. There is nothing wrong with knowledge and experience in themselves. The Book of Proverbs[49] advises that: "Zeal without knowledge is not good; a person who moves too quickly may go the wrong way". We need and value knowledge and experience!

This cluster of thinking errors, however, focuses on the misapplication of past learning and overreliance on expert knowledge, and comes into play when we:

- Categorise a situation on the basis only of past experience
- Interpret a situation from the vantage point of our own worldview or expertise.

When Knowledge is a Curse

Have you ever tried to teach someone something about an area in which you are expert and they aren't? It's tough and this is where the skills of great teaching stand out. What great teachers and trainers do really well is to put themselves into the shoes of the learner. They remember what it was like not to have this knowledge and identify with the person's circumstances.

The challenge for many of us is that we aren't great teachers. We have forgotten what it was like to be the student and inaccurately assume that other people know the things we do. An example of this was illustrated through a famous psychological experiment involving tappers and listeners. The tappers were asked to tap out the rhythm of a well-known song they were familiar with; and the listeners needed to listen and figure out what the song was. On average the tappers were 50 percent certain that the listeners would identify the song (and were therefore confident in their ability to tap in a recognisable way). The actual results were quite shocking: only 2.5 percent of songs were recognised by listeners.[50]

Extrapolating these results, this means that we think people understand what we are saying a great deal more than they actually do. As we are so used to knowing the things we know, we expect others to know them as well. This is also always a challenge for anyone who sells their expertise and for teachers, trainers and indeed authors!

Thinking Inside of the Box

One of the reasons we find it hard to think outside of the box is because there are thinking errors that keep us fixed to what we have learnt inside the box. Gestalt psychologist Karl Duncker explored this notion of *functional fixedness* many years ago. In a test, known as the candle problem,[51] published posthumously in 1945, Duncker gave participants a box of matches, a candle and a box of thumbtacks and tasked them with fixing a lit candle on a corkboard wall in a way that wouldn't result in candle wax dripping onto the table below. Duncker observed how most people tried to attach the candle to the wall using the tacks or by melting wax to secure the candle. Very few of them thought of using the inside of the box as a candleholder and tacking this to the wall. In Duncker's terms, people were fixated on the box's normal function as a tack holder and failed to re-conceptualise alternative uses.

This idea of *functional fixedness* explains some of the issues we often encounter in organisations. There are many examples, including:

- The engineer who only visits client sites to fix problems but isn't encouraged to identify new sales opportunities
- The top sales person who is rewarded through bonuses on sales but not for making time to mentor colleagues
- The finance team that has captured insights about customers but is not encouraged to share these with their customer-facing sales teams
- The junior member of staff who coaches and trains a local rugby team but isn't given responsibility at work because he or she is too young and experienced
- The new apprentice who has only ever known how to communicate using social media but isn't able to influence the organisation's social-media strategy.

This list could go on and we are sure you can think of many of your own examples. Pigeonholing knowledge and experience keeps thinking firmly inside the box.

When You Know too Much to Innovate

Andy Zynga, writing for the HBR blog,[52] notes: "It is a profound irony that the more you know about a particular industry, and the more experience you gain in it, the more difficult it can be to move it forward with truly meaningful innovation." In seeking to understand why this is the case Zynga points conclusively to the *curse of knowledge* and *functional fixedness* thinking errors as an explanation. This is because we filter information through the context of our past experiences. As we respond to new challenges, we fall back increasingly on our memories of how we have always done it.

We encounter this thinking error time and again in the course of our work. A good example is the 'request for proposal' process adopted by many public and increasingly private-sector organisations. The concept is sound – you specify what you want and ask consultancies to submit their response. What tends to happen is that the procurement process is managed by procurement specialists who have an interest in defining the requirements in such a way that they can measure and assess responses and internal experts who frame the problem. The question is always, what if the way the problem is framed doesn't give the whole story? Experts make limiting assumptions about what the problem is and what the solution should be. They write detailed specifications based on what has worked in the past and set selection criteria linked to their experience. A consequence is that many, and potentially more innovative, suppliers rule themselves out (or are ruled out by the process) because procurement specialists don't think their offering is relevant.

An example of this is given in Zynga's blog when he tells the story of the International AIDS Vaccine Initiative (IAVI), which launched an open challenge to the scientific community to propose an effective inoculation against AIDS. The request for proposal was defined as a "vaccine challenge" and didn't elicit many quality responses. When the issue was re-framed as a "protein stabilization challenge" over 34 high-quality proposals were received from scientists in 14 countries, most of whom wouldn't see themselves as vaccine specialists. Of these, three were considered promising enough for further development with significant IAVI funding.

Another example of too much knowledge being a dangerous thing comes from the world of information technology. Writing in the *MIT Sloan Management Review*,[53] Andrew McAfee addresses both the scale of investment in information technology and the disappointment that 30–75 percent of this investment results in new systems that don't live up to expectations – financial impact, improved work processes or organisational change. This is a statistic that hasn't changed much over the past two decades despite the amount of experience we now have in implementing large-scale systems and change management. Why is this?

McAfee points to knowledge and experience. He notes that typically the quality of people working on large systems implementations is very high, whether it is internal management or external consultants, IT vendors or academics. He even notes that managers tend to take on board advice and are attentive to understanding 'best practices'. He also points out that this combination is also a contributory factor to poor implementation. It isn't the lack of brainpower or advice that is the problem, or the lack of checklists. The fundamental problem is that a one-size-fits-all approach is often taken without recognising that the circumstances of implementation are different for every project and that experts are not flexible enough in adapting their thinking. What may have been a 'best practice' in organisation X may require a different practice in organisation Y. An example McAfee gives is of the advice to "secure top-level management support". You can't argue with that. Yet the type and level of support needed varies enormously from project to project, even within an organisation.

McAfee adds that "successful leadership of an IT implementation will continue to be a subtle craft" and concludes that IT-enabled business transformation will continue to be plagued by catastrophes and high rates of failure and disappointment because technology can never trump the unique human, organisational and process considerations in each organisation. Knowledge and experience only gets us so far. Being able to apply this knowledge in uncertain environments requires us to explore what we don't know.

The Dangers of Adjacent Moves

Adjacent moves stem from our belief that experience and success in one area fully equip us to be successful in an adjacent area. There are some notable examples and failures from the world of business.

In the 1980s and '90s, Sir Clive Thompson, CEO of Rentokil, was the darling of British business. Known as 'Mr Twenty Percent' due to his track record of 20 percent growth in profitability each year, Thompson not only had longevity at the helm of a leading business but experience of leading 130 acquisitions. Under pressure to maintain this extraordinary pace of growth, Thompson had to seek larger deals. In 1994, he acquired Securiguard and increased the size of Rentokil by 30 percent in one stroke. This was followed in 1996 by the acquisition of BET. This acquisition more than doubled the new business and led to the creation of the current organisation, Rentokil Initial.

The deals were not a success and the share price tumbled. More importantly the culture created in Rentokil was compromised.

Thompson was asked to resign his position shortly afterwards. What went wrong? There are many possible explanations but the two that stand out the most were Thompson's fixation with 20 percent growth (it would have been hard to become 'Mr Ten Percent' after such a long run) and his own reflection that he was misled by his experience. He realised afterwards that just because he had successfully led 130 small acquisitions he could also lead big acquisitions. He treated them as equal challenges when they weren't. It is fair to say too that Thompson had a strong emotional attachment to deal making and acquisitions – it gave him a buzz and he is quoted as saying: "Better to live like a lion for a day than a lifetime as a lamb".[54]

What happens when we encounter situations that are similar to others we have encountered is that the brain makes a connection. We focus on the familiar and notice the similarities. We convince ourselves that just because we did something similar successfully, we can also address the new situation successfully. Sometimes we can, but we shouldn't assume it! This effect is called the *availability heuristic*[55] by psychologists and is associated with a number of other thinking errors. The *recency and vividness bias* highlights our tendency to access more recent and vivid information before older and less vivid information, even when digging deeper into our memory may be more relevant. The *retrievability bias* spotlights easier-to-access information and memories over harder-to-access information, even when the latter is more relevant. The *presumed association* bias searches and amplifies the associations between two situations instead of accepting that there are times when there are no associations.[56]

Missing the Solution in Front of Our Noses

When the *Titanic* hit the iceberg, an obvious route to survival was missed. Fixated by the fact that the iceberg was the cause of the disaster and the knowledge that icebergs can sink ships, people overlooked the possibility that the size, shape and stability of the iceberg meant that it offered them one of the safest options for survival. With an estimated height of between 50 and 100 feet and length of between 200 and 400 feet, the *Titanic* could have pulled aside the iceberg and offered people a flat place to stay for a few hours before help arrived.[57] Why was such an opportunity missed? Put simply, it's possible that the people in charge didn't manage to think beyond the horizons of their own experience.

The poet Alexander Pope once wrote that "a little learning is a dangerous thing".[58] This is a very insightful statement: a little learning can easily persuade us that we are more expert than we really are. Pope's verse has since been adapted over the years into the expression "too much knowledge is a dangerous thing". Perhaps the voice of the people has long understood the downside of knowledge and experience, recognising that with deep expertise comes a narrowing of focus that excludes solutions that exist outside of the experts' field of vision. We could say that psychology is only now catching up with the science to explain this popular understanding.

PART 2

The Characters in Our Heads

"To effectively communicate, we must realise that we are all different in the way we perceive the world and use this understanding as a guide to our communication with others."

Tony Robbins

7

Breaking Patterns of Thinking

"We are what we repeatedly do. Excellence, then, is not an act but a habit."

Aristotle

In 2005, the late writer David Foster Wallace told the following tale at a graduation ceremony at Kenyon College:[59] "There are two young fish swimming along and they happen to meet an older fish swimming the other way, who nods at them and says 'Morning boys, how's the water?' The two young fish swim on for a while and then one turns to the other and asks, 'What the hell is water?'"

For much of our life we operate on automatic pilot with routines that require virtually no thought. We stand in the same place on the station platform each morning or take the same route to work, visit the same coffee shop on the way in and so it goes on. Throughout the day habitual patterns of behaviour guide our actions. Our habits are like familiar, comfortable clothes. Many practical habits are helpful and don't require us to think too deeply. But some habitual thought patterns and responses can be destructive and unhelpful.

Wallace used the tale of the two young fish to remind his students of this – that our lives are influenced by many factors we do not tend to notice. For the fish, the water represents the unconscious choices and invisible decisions at work in our everyday lives. Wallace wanted to encourage students to be more attentive to their environment and these unconscious, invisible forces that shape our habits. He hoped students would consciously choose how to perceive others, think about meaning and act appropriately in everyday life. His message was that we do have a choice about what we think and what we pay attention to: that there are other options to our habitual routines.

In Chapters 3 to 6, we highlighted research that has helped us to understand the unconscious forces in our choices and how thinking errors identified through this research could be clustered into four substantive categories – **R**elationships, self-**I**nterest, **S**hortcuts and **K**nowledge & experience (our Hidden R-I-S-K™ framework). Chapters 9 to 16 take the Hidden R-I-S-K™ framework to a deeper level, introducing you to eight characters that embody clusters of thinking errors. Before we move on we need to recognise that many of our choices, and underlying thinking processes, are products of habit – whether made by individuals or groups (large and small). To make better choices, we also need to break unhelpful patterns of thinking and establish new, generative habits.

In his excellent book *The Power of Habit*,[60] Charles Duhigg sets out how habits form in individuals, companies, organisations and societies. He notes that habits are "the choices all of us deliberately make at some point and stop thinking about but continue doing, often every day".[61] Research published by Duke University in 2006[62] found that more than 40 percent of the actions performed by people each day weren't actual decisions, but habits. The Hidden R-I-S-K™ framework needs to be understood through this lens of habit formation. Our unconscious is actively at work in the many choices we make each day and thinking errors will be an inherent part of these choices. Knowing how we form habits means we also acquire the key to unlock them.

As Charles Darwin so eloquently observed, our ability to change is a key element to our survival, not our fitness. Yet our habits are hard to break. How often do you stick to your New Year resolutions, or that revolutionary new diet, or that fitness regime, or that new hobby you always wanted to take up, or to getting up 30 minutes earlier for some 'me time' before the day really kicks in? Habits are indeed hard to break – but not impossible.

Received wisdom suggests that changing habits is simply a matter of willpower. Willpower certainly has its place, but scientists are discovering that the greatest obstacle to shifting a habit is not a lack of willpower but a lack of understanding of how a habit works.

How Habits Work

During the 1990s, researchers at the Massachusetts Institute of Technology Brain and Cognitive Sciences Department[63] discovered a simple neurological loop at the core of every habit. They called it the *habit loop* and it comprises the following three steps:

- **Trigger** – a cue that tells our brain to go into automatic mode and which habit to use
- **Routine** – a physical, mental or emotional response to the trigger
- **Reward** – an outcome that helps our brain to figure out if this particular loop is worth remembering.

As the researchers studied people and organisations, they realised that the *habit loop* not only helped us to understand how habits are formed but also how habits could be broken or reset. What researchers found was that people who had successfully changed their habits had done four things:

1. Successfully identified the *routine* around their habit

2. Experimented with different *rewards* to satisfy the craving the routine was trying to meet
3. Isolated the *trigger* that initiated the habit in the first place
4. Put a *plan* in place that would help them respond differently to the trigger that initiated the routine.

A 2015 BBC documentary *What's the Right Diet for You?*[64] demonstrated the power of the *habit loop* in tackling one of the biggest problems facing modern Britain today – obesity. In the UK, 67 percent of men and 57 percent of women are considered to be overweight or obese. The UK has the third-highest rate of excess weight measured in terms of Body Mass Index in Western Europe, being behind only Iceland and Malta. Yet, as the BBC documentary explored, not all weight issues are a result of constant overeating. There are other factors that come into play and around 30 percent of people who are overweight carry excess weight because they are 'emotional eaters'.

Emotional eaters have a habit of overeating as a response to stressful situations. Most emotional eaters are not aware of their habit and wonder why they are piling on the pounds. To tackle their destructive habit, emotional eaters have to become aware of the routine they unconsciously engage in before they can address their overeating successfully.

In this BBC documentary, a group of emotional eaters (all specially selected volunteers) who were largely unaware of their overeating habit were put through an experiment. The thesis was that people ate more in response to stressful situations. They were therefore given a driving test (which provided a stressful situation to cope with) followed by a buffet-style meal. As the psychologists on the show had predicted, all participants became very stressed indeed when they sat the driving test with some even reduced to tears. Afterwards, all the participants piled their plates high with food at the buffet.

When the participants were shown the footage of themselves eating at the buffet, they could not believe the mountains of food they had just devoured. They had been totally unaware of the way they used food to reward themselves after stressful situations. Through reviewing the footage played back to them, these emotional eaters were able to pinpoint their routine and understand how they used food as a reward following stress.

The psychologists in the programme then set to work with the volunteers. First they helped them to recognise the triggers – understanding when and how they become stressed – and then to understand what triggers their behaviour. The psychologists then replaced food with social support and interaction as an alternative reward for stress. Instead of reaching for the content of the fridge whenever they felt stressed, the volunteers were encouraged to reach for their mobile, laptop or phone in order to contact each other for mutual support. Replacing the reward of food with social support and interaction cracked the habit and proved very successful as the group of volunteers achieved staggering weight loss.

What we see in this powerful example is the habit loop at work:

Figure 3: The Habit Loop of the Emotional Eater

In the same way that the emotional eaters were unaware of their overeating routines, we are also largely unaware of our thinking habits. Our unconscious kicks in and thinking errors play out without a second thought on our part. This is due to a phenomenon in our thinking patterns that we highlighted earlier in this book.

In Chapter 1, we referenced the work of Nobel laureate Daniel Kahneman into System 1 and System 2 thinking. If you recall, System 1 thinking is where fast, intuitive decision making happens. System 2 is where more deliberate, slower thinking happens. Our thinking habits sit very much in the domain of System 1 and, as Kahneman has highlighted, this is fine for straightforward decisions requiring little effort (helpful habits and routines) but is inappropriate when we are faced with more difficult judgements where there may not be a clear-cut answer and where we may need to deal with greater complexity and ambiguity.

Habit formation is therefore tightly intertwined with our thinking errors. Take a recruitment situation through the lens of habit formation. The trigger is the initial judgement made on a candidate. Let's say the candidate is overweight and has prominent and visible tattoos. The role you are recruiting for means that the role holder will be your face to the public. The trigger for the recruiter may be what is already in their mind – negative opinions about tattoos and weight shaped by a prior experience. The person who just walked through the door reminded them of a narcissistic, anarchic bully they had to put up with in their late teens. For them, the routine was not to look beyond those already formed opinions and to focus only on the evidence that confirmed their pre-existing beliefs. The reward was satisfaction that the selected data backed up their underlying belief about people who are overweight and have tattoos, leaving them feeling satisfied that their decision to reject the candidate 'felt right' and that they are skilled in reading people very quickly.

This is only just one simple example of how a thinking error is an unconscious habit. We believe that most thinking errors can be understood as the result of unconscious habits.

In the next chapter we will show how common thinking errors can be embodied in eight characters. Getting to know these eight characters gives us a way to access our unconscious routines. That's where the habit loop comes in and provides us with the key to break out of our patterns of thinking. As we progress through Part 2 and get to know each of the characters in more detail, we will build an understanding of the *habit loop* associated with each so that we can change the way we think – not just for today but permanently. What we now know from the field of neuroscience is that, contrary to conventional wisdom, you *can* teach that old dog a new trick!

One of the most significant scientific findings of the last fifty years is that of brain plasticity. Brain plasticity, also known as neuroplasticity or cortical remapping, is a term that refers to the brain's ability to change and adapt as a result of experience. Up until the 1960s, researchers believed that changes in the brain could only take place during infancy and childhood. By early adulthood, it was believed that the brain's physical structure was permanent. Modern research has demonstrated that the brain continues to create new neural pathways and alter existing ones in order to adapt to new experiences, learn new information and create new memories.

Our understanding that the brain we are born with is not fixed, but instead is a mutable organ that is adaptable and can be trained to overcome our deficiencies, has huge implications for the way we view ourselves and our capacity to change. When it comes to making better decisions we *can* train ourselves to form new habits. Our brain *can* create new neural networks that take account of our new understanding of thinking errors.

In the next chapter, we introduce you to eight characters who will help you to make conscious the unconscious forces at work in your choices. Understanding and recognising our unconscious routines is the key to habit change and the eight characters we introduce in our Hidden R-I-S-K™ framework will provide you with a powerful tool to access these **routines**. In the following chapters you will learn how to recognise the ***triggers*** that bring unconscious biases into play and the ***rewards*** associated with each routine. Most importantly, through standing in the shoes of each of the eight characters, you will be able to develop strategies to be more intentional about your decisions so that poor thinking habits can be broken for good.

8

Making the Unconscious Conscious

"Simple can be harder than complex. You have to work hard to get your thinking clean to make it simple."

Steve Jobs

By all accounts, Steve Jobs was not an easy boss. People who worked for him recall that he often responded with verbal abuse to people he considered to be wasting his time. Anyone whom he thought rambled, he cut off. He was also tough in evaluating ideas. Jobs often rejected people's work. Not because it was bad, but because it failed to distil the idea to its essence. His colleagues called it being hit with the "simple stick".

The *simple stick* symbolised a core value within Apple that many believe has been responsible for the global appeal of Apple's products. Jony Ive, who was the head designer for Apple under Jobs, described the importance of simplicity in product design as follows:

> Simplicity isn't just a visual style. It's not just minimalism or the absence of clutter. It involves digging through the depth of complexity. To be truly simple, you have to go really deep. You have to deeply understand the essence of a product in order to be able to get rid of the parts that are not essential.[65]

In the modern world, simplicity grabs our attention. What is true of design is also true of communication. We all suffer from cognitive overload as we are bombarded with the noise of information. We live in a communication blitzkrieg where the sound bite is the message that hits its mark. The sound bite is effective because it is short and crisp. It has visual and verbal dimensions, striking with the precision of a laser beam. Sound bites are memorable; long, convoluted explanations are not. Sound bites represent simplicity in communication because they capture the essence of ideas, thoughts and feelings.

What designers, innovators and communicators are doing through simplifying an idea to its essence is a process Steve Jobs called "getting our thinking clean". We have embraced this principle of simplicity and clean thinking in making sense of the 100-plus thinking errors that have been identified by neuroscientists, cognitive psychologists and behavioural economists. Clustering these thinking errors into the four areas of the R-I-S-K framework was an important first step in simplifying a complex array of biases. In itself, R-I-S-K goes a long way in providing us with a memorable framework to identify thinking errors in ourselves and in others. Remembering the four areas of R-I-S-K is already a more manageable task than trying to remember more than 100 thinking errors.

R-I-S-K doesn't quite get us the whole way there, though. It doesn't quite capture the *essence of the internal processes* at work and it doesn't give us a language to have productive, generative conversations about the unconscious, emotional aspect of our decision making. Being told that you have a few issues with self-interest thinking errors is unlikely to lead to a productive and generative conversation!

The tricky dilemma we have wrestled with is how to get our thinking clean on internal processes and routines which are essentially unconscious – how can we make the unconscious conscious? How can we surface thinking errors in a way that enables us to make better choices?

A Lesson from the World of Therapy

One group of professionals which has had more than a century of experience in dealing with how we think about things and whose very purpose is to make the unconscious conscious is that of psychoanalysts, therapists and counsellors. Their work is to help people understand their internal processes. So how do they do it?

An early technique therapists used to bring the unconscious into conscious awareness is psychoanalysis. Psychoanalysis was invented in the 1890s by Sigmund Freud, a Viennese psychiatrist, and is still widely used today. The essence of psychoanalysis is an "in the moment demonstration" of how the brain can wrongly make assumptions about a current situation on the basis of past experience. The psychoanalyst helps clients first to recognise their unconscious responses, then to realise that these responses belong in the past and, finally, to shift to a new way of being.

Later therapeutic interventions include a technique called 'externalisation'. Externalisation is used widely and successfully in family therapy. Through the use of this technique, internal processes can be externalised through painting, storytelling or even representation with stones. Let me give you an example from the counselling room:

> A woman in her early thirties came to counselling in order to work out what to do. She had been badly let down by a former partner, who had finished their long-standing relationship shortly after she found out that she was pregnant by him. The relationship broke up because the former partner had found another woman. The client was still in the early stages of pregnancy when she came to counselling, so had the option of having a termination. She was very confused about the situation and was hurting badly from the break up. She was in two minds about keeping the baby.
>
> She was asked to use stones in order to represent her family relationships. She chose two stones of equal size to represent

herself and her partner and she placed those stones far from each other. She then selected another stone and placed it near her former partner to represent his new girlfriend and then proceeded to arrange a series of stones in a circle around the stone representing her: these were close family and friends who were supporting her at this difficult time. Finally, she found the tiniest stone in the box of stones and used this to represent the foetus.

As she placed this tiny stone on top of her stone she burst into tears. Later on she said that when she placed the tiny stone on her stone she realised that she was already attached to the baby and never wanted to let go of this little life, which was already part of her.

Here, externalising relationships and emotions through the use of stones was a powerful and effective technique in making the unconscious conscious.

Another approach to externalisation is used when a child comes into therapy with anxiety issues. In these cases, the child will frequently be unable to express exactly how he or she feels. The feelings are only understood in a very nebulous fashion, if at all, as being 'odd' or 'weird'. Alternatively, they might be described in terms of the behaviours they induce, such as 'hiding behind mummy' or expressions they use such as 'being a bad girl or boy'.

In these situations, therapists respond by encouraging children to give their anxious feelings a separate identity, such as the 'worry bug'. The worry bug becomes the vehicle through which the child can express all those confusing feelings they are experiencing; it boils these anxieties down to their essence. The child is able to talk about the worry bug: when it appears; when it is strong; when it is less strong; what it is feeling and so on. This gives the child a measure of control over their anxious feelings and enables them to talk about what they are experiencing at the unconscious level.

We know that choices are made invariably at the emotional level. Regardless of how well our logical and rational thinking processes operate, it is at the level of emotions and feelings that the final calls are made. The clustering of cognitive biases into the four areas of R-I-S-K gives us a powerful framework to help us locate potential thinking errors. But our understanding of these thinking errors is still operating largely at the logical–rational level. We know about them but we still aren't really tuning in to what is really happening at the unconscious, emotional level of decision making.

To bridge this gap between the logical–rational and the emotional levels, we have learnt from the technique of externalisation and simplification to distil these thinking errors into eight characters. These characters each embody a sub-cluster of thinking errors and help us to understand our habits and tune into our unconscious, emotional–feeling responses to the choices we face.

The Essence of Our Thinking Errors: Introducing Eight Characters

Our eight characters each represent the hidden risks in our decisions. They embody different biases within the four areas of R-I-S-K: two characters for each cluster of thinking errors. These eight characters each embody different facets of their respective thinking errors. Through these characters we are able to see more clearly the unconscious forces at work in our choices and their consequences. In Steve Jobs' terms, the combination of our eight characters with R-I-S-K gets us to the essence of thinking errors in decision making. This Hidden R-I-S-K™ framework simplifies the complex and, as we shall see, provides us with a language that enlarges the open space of effective decision making.

Chapters 9 to 16 explore each of the eight characters in detail. The rest of this chapter gives a brief introduction to each.

Hidden R-I-S-K™ Framework

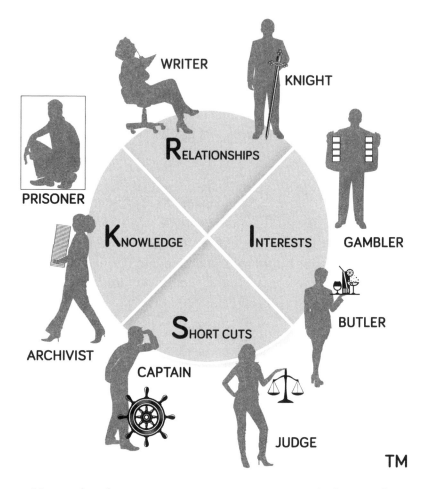

How thinking errors are expressed through EIGHT characters we find in all of us

Each of these characters is present in all of us. One or more of the characters will come to the fore in any decision we have to make. Sometimes, all eight characters might be active in a decision. On other occasions maybe only one or two of the characters will surface.

Each of these characters embodies a cluster of unconscious biases. We improve our decision making through being mindful of which characters are at work in our decisions and taking actions to mitigate their work.

Relationship Thinking Errors

In Chapter 3 we noted how attachment was both central to our functioning as human beings and also the source of thinking errors in decision making. There are two main manifestations of thinking error linked to relationships and these are embodied in the following two characters:

The Writer

The Writer in us uses past relationships as a reference point for current choices. As a result the Writer writes scripts about people, situations, ideas, things, organisations and so forth that may or may not be true.

It is important that we understand how the Writer works – confusing reality with the narrative we are writing based on past relationships.

Can you think of an occasion when you wrote a script about someone or something in your mind that later turned out to be incorrect?

The Knight

The Knight in us defends attachments and relationships that we have forged.

It is important that we understand how the Knight works – defending relationships of all kinds even in the face of compelling evidence that suggests we are wrong.

Can you think of an occasion when you have defended a relationship with a person, idea or course of action even when there was evidence that such a defence would not have a positive outcome?

Self-Interest Thinking Errors

In Chapter 4 we noted how self-interest can be a dynamic and positive force for good in our world but when misdirected it becomes a significant source of thinking errors. We also observed that the impact of misdirected self-interest is pervasive and affects the choices of the most thoughtful and upstanding people and that it creeps into our choices even if we are actively trying to be unselfish and collaborative. There are two main manifestations of thinking error linked to self-interest and these are embodied in the following two characters:

The Gambler

The Gambler in us manipulates situations to our own advantage through displaying overconfidence and over-optimism concerning the outcomes of the situation.

It is important that we understand how the Gambler works – accentuating the positives and failing to assess correctly the downsides of a choice.

The **GAMBLER** Can you think of an occasion when you have been over-optimistic or have made unrealistic forecasts for particular projects or situations?

The Butler

The Butler in us assumes a passive role, by adopting a subservient stance in relation to those who have power over us.

It is important that we understand how the Butler works – serving up what we think people want to hear rather than what needs to be said.

The **BUTLER** Can you think of an occasion when you have gone along with the majority, or your boss, even when you have believed that course of action is not the right one?

Shortcut Thinking Errors

In Chapter 5 we noted that psychologists have long understood that humans use cognitive shortcuts to expedite decision making. As a result, we are often lazy thinkers who value speed over the quality of our decisions. There are two main manifestations of thinking error linked to shortcuts and these are embodied in the following two characters:

The Judge

The Judge in us is more like a reality TV judge and focuses on information that elicits an emotional response from us and rates this information as more significant.

It is important that we understand how the Judge works: placing significance on what stands out – whether it is a person's reputation, specific information or features – and connects with us emotionally.

Can you think of an occasion when you have agreed with someone's ideas just because of their reputation or have connected emotionally with the way they put their ideas across?

The Captain

The Captain in us selects information in order to confirm an already predetermined decision.

It is important that we understand how the Captain works – selecting information that steers us in a particular direction.

Can you think of an occasion when you have made your mind up about a decision before you looked at the evidence?

Knowledge and Experience Thinking Errors

In Chapter 6 we noted that the application of our knowledge and expertise is crucial and that the misapplication of past learning and overreliance on expert knowledge can be a source of thinking errors. There are two main manifestations of thinking error linked to knowledge and experience and these are embodied in the following two characters:

The Archivist

The **ARCHIVIST**

The Archivist in us categorises a situation on the basis of past experience only.

It is important that we understand how the Archivist works – relating the current decision to similar ones experienced in the past.

Can you think of an occasion when you fell back on past experience to make sense of a situation and it turned out to be quite different?

The Prisoner

The **PRISONER**

The Prisoner in us interprets a situation from the vantage point of their own worldview or expertise.

It is important that we understand how the Prisoner works – seeing the world through a narrow lens of their expertise.

Can you think of an occasion when you were so fixed on looking at a problem in a particular way that you failed to see alternative ways to solve that problem?

Summary: The Story so Far

Our starting point is that no-one makes bad decisions out of choice but researchers have found that we are all prone to unconscious biases – the hidden risks in our decisions.

The effect of unconscious biases will be situational. Not noticing and addressing them can have a significant impact on the effectiveness of our decisions.

The difficulty in making better decisions is that we simply cannot attend to 100-plus thinking errors. We need a simpler, more memorable way to help us identify and address our thinking errors.

The Hidden R-I-S-K™ framework addresses this gap. Thinking errors are clustered into four areas around the most common sources of error: **R**elationships, self-**I**nterest, **S**hortcuts and **K**nowledge. The acronym R-I-S-K is not only easier to remember but also accurately describes the impact of thinking errors on our environment as risk is inherent in our choices and becoming aware of these downsides is the first step to breaking patterns of thinking in decision making.

Within each of the four areas of R-I-S-K we identified two main manifestations of unconscious biases. The eight characters – the Writer, the Knight, the Gambler, the Butler, the Judge, the Captain, the Archivist and the Prisoner – each embody different unconscious biases. Understanding how the different characters work – in ourselves and others – will help us to recognise and mitigate sub-optimal decisions. The characters also provide us with a neutral, non-judgemental language to challenge unconscious biases and open the possibility of dialogue about these complex psychological processes with others.

Unconscious biases can also be understood through the lens of habit formation. Unconscious biases are played out through the habit loop and have a trigger, a routine and a reward. In chapters

9 to 16 we will explore the character-specific habit loops and these character-specific habit loops will form the starting point for a systematic approach to the mitigation of thinking errors.

Hidden R-I-S-K™ framework

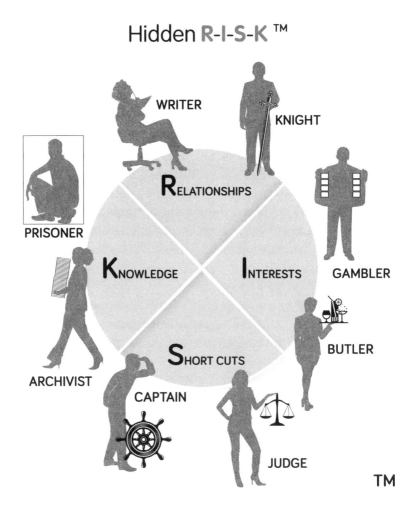

The eight chapters that follow focus on each of the characters that embody unconscious biases. We have written the chapters so that you get to know the character through stories and examples of how they influence our decisions at the unconscious level. In introducing each character we:

- Write a short sketch describing the character and how they influence our choices
- Give a motto the character might use
- Provide a summary of what you need to remember about each character
- Suggest pointers to what smart deciders do to counteract the influence of the character.

We have already stressed that each of our eight characters embody the essence of the 100-plus unconscious biases identified through research in the fields of neuroscience, cognitive psychology and behavioural economics.

We also explore the eight characters from the vantage point of habit formation. We develop character-specific habit loops that help us to understand the mechanisms underlying our unconscious biases.

Finally, at the end of each chapter we have set out a summary of key points along with some questions for you to use to reflect on how the respective character may be at work in your choices.

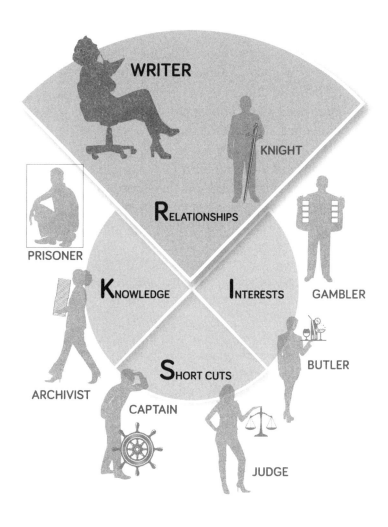

WRITER

KNIGHT

RELATIONSHIPS

PRISONER

GAMBLER

KNOWLEDGE

INTERESTS

ARCHIVIST

BUTLER

SHORT CUTS

CAPTAIN

JUDGE

9

The Writer

The
WRITER

"And as imagination bodies forth
The forms of things unknown, the poet's pen
Turns them to shapes and gives to airy nothing
A local habitation and a name."

William Shakespeare,
A Midsummer Night's Dream

The Writer's Tale

I am the Writer. I try to make sense of unfamiliar people, situations, ideas or things by writing a script about them. I create a story by filling in the gaps with information I have gathered in my memory bank. These stories can reflect my own self, project my past associations or simply be pieces of random information I have picked up over time. I think that my stories are true even though they are often not an accurate representation of reality.

The Writer's Motto: **"You must have a story."**

What You Need to Remember about the Writer

The Writer in us is triggered when we encounter unfamiliar situations, people and ideas.

The Writer:

- ✓ Writes scripts about people, situations, ideas, icons
- ✓ Fills in information gaps by using past associations, their own projections and random facts to create a story about a person, situation, idea or icon
- ✓ Rewards us through emphasising speed of decision making and through reinforcing our prevailing view of the world.

What Do Smart Deciders Do?

Smart decision makers:

- ✓ Understand that the Writer is at work in all of us and tune in to the stories being written in our minds
- ✓ Proactively check out these stories in the mind against the evidence
- ✓ Use these stories as a basis on which to ask deeper questions
- ✓ Are mindful of the Writer at work, particularly in conflict situations where unconstructive narratives can be written that hinder an effective resolution.

It is the CEO's first day in a new role. The business isn't performing well and the board has prioritised the need to rid the company of all slackers. At lunchtime the CEO is given a tour of the facilities and notices a guy leaning against a wall while others are busying themselves. The CEO walks up to the guy and asks, "How much money do you make a week?" Undaunted, the young fellow looks at him and replies, "I make $300 a week. Why?" The CEO then hands the guy $300 in cash and screams, "Here's a week's pay, now GET OUT and don't come back!" Feeling pretty good about his first firing, the CEO looks around the room and asks, "Does anyone want to tell me what that loafer did here"? With a sheepish grin, one of the other workers mutters, "Pizza delivery guy from Domino's".

This joke illustrates not only the dangers of making up our minds too quickly about others, but also how the Writer is activated. The CEO has been given a background narrative about poor productivity and meets an unfamiliar person. This triggers the Writer in him. He picks out one salient characteristic that aligns with the narrative of poor productivity. Namely, the person is idle. The CEO then connects the idleness he observed in the stranger with his mandate that idle people in the company must be removed. In his mind, he writes a story that is in line with his own expectations in order to make sense of the unfamiliar person's behaviour. The reward for making such an impulsive decision is speed of decision making, being seen as decisive by others and in making a 'quick win' against the mandate he had been given. The joke makes us laugh because the arrogant CEO gets it so spectacularly wrong and we can even feel a degree of schadenfreude as the pizza delivery guy gets the last laugh.

Yet we all make assumptions about others all the time and base our judgement of others on those assumptions. Our unconscious tries to find patterns in situations and behaviours based on a very narrow selection of experience. We have called this tendency to find patterns and extrapolate those patterns to fit new situations the work of the Writer in us, because just like a Writer we make sense of new situations by weaving a story through connecting disparate pieces of information. Our mind 'connects the dots' by writing a script.

When it comes to decision making, the Writer's scripts are unreliable. The stories the Writer crafts may or may not be true and the consequences of making choices based on an unreliable narrative are, as we will see, significant.

The work of the Writer is brilliantly described in the famous John Godfrey Saxe poem 'The Blind Men and the Elephant', which itself is based on an ancient Indian folk tale.[66] This poem tells a tale of how six blind men of Indostan encounter an animal they have never seen before (the elephant). Each tries to make sense of this alien creature by touching different parts of the elephant's body. Depending on which part of the body a man touched, the elephant was to him a wall, a spear, a snake, a tree, a fan or a rope. Each made sense of the elephant through writing a script based on experiencing only one part of the whole picture. As Saxe concludes:

> And so these men of Indostan
> Disputed loud and long,
> Each in his own opinion
> Exceeding stiff and strong,
> Though each was partly in the right,
> And all were in the wrong!

Again we see how the unfamiliar – in this case an elephant – triggers the Writer and how the Writer in the men of Indostan uses the familiar to explain the unfamiliar. This ancient wisdom strikes a chord with us because the scripts we all write about ourselves, the people we meet and the situations we face are a central part of what it means to be human. All of us, like the blind men, are trying to make sense of the world by writing scripts about the unknown using past knowledge and experience as reference points. As Steven Pinker writes, "cognitive psychology has shown that the mind best understands facts when they are woven into a conceptual fabric such as narrative, mental map, or intuitive theory. Disconnected facts in the mind are like unlinked pages on the Web: they might as well not exist".[67] It is our internal Writer who does the connecting and the linking for us.

The Habit Loop of the Writer

In Chapter 7, we explained how our thinking habits are formed and how understanding the *habit loop* is our key to unlocking more effective choices. When it comes to the Writer, the habit loop tends to be this:

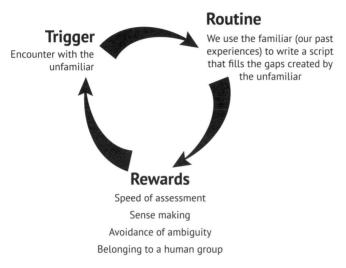

Figure 4a: The Habit Loop of the Writer

In this chapter, we will highlight how the work of the Writer impacts typical areas of decision making in organisations that have a strong people focus – like hiring decisions; decisions about who gets rewarded (whether promotions, development or remuneration); how conflicts arise; and how our scripts about ourselves and others affect how well we perform. An undercurrent in all these areas is that of inclusion and diversity and we will see throughout how the Writer's scripts skew our thinking about gender, ethnicity, age and other ways we discriminate between people. The research that helps us to understand the work of the Writer comes from a variety of sources and includes some significant studies from outside the corporate world. Although these studies have a different setting to that of the typical organisations, their findings are highly relevant and transferable, offering great insights into the impact of the Writer on our choices – whatever the context.

Having read this chapter, you will be familiar with the work of the Writer in distorting typical people-management decisions and will be able to use these insights to spot the Writer at work in other areas of decision making.

Our Choices in Hiring

Imagine you are about to be interviewed for a new job. You have done your homework and prepared well. You have researched the company, looked up on LinkedIn the bios of key people you might be working with and have thought carefully about the key points you want to get across. You are ready to make a big impression. You have been told that your meeting will last up to ninety minutes, but how long do you think you have to impress the person you will meet – ninety minutes, until you have answered their first question or some other timescale?

Research into hiring decisions (and indeed speed dating!) suggests that the amount of time you have to make that powerful impression is actually the blink of an eye. Your prospective new boss has probably made up their mind before you have even finished introducing yourself properly. The Writer in us leads us to form impressions about a person or group in split seconds. Startling research from Princeton University suggests that it takes just one tenth of a second for us to make a good first impression before someone has formed an opinion of us.[68]

Whether it is tenths of a second or slightly longer, high-speed judgments are made because the Writer in us works through associations. People we come across are automatically assigned to categories associated with age, gender, race, looks, status, wealth, class and so on. Once an individual is categorised, specific meanings associated with that category are automatically activated. These associations become the Writer's script and, in turn, shape both what we think about particular individuals and also how we treat them. As this process happens so quickly we are often unaware of the scripts the Writer is writing and we can easily fall into the trap of ruling someone out for a particular position just because their physical appearance, accent, weight, age or the like doesn't fit.

Here are some of the most common scripts of the Writer, identified through research undertaken in the USA and Europe:

What the Writer sees: *Characteristics*	The script the Writer writes: *Associations*
Obesity	• Lack of self-discipline • Lazy • Unattractive • Lack of motivation
Older people	• Outdated • Incompetent • Kind, friendly... but frail • Unproductive and slow
Men	• Strong • Task orientated • Assertive • Less emotionally intelligent
Women	• Weak • Needing support • Unassertive • Nurturing
Race – (African–American heritage)	• Poorly educated • Ignorant • Violent & aggressive (males) • Uncooperative • Lazy

These are very powerful (and often toxic) stereotypes that work at the subconscious level in our choices. When we follow the Writer's lead without checking out our script against hard evidence, discrimination can happen inadvertently. The scripts listed above are to a greater or lesser extent part of our collective psyche and therefore will have an impact on how we view and even treat others.

In the UK, weight discrimination is more prevalent than other forms of discrimination, including gender and race. Doctors will treat patients less sympathetically than their thinner counterparts[69] and research in the corporate world has shown that weight discrimination occurs at every employment stage – hiring, placement, promotion, compensation, discipline and firing.

Our narratives about people who are considered to be overweight are written when we actually see them. Other research suggests that the Writer is in full flow before we even have sight of a person. In hiring situations, we start to create narratives about people from the moment we read their name.

In the United States, racial/ethnic disparities are particularly prevalent. Professors Mullainathan and Bertrand[70] examined the level of racial discrimination in the labour market by using a randomised field experiment. Nearly 5,000 CVs were sent in response to over 1,300 newspaper ads for sales, administrative and clerical jobs in Boston and Chicago. CVs were randomly assigned either a black-sounding name (such as Lakisha Washington or Jamal Jones) or white-sounding name (such as Emily Walsh or Brendan Baker) to imply the applicant's race. CVs with white-sounding names received a staggering 50 percent more call backs than those with black names. There were no statistically significant differences in discrimination across the tested occupations, industries and employers, and the level of discrimination was very similar in both cities. Federal contractors and employers who list "Equal Opportunity Employer" in their advertisements discriminated as much as other employers.

Our subconscious scripts can also be shaped by current news stories. In the aftermath of 9/11 for example, job applicants with Muslim-sounding names had a particularly tough time in the US job market, with many managers not even giving applicants an opportunity to interview.[71] Following the July 2005 London bombings by Muslim extremists, a study of Australians who played simulated computer games found that they were more ready to 'shoot' someone wearing Muslim headgear.[72]

Similar unconscious forces also prevail when it comes to age. In the UK, there was huge controversy when older women were not being employed in high-profile, prime-time television roles such as newsreaders and presenters. The letter to the UK newspaper *The Times* summarised the anger felt by many about the way we perceive age and aging:

Letter to *The Times*, 18th May 2013

Negative stereotypes of older women — and particularly successful ones — remain deeply entrenched in our collective psyche

Sir, It does not surprise me in the least that television struggles in its quest to put more older women on our screens ("TV grows up (slowly) to real women", May 16). Negative stereotypes of older women — and particularly successful professional women — remain deeply entrenched in our collective psyche. My research has shown that they get caricatured in at least three ways. There is the Battle Axe (think Margaret Thatcher before she was canonised after her death), the Seductress (Carol Vorderman or Nadine Dorries) and the Schoolmarm (Harriet Harman or Theresa May). The only stereotype that escapes this negative tag is the Pet — a woman who is nurtured by a male boss and plays on her girlish charm. The value of the Pet is that she is young, gracious, elegant and charming but wholly unthreatening. Most weathergirls fall into this category, but so do certain female presenters. Much as I love the grace and intelligence of Fiona Bruce and Sophie Raworth, they remain Pets of the institution. Until they grow old, of course, and then they are right to be cautious.

Let's hope that the campaign for real women in the media wins the public round before any more of our presenters resort to facelifts.

Professor Judith Baxter, Aston University

What this research suggests is that we need to attend very carefully to the work of the Writer in making hiring decisions. Whilst we may think we are looking objectively at the information presented to us (whether on a CV, a psychometric assessment or some other form of assessment), the chances are that our opinions about someone have already been formed through the work of the Writer. Other research suggests that the Writer's work doesn't stop at hiring. It also informs decisions about who gets promoted, developed and remunerated well.

Who We Choose to Reward and Recognise

In 2015, the boards of FTSE 100 companies were less than 25 percent women, 6 percent from ethnic minorities and only five were led by female CEOs. Seventy percent of FTSE 100 companies had no non-white person on their board and 73 percent had no women holding senior executive positions.[73] Across other European countries and in the USA, the situation was not much different.[74] Differences in who gets ahead don't just impact the boardroom (about which we have more data than for other areas, as a result of mandatory company reporting). A 2012 European Union report suggested a 16.4 percent average pay gap between men and women across EU countries.

In a recent conversation we had with a director of a global professional services firm, she recalled how their analysis of performance ratings showed top rankings dominated by white males, and bottom rankings showing a high proportion of people from ethnic minorities.

A recent article in the *Economist*[75] drew parallels between hierarchies in gorilla societies and the characteristics we put a value on that elevate mainly men into senior roles. The article noted that "the typical chief executive is more than six feet tall, has a deep voice, a good posture, a touch of grey in his thick lustrous hair and, for his age, a fit body. He stands tall when talking to subordinates". Despite changes in society that have seen more women reach senior levels and where half the world's largest 2,500 public companies have their headquarters outside the West, this image of what a successful and powerful man looks like persists. The article concludes that selection committees continue to look for that X factor and continue to find it in people who look remarkably like themselves.

There will clearly be many reasons why these statistics are the way they are and the good news is that they are improving. Our point though in highlighting these statistics is to challenge us to understand better why we reward and recognise the way we do – who we promote, invest in developing and remunerate better – and in particular to catch the Writer at work in our decision making.

Another source the Writer uses to create scripts is our childhood experience. As children we absorb very powerful messages that shape much of our worldview. Another great poet, Rudyard Kipling, explained these subconscious influences well in his poem *We and They*:

> FATHER, Mother, and Me
> Sister and Auntie say
> All the people like us are We,
> And every one else is They.
> And They live over the sea,
> While We live over the way,
> But – would you believe it? – They look upon We
> As only a sort of They!

You can read the whole poem through the link in the endnotes[76] but the point is clear – subconsciously, we create positive associations with people who are like us.

Research shows that early imprinting is particularly powerful and less likely to be overwritten by new information.[77] Associations learned in childhood tend to provide consistent material for the

Writer throughout a person's lifetime. The most basic association is 'good' or 'bad' and children learn early that their family and community are 'good' whereas outsiders who are not like their family may pose a threat. So the Writer in us will write a positive story for those people who are like us and sound like us. There also seems to be a connection between how a person has been raised and the strength of these associations. Salvatore Maria Aglioti,[78] of the Sapienza University in Rome, led a study to measure empathy for people of a different race. He and his team discovered that people feel less empathy when they see pain inflicted on a person of a different skin colour. The study involved volunteers watching a video of hands being spiked with a needle whilst having a brain scan. The study found that an empathic brain response did not show up on a brain scan when the hand was a different skin colour to viewer's own. The effect was observed in both 'black' and 'white' participants – each showing a preference for their own skin colour. The scientists behind the study maintain that their findings have no biological foundation. They are attributing the response to conditioned cultural prejudices i.e. associations from early childhood which then have become hard wired rather than inherent traits.

So what are the implications of this research and what does it tell us about the Writer at work?

The research suggests that because we tend to have greater empathy with those who are like us, the likelihood is that we are more helpful to people we consider to be like us than those who are different from us. This helps to explain why in a work situation we are more disposed to people who are like us. Much of the time we are unaware of these forces at work.

How Conflict can be Stimulated by the Writer

The Writer in us has a long memory and frequently writes the script about people we meet in the here and now, using experiences we have had with people in the past. Psychologists call this 'transference' because the Writer literally transfers the feelings associated with one relationship directly onto another. This is particularly true of feelings we have unconsciously retained from childhood. For a transfer to take place, all that is needed is for a person we encounter to remind the Writer within us of a particularly significant person we have experienced in the past. What then happens is that we deal with the person in the here and now through the experience of that past relationship.

The result is that we don't see the person for who they really are but deal with them in terms of who we think they are. A colleague may say something that triggers memories of a bad experience at school and you react as if you are back in the playground rather than in the workplace; your salsa dancing class instructor reminds you of a strict teacher with a particularly hurtful tongue, so you avoid her at all costs; the new recruit reminds you of your college friend so you crack a joke that your college friend would find funny – but it draws a blank and you think there's something wrong with this guy.

Many conflicts at work are the result of the Writer modelling a script based on someone from the past. Authority and power relationships in the workplace share some important psychological commonalities with parent–child relationships and the Writer within us is quick to pick this up. So the boss sometimes gets confused with a parental figure and negative, self-fulfilling cycles can occur when boss and employees bring unresolved childhood conflicts to the table such as hostility, expectation of failure and criticism.

Let's look at some examples of how this dynamic can play out at work:

Gordon is a 45-year-old middle manager and harbours resentment that he now has to answer to his new female boss. He constantly expects special treatment from her and is appalled when his efforts do not get the accolades he thinks they deserve. He shows his anger by showing up late or making up far-fetched excuses for not meeting the boss's deadlines. He constantly criticises her behind her back. As the new boss unconsciously reminds Gordon of his mother, the Writer in him is crafting a script that reflects that past mother–son relationship. Gordon's mother was a very strict and authoritarian woman who liked things done her way and only rewarded him on that basis. Gordon is unaware that the script he is writing for his new boss is leading him to rebel against her authority and perform poorly.

John is a 28-year-old salesman. He is highly competitive and has a high need for approval from his manager. He goes out of the way to befriend his manager and often suggests they meet up socially. Although he thinks highly of John, his manager doesn't see the need to have high levels of out-of-office social contact. As a result, John feels rejected and wounded and concludes that his manager really does not like him. John is unaware that the Writer in him has confused his boss with his father and that he is really looking for the fatherly affirmation he didn't receive as a child.

Sofia, a newly qualified accountant becomes quiet and shy when interacting with her boss. She loses all confidence when she is with her boss and avoids speaking up directly, hoping instead that her boss will be able to read her mind. When her boss does not rate her highly in the annual salary review she feels cheated, confirming her impression that he did not make the effort to get to know her. Sophia is unaware that the Writer in her is confusing the boss with her father who had a very domineering and intimidating personality.

Treating your colleagues as though they were your siblings can also be a source of conflict at work. Co-workers can feel a positive sense of common identity and destiny, but at times, interactions in teams can take on a negative, sibling-rivalry-like quality. This can become apparent when resources have to be shared out. Fights can often break out which are akin to 'sharing out the last slice of the cake'.

The habit loop in Tranference situations looks like this:

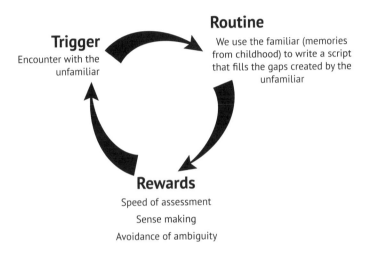

Figure 4b: The Habit Loop of the Writer

Gaining a greater understanding of our own internal Writer's scripts is an important first step in self-awareness. Psychologists at a number of American Universities – Harvard, the University of Virginia and the University of Washington – have developed Implicit Association Tests (IATs) to measure unconscious bias. The tests are free of charge and give people useful insights into their own ways of thinking.[79] *But...* 'buyer beware'! Although IATs can be helpful as an exercise in increasing our own self-awareness, they can never cover all the associations our internal Writer uses to create the scripts we write as these will be personal – as in the case of transferences, for example – and also culturally specific and situational.

Our Scripts are Situational and Different Situations will Produce a Different Script

Consider a tattooed woman. How do you feel about it? Cool, catastrophic or couldn't care less? Tattoos are currently very fashionable. Despite this, getting a tattoo does not appear to be a good move, particularly for a woman.

A laboratory-based study by Swami and Furnham[80] showed that tattooed women were associated with being less physically attractive, more sexually promiscuous and heavier drinkers than women without tattoos. A follow-on study by a different researcher[81] was carried out on a beach. Women were instructed to read a book while lying flat on their stomachs. At times they had a temporary tattoo on their lower back and at other times they didn't. More men approached the tattooed participants and in follow-up interviews men reckoned that tattooed women were indeed more promiscuous than their non-tattooed counterparts. However physical attractiveness ratings in a beach situation differed little between the tattooed and the non-tattooed. This suggests that the Writer in us makes different associations in a beach situation than in a laboratory situation. What is okay in one situation is rated differently in another situation and, as the following account portrays, can even have deadly consequences.

Professor Dr. Michael Antonio has some advice he believes can save a person's life. It's this: "Do not look bored or frightened if you are on trial for murder and are facing a jury"! Michael Antonio is Professor of Criminal Justice at Northeastern University in Boston, USA. There he led research (the Capital Jury Project – CJP) focused on how people who serve as jurors on capital cases make the life or death sentencing decision. He interviewed 80 jurors in the USA during their involvement in real-life murder cases and discovered the shocking news that whether jurors decided to hand down a life sentence or death penalty depended in part on their *perception* of the defendant's demeanour.

Even after taking into account the nature of the murder, defendants who were perceived by jurors to be sorry and sincere were more likely to be sentenced to life imprisonment than the death penalty. On the other hand, defendants who appeared bored or who looked frightening were more likely to be given the death penalty. That is despite jurors being instructed to make their decision based only on the legal facts of the case.

These findings caused a stir when they were first published and point to the persuasive powers of our internal Writer to overlook evidence in favour of the subjective impressions that shape our script about the defendant. Michael Antonio commented: "Finding that trial outcomes are not solely the result of legal facts and evidence brought out during the trial, but are attributable to extra-legal factors, including the defendant's appearance, may be disturbing to many who believe in the integrity of our criminal justice system."[82]

The Writer's script can even rewrite our memory and perception of events or people. In trying to make sense of the world, the Writer can override facts and create storylines that better align with our unconscious views about how things ought to be. For example, people remember successful black people as being 'whiter' than they really are. A study[83] suggests that when we meet someone who challenges our internal racial bias, the Writer in us sometimes edits our memory, rather than revising our original story. The research, which involved American participants, suggests that educated black men risk being remembered as paler than they really are. "Uncovering a skin tone memory bias, such that an educated black man becomes lighter in the mind's eye, has grave implications," said Professor Ben-Zeev who conducted the study.

We already know from past researchers about the disconcerting tendency to harbour more negative attitudes about people with darker complexions (e.g. the darker a black male is, the more aggressive he is perceived to be). A skin tone memory bias highlights how memory protects this 'darker is more negative' belief by distorting counter-stereotypic black individuals' skin tone to appear lighter and perhaps to be perceived as less threatening. These findings might have serious implications for any kind of witness statements, suspect descriptions or police line ups where picking out the right suspect is crucial.

Implications for Conflicts at Work

The Writer often spins a yarn when there is a discrepancy between the *expected* and the *real*. In the case of the American jurors there was a gap to be bridged – an expectation of what a remorseful defendant should look like and what the defendant actually looked like. When there is a discrepancy like this between expectation and reality, the Writer in us kicks in – in this case, demoting the importance of evidence in favour of their own narrative as to what constitutes a guilty or innocent person.

Script violations in the work place will often badly hurt people who have been the subject of the script. A study, published in the *Academy of Management Perspectives* journal, found that when a scenario depicted a conflict between two women, people considered the implications more negative and serious than a conflict involving two men or a man and a woman. The reasons why disputes between two women are considered to be more serious is that the Writer associates females with nurturing and the existence of conflict between two women threatens that nurturing image.

When participants in this study were asked to judge the likelihood of two managers repairing a frayed relationship, they rated the chances of repair 15 percent lower when both managers were female, compared to conflicts involving just men or a man and a woman. Participants also believed all-female conflicts had a stronger negative impact on job satisfaction. Interestingly, there was no difference in the way male and female participants in the study rated the different scenarios.

For the work place, such perceptions have implications. As the authors of the study noted:

> A manager might decide against assigning two female subordinates to a task that requires them to work together if he or she suspects that they cannot set their interpersonal difficulties aside or even might decide against selecting a woman for a coveted position in a work group if there is already a female member in the group, for fear that the cohesion of the group will decline as a result.[84]

These examples suggest that the Writer's work can be a powerful stimulus to conflict in the workplace. Whether it is through confusing past relationships with current ones or through distorting and misrepresenting the visual cues we pick up, the Writer puts us in a place where fact becomes confused with fiction and where misunderstandings and conflicts arise as a result.

How the Writer in Others can Limit our own Beliefs

We recently attended a baptismal service. It was quite a special occasion as one of the baptismal candidates was Alan. Alan had spent most of his life in and out of prison. Although he had most recently been given a life sentence for grievous bodily harm, he had now been released on licence (a special provision in UK law for people to serve their sentence in the community rather than prison).

The story Alan told about his life and faith journey was compelling, but one thing really stuck out. His mother had died when he was young and his father was an abusive alcoholic. At the age of seven, he said that he was told in no uncertain terms by teachers that he was a "problem child". He said that at that moment he decided that if he was a problem child, he would be a really big problem child.

In Alan's case, someone wrote a narrative about his life that would have huge consequences on how he saw himself and defined his identity. It was a script Alan himself embraced and made his own. What changed for Alan was the realisation that there was an alternative script that could be written and, when he embraced that, it also had a profound impact on his behaviours, attitudes and life chances.

A couple of years into his first job at Shell, Mark (along with all other graduate entrants) was given what was called a "current estimated potential" (CEP). This was his manager's best estimate of the level/grade Mark would reach at the end his career at Shell in his mid-fifties. The process assumed many things – not least that people would stay with Shell for their whole career. However, the biggest assumption in this process was that the manager had gained sufficient insight into someone's ability and aptitude within the first few years of work to write a narrative about their career trajectory over the next 30-plus years. We will never know whether these judgments of people early in their careers were sound or not as a high correlation between CEP and ultimate career peak could as easily be attributed to a self-fulfilling prophecy as good managerial judgement. What was certain was that those people given high CEPs quite liked the narrative that was being written about them, whilst those rated lower didn't.

There is a complex dynamic between potential and performance, and what we tell ourselves and what we tell others can have significant consequences on how well we do. Take the example of female competence at mathematics. Studies have shown that when female participants in a maths test are reminded of the stereotype that women are innately inferior at maths compared to men, they unsurprisingly perform sub-optimally at a maths task, especially when in the company of men. This effect, known as *stereotype threat*, occurs at least in part because of the anxiety that one's own poor performance will be used by the ignorant to bolster their prejudicial beliefs.

Are You the Writer?

Figure 4c: The Habit Loop of the Writer

The Writer is triggered when we come across someone or something unfamiliar. To make sense of it we will draw on our database of past experiences to write a script to predict outcomes.

Imagine going to the cinema with your partner to watch a favourite movie. You go to the ticket office and collect your ticket and then you make your way to the cinema where the film is showing. As you enter the cinema you look around in the twilight to find your seat. Slowly it dawns on you that the cinema is not only completely packed with only a few seats available, but that everyone else in the audience is a fierce-looking, big-muscled, tattoo-covered, hairy, leather-clad male biker. What would you do?

Would you make for a quick exit or stay and find your seat?

In an ad campaign devised by the Brussel's ad agency Duval Guillaume Modem for Carlsberg beer, you can see how other people reacted when they were faced with this unfamiliar and unexpected situation. Couples were secretly filmed when they walked into the cinema. While many stormed out looking annoyed, afraid and shocked, those few couples who took their seats were greeted with a huge cheer by the bikers and were handed a bottle of Carlsberg as the message "That calls for a Carlsberg" came up on the big screen. If you have not seen it, go to YouTube and join the millions who have, and watch the Writer in people writing a script about the bikers in the audience.[85]

Reflection Point

Can you think of recent examples where the Writer in you has written a script about another person or idea or thing?

What was the context in which this happened?
What was the trigger?
Where did you get material to write the script?
Did you observe a reward?

What We Have Learned in this Chapter

- The Writer reflects our tendency to write a script about unfamiliar people and situations.
- The encounter of something unfamiliar is the trigger for the Writer in us.
- The Writer's routine takes the form of us using the past to fill in a gap created by the unfamiliar.

- Seeing our decisions through the lens of the Writer helps us to understand more deeply the scripts we are writing about others as well as how we try to fill the gaps in our knowledge when faced with unfamiliar situations.
- Talking about the Writer in us writing a script for others stops us from finger pointing and provides a blame-free language to address bias in one's self and others.

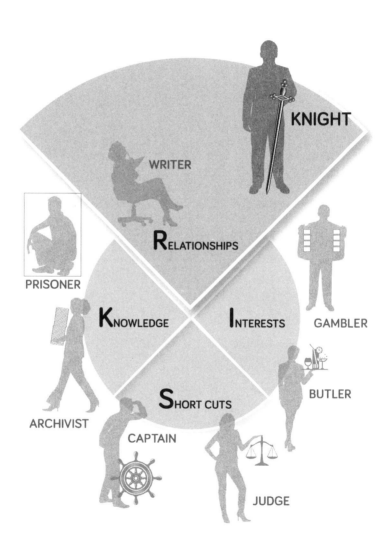

KNIGHT

WRITER

RELATIONSHIPS

PRISONER

KNOWLEDGE

INTERESTS

GAMBLER

BUTLER

ARCHIVIST

SHORT CUTS

CAPTAIN

JUDGE

10

The Knight

The
KNIGHT

"The More Important Your Cheese Is to You, The More You Want To Hold onto It."

Dr. Spencer Johnson,
Who Moved My Cheese?

The Knight's Tale

I am the Knight. I form strong attachments with people, situations, ideas and things. I defend against loss valiantly, even if it means that I ultimately lose out. I stick to set courses of action, ways of thinking and ways of working. I dislike and often resist change. I will do my utmost to save face and I will ride a dead horse if need be. When the Knight in me is strongest, I can be a fighter of lost causes.

The Knight's Motto: **"Hold on to what you have."**

What You Need to Remember about the Knight

The Knight in us is triggered when attachments we have to people, situations, ideas and things are threatened.

The Knight:

- ✓ Defends against loss
- ✓ Resists change
- ✓ Uses defensive strategies to protect that which is threatened. Typical defensive strategies include holding on, increasing investment and directly attacking the perceived threat.

What Do Smart Deciders Do?

Smart decision makers:

- ✓ Are mindful that the Knight's work is all about dealing with loss and see defensive impulses in terms of loss
- ✓ Focus on how to deal with their perceived or actual loss in constructive ways
- ✓ Understand how inappropriate attachment presents a risk to health, wealth and happiness
- ✓ Marshal the Knight at work in others to their advantage.

Why is it that we find change so difficult even in situations when we know it will be good for us? As professionals who have worked in the field of change for over 30 years, we know that this question is one that keeps puzzling anyone who is tasked to change something. As we have come to understand the unconscious working of the Knight in us, we now have a much deeper awareness of why changing anything is tough and what can be done to mitigate the workings of the Knight. Let's look at some examples.

Few people are unhealthy intentionally. Ask people on 1st January what they resolve to do in the coming year and a high percentage will say get fitter and eat healthier. Gym membership soars during that post-New Year rush to make this year the one that gets us onto that healthy-living pathway. Yet, despite knowing healthy living is good for us and despite wanting to be healthy, one of the most pressing challenges in public health is still for people to be proactive in staying healthy – to take responsibility for their own health and wellbeing. This isn't just about exercising regularly and eating healthily. It is also about people taking their medication or seeing their doctor for regular check-ups. Although most people are well aware of the consequences of their failure to perform these simple tasks to stay healthy, too many people still choose not to take proactive action. In the USA alone, the estimate cost of medical non-compliance is estimated to be as high as $100 billion per year.

Health experts have a name for this behaviour. They call it 'patient inertia'. Patient inertia has been puzzling health experts for a long time. This behaviour is hard to explain simply in terms of laziness. Research[86] has now shed new light on this baffling phenomenon. Researchers have found the reasons for this inertia to be closely aligned to the thinking errors embodied in the Knight. This research clearly demonstrates that when a large number of patients are faced with a choice that requires them to change their patterns of behaviour, most opt to do nothing, even when actions are easy to perform and could make a noticeable improvement to their current situation. The research also noted that people are also unlikely to break this habit of inertia without establishing new patterns of behaviour for a period of time. After that period of new routines, patients are more likely to choose to be more proactive about the new regime.

These findings point out the strong unconscious impulses within us to defend what we have even when we know that the alternatives are more beneficial. Paraphrasing Samuel Johnson, the multi-billionaire investor Warren Buffett cautioned that "chains of habit are too light to be felt until they are too heavy to be broken".[87]

In business, the defence of the status quo can lead to serious losses and even bankruptcy. In a *Financial Times* article,[88] John Kay posed a question: "So why didn't Sony launch their version of the iPod?" Sony was the company that created the Walkman – an analogue predecessor to the iPod. For a generation Sony was the world's most successful electronics business and the Walkman was a market leader and an iconic brand. Kay concludes that Sony executives did not rush to embrace new opportunities offered by new channels of distribution because "they saw these technological developments as threats to well established business models in which they had large personal and corporate investments".

The demise of the Walkman and the rise of the iPod and other digital alternatives are well known. As these stories are well known we may even assume that the outcome was all rather inevitable. The question posed by John Kay underlines that there was no predictable outcome here. Sony executives could have made other choices but decided to defend what they had rather than embrace a new and unfamiliar disrupter – digital technology. For them, they had an iconic global brand that was dearly loved by their customers. Their choice to defend this iconic brand illustrates well the Knight at work in decision making and a trap many business leaders can easily fall into.

The trigger for the Knight in us occurs when events threaten someone or something we hold dear and are attached to. In the case of Sony, the threat came from technological innovation. The attachment Sony executives were defending was their business model and iconic brand that had served them well in the past. Sony executives were fearful of change because they were fearful of losing what they had built up over many years.

The Habit Loop of the Knight

In Chapter 7 we explained how our thinking habits are formed and how understanding the *habit loop* is our key to unlocking more effective choices. When it comes to the Knight, the habit loop tends to be this:

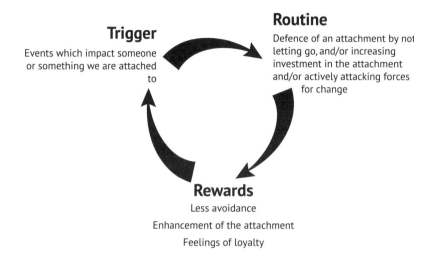

Trigger
Events which impact someone or something we are attached to

Routine
Defence of an attachment by not letting go, and/or increasing investment in the attachment and/or actively attacking forces for change

Rewards
Less avoidance
Enhancement of the attachment
Feelings of loyalty

Figure 5a: The Habit Loop of the Knight

In this chapter we will particularly focus on how the work of the Knight hinders our ability to anticipate and embrace change – personally, organisationally or within groups or teams. The research that helps us understand the work of the Knight comes from many sources. There are also a number of high-profile corporate examples such as Sony's to which we can point. As practitioners in the field of organisational change, we will also draw on some examples we have encountered that illustrate the Knight at work. Having read this chapter you will be familiar with the work of the Knight in defending attachments and will be able to use these insights to examine key choices you have to make through the lens of loss and defence against loss.

Sony is by no means an isolated example of an organisation failing to respond to external changes. The story of Polaroid almost mirrors that of Sony. Senior executives at Polaroid were so committed to their strategy of making money through selling film that they failed to respond to technological developments in digital photography. Whilst competitors powered ahead in embracing the new technology, Polaroid only released their first digital camera in 1996, four years after the prototype was ready. By that time more than three-dozen competitors had already launched theirs. Despite this, executives remained committed to their losing strategy and this eventually sent Polaroid on the road to bankruptcy, costing many employees their jobs. Every organisation, whether business, government, not for profit or voluntary, can cling on to old models that have hit the end of their shelf life or even expired.

The tribal wisdom of the Dakota Indians, passed on from generation to generation, says that: "When you discover that you are riding a dead horse, the best strategy is to dismount".

In the corporate world more advanced strategies are often employed, such as:

1. Buying a stronger whip
2. Changing riders
3. Appointing a committee to study the horse
4. Arranging to visit other countries to see how other cultures ride horses
5. Lowering the standards so that dead horses can be more productive
6. Hiring outside contractors to lift the dead horse and move its legs
7. Harnessing several dead horses together to increase speed
8. Providing training to improve the dead horse's performance
9. Running a productivity study to see if lighter riders would improve the dead horse's performance
10. Rewriting the expected performance requirements for horses, especially dead ones
11. Promoting the dead horse to a supervisory position.

The cases of Sony and Polaroid reveal that the Knight can spell disaster in terms of material and reputational loss for organisations and individuals. Recent research[89] by cognitive psychologists has made a very interesting discovery about our propensity to hold on to what we have.

This research uncovered two important insights into how the Knight in us works. First, *we tend to demand much more to give up something than we are willing to pay to acquire it.* Second, the price we are prepared to pay to hold on to something can rapidly escalate. Psychologists have found that decision makers who commit themselves to a particular course of action have a tendency to make subsequent decisions that reinforce that commitment beyond the level that can be seen as reasonable. As a consequence, resources are often allocated in a way that justifies previous commitments irrespective of whether such a commitment remains valid. Although the Knight can display exceptional bravery in the face of adversity, this bravery can easily turn to foolhardiness. Psychologists have a term for this and call it 'irrational escalation'.

Throwing Good Money after Bad: The Knight's Response to Monetary Loss

Many of the recent trading scandals such as the Swiss bank UBS's loss of $2 billion due to their star trader Kweku Adoboli's investments in 2011 or Societé General's loss of €4.9 billion in 2008 by another successful trader, Jerome Kerviel, are the result of the Knight at work. In these examples traders continued to justify increased investment in a decision even when the mounting evidence suggested that the original decision was wrong. Their rationale was that the cumulative value of the investment was now so great that the position had to be defended.

In 2006 Brian Hunter, a trader with the hedge fund Amaranth, held a financial position that predicted the rise of natural gas prices. Despite mounting evidence that natural gas prices were likely to fall, he stuck to his position. Within a week he amassed $4.6 billion in losses. This precipitated the largest hedge-fund collapse in history.

In retail banking the Knight can also cause considerable losses. Data collected from 132 Californian banks over a nine-year period[90] showed that even after their clients had already defaulted, banking executives still believed they could turn things around by giving second loans. They firmly believed that the debtors would come through their "initial financial difficulties". Only when new managers, who weren't attached to the clients or to the original decision, took over the accounts could a more objective view be taken to cut losses and write off the loans.

A famous example of the Knight holding on to a failing project is the Concorde project. Concorde was a turbojet-powered supersonic passenger airliner, developed jointly by the British and French governments. Concorde was allowed to operate for reasons of 'prestige' for 27 years, incurring huge losses to the public purse. As early as 1981, a parliamentary report suggested that Britain should drastically cut expenditure or scrap the project altogether. By that time Concorde had been flying for five years and had already incurred huge losses: Britain had paid $1.2 billion in development costs and it was estimated that another $2.7 billion were needed to keep Concorde flying for the next few years. No decision was taken to pull the plug on Concorde and to save face: the aircraft was allowed to operate for another 22 years, leaving taxpayers on both sides of the channel considerably out of pocket.

The prize for the most costly project goes to the Long Island Lighting Company. In 1965 this company set out to build the first commercial nuclear power plant. It was scheduled to commence operations in 1973 at an estimated cost of £70 million. Despite cost overruns, regulatory setbacks and evidence of economic infeasibility, the company pressed forward. In 1983, the plug was finally pulled on the project. Never having seen a day of commercial operation, expenditures had mushroomed to over $6 billion.

How Competition Feeds into the Knight's Determination to Hold On

Competition can reinforce the Knight's desire to hold on, as competition itself can be interpreted as a threat.

At the start of his course on decision making, Max Bazerman, a professor at Harvard Business School, auctions off a genuine $20 banknote to his students. How much would you expect people to pay for it – less than twenty dollars, twenty dollars exactly or more than twenty dollars?

You may be surprised to learn that the $20 banknote typically sells for more than $100. This generally causes enormous hilarity (you can only laugh or cry) once people realise how their desire to win the auction has been so great that they abandoned their 'right mind' in decision making – who in their right mind would pay more than $100 for a $20 banknote? With an average IQ of 150, Harvard undergraduates are hardly stupid. Yet the work of the Knight even misleads the brightest and the best.

Research on how we react to the prospect of losing an auction suggests that it creates a flurry of activity in the part of the brain that deals with feelings of reward and punishment. The stronger this activity in a person's brain when they lost, the more likely they were to overbid in order to win auctions on future occasions.

On a much larger scale the Knight's desire to hold on in the face of stiff competition is seen when companies pursue a takeover target. This can lead to the pursuit of reckless and ruinous bidding strategies. A high-profile example of this was the collapse of Robert Maxwell's publishing empire during the 1980s. This collapse can be attributed to a desire on Maxwell's part to outbid Rupert Murdoch, a life-long rival, in purchasing America's Macmillan publishing company. Maxwell pursued this rivalry so far that he even illegally diverted resources away from the UK pension fund in order to service the debt to finance the acquisition. The story ended tragically with Maxwell allegedly committing suicide before the true magnitude of this failed strategy unfolded with his business empire collapsing under a mountain of debt.

Other examples from the world of acquisitions include the bankruptcy of real-estate magnate Robert Campeau, who ended up buying Bloomingdale's department store for an estimated $600 million more than it was worth. Another was the ruinous bidding battle between Royal Bank of Scotland (RBS) and Barclays Bank over the acquisition of ABN-Amro Bank. Although Fred Goodwin (CEO of RBS) sealed the deal and won the battle, it ultimately contributed to his downfall and the subsequent sale of ABN-Amro to Barclays.

The Knight Defends Personal Relationships

The Knight in us is equally defensive of our relationships with people. In June 2014 the British Prime Minister, David Cameron, made a public apology for his employment of Andy Coulson.[91] Cameron had appointed Andy Coulson (a former editor of the *News of the World* newspaper) as the Conservative Party Communications Director in 2007 and then took him into government in 2010 as his Director of Communications in Number 10 Downing Street. Despite regular warnings about Coulson's involvement in phone hacking at the *News of the World*, Cameron chose to back his man. It wasn't until Coulson was convicted of conspiring to hack into phone messages that Cameron confessed to making "the wrong decision". It was noted at the time that Cameron put his relationships ahead of doing the right thing.

In Chapter 3, we recalled the story of how a sexual relationship between then World Bank Chief, Paul Wolfowitz, and a colleague led to his downfall. Despite the matter being referred to the Bank's Ethics Committee and despite Wolfowitz using his position to negotiate a substantial salary increase and promotion guarantees for his mistress, he defended both the relationship and his actions to the last. You may want to refer back to Chapter 3 to review other good examples of how we defend our attachments.

The Knight in us is willing to risk a great deal in order to hold on to and defend people with whom a relationship has been forged. For the Knight, the rewards gained through this defence are feelings of loyalty to a trusted friend or lover, and an enhancement of the relationship. This is why our unconscious can trick us. It isn't wrong to feel loyal to the people we love or our friends, and it isn't wrong to want to enhance and deepen those relationships. In many ways, the value we put on our personal relationships can be seen as heroic, particularly if we are prepared to put ourselves on the line for them. However, our understanding of the Knight at work in us also needs to trigger warning signs particularly as the defence of personal relationships has been identified as the cause of some spectacular corporate failures.

More concerning is the curse of misplaced loyalty. Randall Morck explains: "misplaced loyalty lies at the heart of virtually every recent scandal in corporate governance. Corporate officers and directors, who should have known better, put loyalty to a dynamic Chief Executive Officer above duty to shareholders and obedience to the law. The officers and directors of Enron, Worldcom, Hollinger, and almost every other allegedly misgoverned firm could have asked questions, demanded answers, and blown whistles, but did not. Ultimately they sacrificed their whole careers and reputations on the pyres of their CEOs."[92]

A case in point is that of AIG. The AIG board had been handpicked by Hank Greenberg over his years as a dominating CEO and mainly comprised two types of people: loyal friends and colleagues, and distinguished former politicians and government officials who were chosen 'to add prestige to the board'. Such a board was unlikely to be capable of challenging a dominant long-standing CEO even if it had the technical skills to understand the business – which is doubtful. This created a weakness in AIG that left important CEO decisions such as the business model unchallenged. The business model assumed 15 percent revenue growth, 15 percent profit growth and 15 percent return on equity and those who did not deliver were 'blown up'. In 2005, it emerged that AIG had 'hidden' significant underwriting losses by using creative 'reinsurance'. AIG was obliged to restate more than four years' earnings. Greenberg resigned following allegations of fraudulent accounting and the use of an offshore entity to conceal losses. AIG never recovered and in 2008 the loss was $99 billion. AIG was eventually rescued by the US Federal Reserve in an operation that required $182 billion of funding to cover debts.

Swissair is another example of how the Knight ruined a national symbol of solidity and financial propriety. We mentioned Swissair briefly in Chapter 1 as we recounted how a network of powerful relationships led to its demise. Swissair was the national carrier of Switzerland and in its heyday of the 1960s and '70s greatly profited from an excellent reputation as a quality airline and from the fact that the political neutrality of Switzerland allowed the company to fly to exotic, lucrative destinations in Africa and in the Middle East. Swissair was known as the 'flying bank' and was a national institution. Many a Swiss youngster wanted to become a Swissair pilot or Swissair cabin crew. Working for the company was hugely prestigious.

When Swissair collapsed under a mountain of debt in 2002, Switzerland went into a period of national mourning and recrimination. Many books have been written on the demise of the company and a film has even been made about this story. Although there are many factors which contributed to the collapse of the company, two errors played a pivotal part in this Swiss tragedy which can be attributed to the Knight at work: first, the emotional connections between the CEO and the McKinsey Company; second, the emotional connection of Swissair staff to their own brand.

The story goes as follows. With European deregulation of the airline industry, Swissair needed a new strategy to survive increasing competition. Together with McKinsey & Company the then CEO, Philippe Bruggisser, formulated what was to become known as the 'Hunter' strategy. It was a disastrous expansion plan. Swissair Group invested heavily in second-tier, unprofitable aviation companies, many of whom were in serious trouble with large debts, low revenues and large losses. In many cases, the acquisitions were overpriced. Also, the speed and reach of the acquisitions were too great, making it impossible for Swissair Group to properly restructure and improve the loss-making companies. Another problem with this strategy was its method of financing, which caused a huge accumulation of debt, overburdening the company. Bruggisser was fired when the extent of the debt was revealed in 2001.

> The lack of ample financial resources to pursue additional acquisitions and to carry out the required refinancing plans in Germany, Belgium and France forced the abandonment of this strategy. The Board felt that it would have been unreasonable to expect Philippe Bruggisser to carry out this new policy because of his personal commitment to the previous strategy.[93]

Bruggisser's dedication to the job and his personal commitment to the strategy were never in question. He worked 18-hour days to bring about business success through this ill-fated strategy. His personal commitment stemmed from a close association with Lukas Mühlemann, a former Head of McKinsey Switzerland, who was then head of Credit Suisse. Mühlemann sat on the Swissair Board. He had played a central role in Bruggisser's appointment and he coached Bruggisser throughout his time as Swissair CEO. The connection with McKinsey, via Mühlemann, was strong and Bruggisser even created a separate function within the organisation staffed with McKinsey people in order to implement the Hunter strategy.

So why was there not more pushback from inside the company? A PhD thesis investigated this question and concluded that it was the positive attachment Swissair's staff had to the firm. This strong attachment with Swissair stopped employees questioning why McKinsey virtually took over its strategic function, and their unwavering belief in the brand as 'the flying bank' stopped employees from questioning the financial health of the organisation.

The Swissair example again reveals the dark and light sides of the Knight. The dark and dangerous side of the Knight leads us to a place of unquestioning loyalty to people and brands. The light and positive side of the Knight engenders loyalty, pride and commitment to relationships.

Attachments Fuel the Knight's Defence

We know that one of the constants in life is change. The Knight often fights a rear-guard action in our lives in order to undermine change and protect the status quo. In organisations, the Knight's belligerence in the face of change can be a real drag on morale and productivity and can have disastrous consequences in terms of the bottom line. The work of the Knight can be held responsible for the resistance so widely encountered when trying to change things.

William Bridges[94] has spent much of his working life looking at how people deal with change. He differentiates change (a change in a situation) from transition (the psychological process we each go through to make sense of this new situation). His three-step model to explain personal transitions suggests that change does not start with beginnings but with endings.[95] Bridges sees resistance as our "coming to terms with endings" and "our attempts to reconcile loss". Every beginning ends something.

Bridges presents an important insight. He recognises that the Knight is hard wired in us and will certainly surface when we are faced with change. Understanding that this resistance is normal – inevitable even – will help us to see resistance through a different and softer lens.

A statistic that hasn't changed very much over the years is that 55 percent of all change efforts fail due to resistance and only 45 percent of those that do deliver benefits succeed in sustaining them.[96] The Knight's rear-guard actions are many and the most significant are:

- Confusion – obfuscation about what will and won't change
- Immediate criticism – rejecting the change prior to understanding the details
- Denial – refusing to accept that things must change or have changed
- Sabotage – taking deliberate actions to undermine change
- Passive–aggressive resistance – apparently agreeing but actually not changing at all
- Easy agreement – saying 'yes', without fully realising to what one has agreed
- Deflection – using diversionary tactics in the hope that change will go away
- Silence – refusing to give any input.

During our own experience as practitioners in the field of organisational change, we have observed all these rear-guard actions used by the Knight.

Bill had recently been appointed CEO of a government agency and was tasked with modernising the organisation. In many ways, the organisation had been successful and had a decent reputation, both in the UK and internationally. However, feedback from 'customers' identified a number of significant areas for improvement including those of culture and behaviour. As part of this strategic review, we were asked by the executive team to help the organisation identify its values. This step was completed and we then turned to embedding these values into the day-to-day operations of the organisation. In many areas of the organisation, we had very purposeful engagement. But there was one function in particular where we hit a brick wall.

There was one memorable meeting when we set aside a couple of hours with this team to consider how they could bring the values to life through their work. Despite customer feedback that identified a number of areas that could be improved, we were met with both denial and silence. During this meeting not one person could think of one thing they might do differently or better to improve the way they worked.

We later discovered that the message the head of function had given this team was that they were an elite, the cream of their profession and that they should consider the role they were performing as the pinnacle of their career. It was no wonder they defended what they had. They were attached to an idea of themselves which wasn't actually true but which was very appealing.

In one of our client organisations, we worked with a team that was in trouble. Relationships had broken down badly and large fissures appeared between a sub-group and the rest of the team. One of the factors that fuelled this divide was the way offices were configured. The sub-group was located in one corner of the office and the rest of the team located far enough away for there to be a physical, as well a relational, divide. The team leader rightly decided to integrate the team physically and reconfigured office space to enable the whole team to be co-located. What followed was a great example of passive–aggressive resistance where the sub-group delayed and delayed acting upon the office changes. Excuses used included misunderstanding what they had been asked to do, claiming workload prevented them finding time to move, partly moving their office but actually working in their old workspace and going on leave. Whilst nobody was happy with the poor working relationships in the team, this sub-group were attached to their space and the sense of identity it gave them.

A human resources team had recently gone through a restructuring and one of the major changes had been to create a shared services centre that provided an advisory and employee relations service to managers, as well as the usual personnel administration. The rationale for this change was compelling – it delivered greater quality (as expertise could be concentrated in one place), was more efficient in handling enquiries across the business and was significantly cheaper. The restructuring also changed the role of the HR managers located with management teams, who had traditionally been a one-stop shop for all enquires on people-related matters. Being a one-stop shop had given HR managers a certain status with their business colleagues and a role valued on the basis of their ability to dig managers out of difficult people-management issues.

There was much resistance to this change expressed through confusion (mixed messages about what would or wouldn't change) and denial. Managers liked their 'go to' person who could 'hand-hold' them on people-management issues and HR managers liked the kudos and value gained from that role. In the very short term, neither saw the value in changing – even if it would mean a better service to managers and a more interesting job for HR managers. Both managers and HR managers were attached to a relationship that probably worked well, but was inefficient, expensive and poorer in actual quality of support.

Brand Loyalty: A Different Kind of 'Maiden' for the Knight to Defend

A disappointed salesman from a Cola company returned from an assignment in the Middle East. A friend asked, "What happened?" The salesman explained, "When I got posted to the Middle East I was very confident that I would make a good sales pitch as Cola is virtually unknown there. But I had a problem. I didn't know how to speak Arabic. So, I decided to advertise through three posters. The first poster showed a man crawling through the hot desert sand, totally exhausted and panting. The second showed the man drinking our Cola. The third poster showed our man now totally refreshed. I had these posters pasted all over the place." "That should have worked," said the friend. The salesman replied, "Well, not only did I not speak Arabic, I also didn't realise that in Arabic you read from right to left."

This salesman, to paraphrase the British comedian Eric Morecombe, got all the right pictures, but not necessarily in the right order and therefore failed to create the brand impact he was looking for. We know that getting the brand right has a powerful impact on business performance. In 2004, Kevin Roberts, CEO of Saatchi & Saatchi, wrote a controversial book called *Lovemarks* that has crystallised the importance of emotional branding. Roberts argues that the functionally driven concept of branding has worn thin and that intense competition and more demanding (and cynical) consumers require a more emotionally defined idea of branding – 'super-evolved brands' or what he calls 'Lovemarks'. He defines a Lovemark as a product, service or entity that inspires "loyalty beyond reason", and it represents the next evolution in branding.

The biggest challenge for marketers looking forward, says Roberts, is to create a strong emotional bond for the brand and reinvigorate loyalty. "Lovemarks can reach the heart and gut, as well as the mind, creating intimate, emotional connections... Lovemarks is a relationship, not a mere transaction... you do not just buy Lovemarks, you embrace them with passion", according to Roberts.

Marketers, when building their brands, are not in the business of selling products but in forging close emotional ties with their customers. Sales are an outcome of the emotional connection they create with their customers. Marketers are relationship builders.

A major advance in this area is represented by the work of Susan Fournier[97] who used the metaphor of interpersonal relationships to study relationships between consumers and brands. In her research, a consumer and a brand are conceptualised as being in a relationship like that between two people. Prior to her work, most of the research on brand building was focused on brand loyalty and brand attitude. While these constructs were useful, they were not as rich as the relationship metaphor in understanding long-term brand associations. Fournier's work shows that it is appropriate to think of consumers as being engaged in relationships with the brands they use.

Just as the Knight in us defends relationships with people, the Knight will also defend our relationships with specific brands. This explains why some people feel extremely passionate about a particular brand. Over the years we have witnessed some classic brand wars – think Apple versus Microsoft or Android, Coke versus Pepsi, Unilever versus Procter & Gamble. And there is no doubt that brands become intertwined with our identity – think clothing, sunglasses, cosmetics, cars, phones, food and much more. A sobering thought about the power of brands was explored in a BBC program, *Secret of the Superbrands*, which was screened on 17th May 2011. A team of neuroscientists scanned the brains of Apple fans and discovered that Apple products stimulate the same part of the brain as religious imagery does in people of faith.

Even before we can read, the Knight in us is awakened through relentless advertisements. Children as young as three are able to distinguish between different brands and are known to influence their parents' purchasing decisions in favour of their preferred brand.[98] For corporates, these findings have important implications. If strong attachments are created with their brand, the Knight working in their customers will defend that brand relationship even in the face of stiff competition.

Understanding what aspect of the product their customers are defending will also give businesses important insights into how to design better products for their customers. BMW's research, for example, has shown that the Knight in BMW drivers is defending the BMW experience. Accordingly, BMWs are designed with that sensory experience in mind: it's the feel, the sound, the smell that lets the customer know they are sitting behind the wheel of the ultimate driving machine.

Brand loyalty illustrates how the Knight surrounds us in our decision making on a daily basis. To counteract the negative impact that the Knight can have on our decision making, let us remind ourselves how the habit loop of the Knight works in everyday life:

Are You the Knight?

Trigger
Events which impact someone
or something we are attached
to

Routine
Defence of an attachment by not
letting go, and/or increasing
investment in the attachment
and/or actively attacking forces
for change

Rewards
Less avoidance
Enhancement of the attachment
Feelings of loyalty

Figure 5b: The Habit Loop of the Knight

The Knight in us is triggered when we become aware of events we judge will have an impact on an attachment that is important to us, whether a person, a routine, a brand or even an investment.

Imagine you are offered a £12,000 wage increase to relocate to another city. Such a proposal triggers the Knight in us. The Knight's routine is to protect and defend an attachment from the impact of a threat. In this case, the majority of us are likely to refuse the offer because we are attached to our home, our neighbourhood, our friends and are unwilling to give these up for something unfamiliar, even if it means more money in the bank. (If you live in a lousy home, a bad neighbourhood and don't have any friends then the answer might be different, of course!)

However, how would you react if we turned the question round? Now imagine you lived in that other town and were offered a £12,000 salary cut to move back again into your hometown. Would you take up the offer? After all, you loved that old place.

Many people would be hesitant to take up this offer, as the Knight is again activated. This time the Knight is defending something different to our home, neighbours and friends. This time the Knight is defending the money in our back pocket.

This example illustrates the unconscious reward system that fuels the Knight's response in all of us. The Knight seeks to avoid losses. In our minds, the fact that the question stipulated that we were no longer living in our home town meant that we automatically assumed a loss had already occurred, in turn meaning that we were not trying to reverse the loss, but instead move to defending the next best thing: the money we have in our pocket. The strength of our defence will depend on the strength of our attachment. Generally speaking, when significant others like family or tribe are involved, the Knight defends vigorously and proactively, and that is why nepotism is such a problem in some parts of the world. In those cases, the reward is not just loss avoidance but maintenance and enhancement of significant relationships. Feelings of loyalty will further re-enforce the Knight.

Reflection Point

Can you think of recent examples where the Knight in you has defended a loss?

What was the trigger?
Can you describe the routine?
Did you observe a reward?

What We Have Learned in this Chapter

- The Knight encapsulates our powerful emotional reactions to the loss of an attachment.
- The threat of loss is the trigger for the Knight's habit loop in us.
- The Knight's routine can take many forms of defence ranging from 'holding on' and increased investment into the attachment to more active forms of attacking the perceived threat.
- Externalising our different emotional reactions to loss in the person of the Knight helps us to spot those emotions more easily in ourselves and in others.
- Seeing our decisions through the lens of the Knight distances us from our own strong emotions and invites us to ask ourselves consciously "What is it that I am defending?" so that we are able to put our attachments and the attachments of others under closer scrutiny.
- As the Knight is a strong and positive image, it can help us to explain to others their reaction to loss without being offensive, belittling or disrespectful.

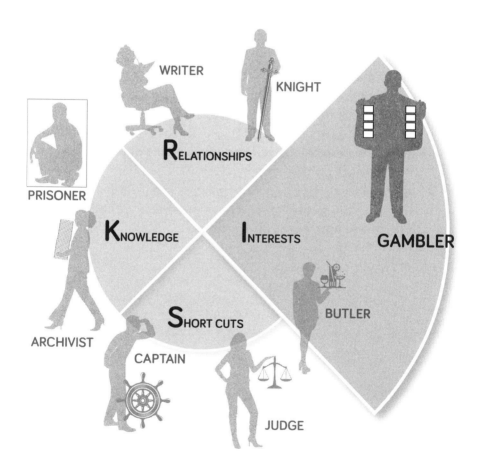

PRISONER

WRITER

KNIGHT

RELATIONSHIPS

KNOWLEDGE

INTERESTS

GAMBLER

ARCHIVIST

SHORT CUTS

BUTLER

CAPTAIN

JUDGE

11

The Gambler

The
GAMBLER

"You got to know when to hold 'em,
Know when to fold 'em,
Know when to walk away
And know when to run.
You never count your money when
you're sittin' at the table.
There'll be time enough for countin'
when the dealin's done.

Now Ev'ry gambler knows
That the secret to survivin'
Is knowin' what to throw away
And knowing what to keep.
Cause ev'ry hand's a winner and
ev'ry hand's a loser,
And the best that you can hope for
is to die in your sleep."

Kenny Rodgers, 'The Gambler'

The Gambler's Tale

I am the Gambler. I will always seek to interpret a situation to my advantage. I am always optimistic about outcomes. Should I lose, it is only bad luck or other people's incompetence, it never has anything to do with my abilities or skills because I am a cut above the rest. Most people agree with my opinions and when I reflect on the past I can only say I did everything right.

The Gambler's Motto: "The future is bright and it's all about me."

What You Need to Remember about the Gambler

The Gambler in us is triggered when we come across a situation we believe will increase our power or reputation, or bring material benefits.

The Gambler:

- ✓ Is overconfident and over-optimistic
- ✓ Tries to manipulate situations to his/her own advantage.

What Do Smart Deciders Do?

Smart decision makers:

- ✓ Are mindful that the Gambler can be at work in anyone
- ✓ Understand the Gambler's game by factoring the Gambler into the overall management picture and decision-making approach
- ✓ Call the Gambler's bluff by introducing systematic downward adjustments to estimates that are likely to be optimistic
- ✓ Ask the Gambler to suggest alternative solutions.

'The Gambler' is the signature song of the American country-music artist Kenny Rodgers.[99] Written by Don Schlitz and released in 1978, it won Rodgers the Grammy award for best male country vocal in 1980. The song itself tells the story of a late-night encounter on "a train bound for nowhere" where the narrator meets a man who is a gambler. The gambler observes that the narrator is down on his luck and offers him a life lesson he has learnt the hard way in exchange for the dram of whisky left in the narrator's bottle. After the gambler takes the drink and a cigarette, he gives the following advice, which the narrator regards as "the ace that I could keep":

> You got to know when to hold 'em, know when to fold 'em,
> Know when to walk away and know when to run.
> You never count your money when you're sittin' at the table.
> There'll be time enough for countin' when the dealin's done.

Put simply, "the ace that I could keep" is a stern warning against overconfidence. This warning forms the chorus to the song, which reinforces the seriousness of the message. Great songs like 'The Gambler' contain truths we resonate strongly with. Our personal exposure to the world of gambling may be just the occasional punt on a horse or football game or a trip to Vegas, but we all appreciate the point of the song. For the seasoned gambler, the song is a warning bell to stop them from falling into the overconfidence trap. This is the point when they fail to see the real odds or, as Rodgers sang, when they count their money before "the dealin's done".

A significant thinking error at play our character, the Gambler, is distorted perception. Distorted perception leads real-time gamblers to feel that a win, particularly a big win, is more likely than it actually is. At this point they are vulnerable to significant losses as they fail to perceive the reality of the situation.

What we now understand through research by neuroscientists and cognitive psychologists is that "the ace" in the song is not just applicable to card games but relevant to a host of life and business decisions.

The trigger for the Gambler in us occurs when we encounter a situation we believe we can use to our own personal advantage. Self-interest is a powerful driver in human behaviour and the Gambler in us takes advantage of this energy to distort our assessment of the situation. What we see is the opportunity to enhance our personal power or reputation, or to make material gains. A toxic cocktail of chemicals kicks in and our brain screens out other factors that we use to temper the influence of the Gambler. At its most extreme, we end up gambling away the shirt on our back and the keys to our home.

The Habit Loop of the Gambler

In Chapter 7, we explained how our thinking habits are formed and how understanding the *habit loop* is our key to unlocking more effective choices. When it comes to the Gambler, the habit loop tends to be this:

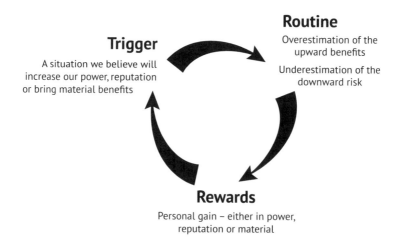

Figure 6a: The Habit Loop of the Gambler

In this chapter we will particularly focus on how the work of the Gambler leads us to make choices shaped and informed by a distorted view of reality. We will explore how overconfidence and over-optimism lead us to overestimate rewards and underestimate risk and how unchecked self-interest convinces us that we each have powers akin to superheroes.

We All Want to be Superheroes

One day, four ants were walking down a road. They saw an elephant coming towards them in the distance. One of the four ants angrily said, "How dare that elephant come in our way". The second ant said, "I will kill that elephant and teach him a lesson". The third ant said, "No, don't do that, he won't realise our glory if he dies," and continued, "I will break his four legs and teach him a good lesson instead". The last ant said, "No friends, let us not harm him. He is alone and we are four. It's not a fair fight."

A meta-study into overconfidence and over-optimism[100] concluded: "The most robust finding in the psychology of judgement is that people are overconfident". This conclusion may not be as obvious as it sounds – research could have told us the opposite. The importance of these studies is that they highlight that the Gambler is at work in all of us. We are all prone to overconfidence in our own abilities and judgements and we all have a tendency to claim more responsibility for our successes than failures. The studies also highlight that we have a deep belief that we have more control over outcomes than we really have. In his bestselling book, *Fooled by Randomness*,[101] Nassim Taleb points out that traders attribute their success to their own good judgements and poor trades to market conditions. The reality, he suggests, is that we are increasingly asked to make decisions through a lens of opacity, trying to make sense of a world we don't understand.

Yet, we are very persuasive and convince ourselves that we are better than we really are. If you were asked how good a driver you are (and assuming you drive), how would you answer – average, worse than average, better than average or probably one of the best? If you think you are better than average then you are not alone. In the UK, 62 percent of young male novice drivers think they are better drivers than the average driver. That means that most young men with little driving experience think they drive better than you! The statistics tell a different story. Young male drivers are more than twice as likely to be killed or seriously injured as young female drivers. A third of car driver fatalities are aged between 17 and 24, despite this age group representing only 8 percent of all drivers. It is this lethal combination of overconfidence and inexperience that delivers such devastating outcomes.

The Gambler in us will also recall the past in a self-serving manner. When married couples each estimate the percentage of household tasks they are responsible for, their estimates typically add up to more than a 100 percent. Politicians can often trip up when recalling the past in a self-serving manner. You may recall the US Republican vice-presidential candidate Paul Ryan who falsely claimed that he once ran a marathon under three hours. It turned out that he was a lot slower than that: 4 hours, 1 minute and 25 seconds, to be precise.

In 2001, the British politician William Hague, then leading the British Conservative Party in a general election, famously misjudged an attempt to appeal to the youth vote. He confidently announced that as a young man he regularly drank 14 pints of beer a day. This is an implausible amount of beer for anyone to drink and was exposed when school mates recalled that in his youth Hague was known as 'Billy Fizz' because his dad ran a soft drinks business and he preferred lemonade to beer. Then British Prime Minister, Tony Blair, took advantage of Hague's outrageous claim and caustically replied: "After 14 pints of beer, everything makes sense... even William Hague as prime minister".

Before we settle into too smug a zone, this tendency to exaggerate and recall the past in a self-serving way is something we all do – whether it is the size of that fish we caught, the length of a drive off the tee, our sporting heroics in school, our sexual conquests, our biggest sales, books we have read or places we have seen. The list is endless and we will let you reflect for a minute and mentally add your own favourite to this list.

The Gambler within us also overestimates how much people agree with us. Our default is to assume that those who say nothing agree with us and those that don't agree with us have something wrong with them. This is rather handy as it reinforces our confidence in our own opinions and our way of seeing and doing things. This reaction is called the false consensus effect. This effect was first discovered through a series of social psychology experiments in the 1970s. These studies found that people are more likely to assume that someone who holds a different view to theirs has a more extreme personality than their own. Whether consciously or unconsciously, we seem to tell ourselves: "all normal, right-thinking people think the same way as me." This, of course, is rather handy as it reinforces our confidence in our own opinions and our way of seeing and doing things.[102]

Above all, the Gambler within us misleads us to see the outcomes of our actions more positively than objective measures would warrant. When it comes to predicting what will happen to us tomorrow, next week or fifty years from now, we overestimate the likelihood of positive events and underestimate the likelihood of negative events. No-one walks down the aisle believing that they have a 50 percent chance of getting divorced and very few people lose sleep over the possibility that they have a one-in-five chance of getting cancer during their lifetime. We also expect to live longer than we can realistically expect. We overestimate our success in the job market and if you talk to primary school teachers they will tell you that the majority of parents believe that their offspring are particularly gifted little geniuses.

The Gambler's swagger can of course be of great value. Looking on the bright side of life guards us from depression and despondency. Confidence in itself is an essential ingredient for success. Overconfidence even has its place because it serves to increase ambition, morale, resolve and persistence, increasing the probability of success. An interesting research study showed that when people were introduced to strangers and then asked what the stranger thought of them, those expressing more confidence in how well they did actually did make a better first impression.[103] Another study that examined the Twitter accounts of sports commentators found that the level of confidence a pundit had in their own opinion was much more important in generating followers than their accuracy.[104] Pundits are overconfident and express strong opinion because that's what the public wants. Uncertainty is understood to generate ambivalent feelings in the audience. In other words, to be popular you need to be unwarrantedly confident rather than right.

The economist John Maynard Keynes famously remarked: "A large proportion of our positive activities depend on spontaneous optimism rather than on mathematical expectations. If animal spirits are dimmed and the spontaneous optimism falters, leaving us to depend on nothing but mathematical expectation, enterprise will fade and die". When moderated, the Gambler at work in us can be a driving force for innovation, creativity and economic growth. Without the cognitive biases embodied in the Gambler, entrepreneurs would not have the chutzpa to invest and start new ventures. In many ways, the attributes of the Gambler are desirable, so much so that Nobel Prize winner Daniel Kahneman once maintained that those biases embodied in the Gambler would be the ones he would like his children to have.

However, there is a flip side to the Gambler. The Gambler misleads us into faulty assessments, unrealistic expectations and hazardous decisions.

Caveat Vendor: The Dark Side of the Gambler

The Gambler is powered by self-interest. It is self-interest that drives the Gambler to play the game in the first place. Without self-interest and its associated rewards (material, reputational, power and self-esteem) the Gambler will not show up at the table. If we return to the story of the ants, what we observe at work is that the ants' overconfidence deflects their actual powerlessness and boosts their own self-image and self-esteem.

Clearly, self-interest can operate at both subconscious and conscious levels. As we encounter different situations, we never quite know if the Gambler's strategies are pursued consciously to advance personal gain or are at work at the subconscious level. The difficulty in determining whether the Gambler is at work consciously lies in the fact that intent is largely unobservable. Intent resides in the mind of the Gambler and is not easily accessed by outsiders, even by smart psychologists with clever research experiments. The waters of conscious and subconscious intent are further muddied by research findings that suggest that whenever individuals face trade-offs between what is best for them and what is morally correct, their perceptions of moral correctness are likely to be skewed in the direction of what is best for them.[105] In other words, we shift our moral compass according to the Gambler's game plan.

Even professional codes and guidelines do not protect us from the workings of the Gambler. Prentice[106] reviewed studies that documented the Gambler at work amongst US professionals. He found widespread evidence that lawyers acted self-interestedly by giving overly pessimistic advice to corporate clients about likely outcomes of litigation cases in order to increase their fees. Auditors, who ostensibly represent the interests of shareholders but are hired and fired by the people they audit, are also blinded to some degree by the incentive for client retention. Researchers found that biases associated with the Gambler are responsible for impasses in negotiations where different parties arrive at judgements of what is fair and right that are skewed in their own interest.[107] The Gambler can be quite stubborn when it comes to giving up self-interest and prefers to believe in the moral superiority of his/her particular cause or claim.

It is not just in lawyers and auditors that researchers have found the Gambler at work. Medical doctors are impacted by the work of the

Gambler too. Doctors were found to order more tests and ensure longer treatments when they were dealing with well-insured patients. When remuneration systems changed, compensating doctors less for testing, the number of referrals for tests dropped. In transplant medicine, transplant surgeons must often decide how to allocate scarce organs between potential recipients. To maintain favourable statistics, it may not be in their self-interest to give a transplant to those who benefit most in terms of increased survival, but instead to those for whom the probability of a successful operation is highest. Research in the US seems to suggest that the transplant surgeon's view of who benefits most from the transplant will be influenced by their interest in maintaining favourable statistics.[108]

The Gambler also influences medical diagnosis. In the UK, a dramatic newspaper headline suggested that one in every six patients is misdiagnosed by their doctor and doctors are found to seldom revise their original diagnosis.[109] Although this frequency of misdiagnosis may be exaggerated, misdiagnosis is a common problem highlighted in research. In general, physicians underappreciate the likelihood that their diagnoses could be wrong. They display extraordinary over-confidence fuelled by professional pride and preservation of self-esteem.[110]

Who Foots the Bill?

The ballad says "if you're gonna play the game, boy, ya gotta learn to play it right" and from the Gambler's perspective playing the game right means understanding the risks associated with displaying the Gambler. Research has found[111] that when the cost of competition is low and the potential gain large, then the Gambler is onto a winning strategy. For instance in recruitment, the Gambler is a good strategy for the candidate to display. Over-optimism and overconfidence in a job interview can play to the candidate's advantage. The worst thing that can happen is that the candidate does not get the job. For the recruiting organisation this is of course another matter. The same holds for politicians.

Politicians can be Gamblers without paying the price personally. In politics, the cost of being wrong might be large for society but almost non-existent for the politician. This is why politicians are content to overpromise knowing that there won't be any real comeback if they under deliver. A great example of this was George W. Bush's "Mission Accomplished" declaration on 1st May 2003 that combat operations in the Iraq war had ended.

The picture changes for the Gambler when there is a shift in risk/reward – when the risks become high. When the risks increase, the work of the Gambler becomes dangerous. As the Gambler in us works predominantly at the unconscious level, our lack of awareness makes the consequences of Gambler-induced thinking errors even more treacherous. For example in mountaineering, the Gambler can lead to fatal accidents. In 1996 five members of an expedition team climbing Mount Everest lost their lives because of the Gambler at work in their decisions. The Gambler caused them to break their own safety rules.[112] Hermann Buhl, one of the most iconic European mountaineers of the last century put it like this: "Mountains have a way of dealing with overconfidence." The same holds for other hazardous activities such as firefighting. Richard Gassaway is a retired fire chief who has been training fire fighters for many years. On his website[113] he warns against the danger the Gambler poses to the lives of firefighter:

> In my Firefighter Safety: Mistakes & Best Practices class where I'll ask a young firefighter (typically with less than 2 years' experience) how comfortable they would be commanding a fire incident if they found themselves being the most senior person on the scene. Remarkably, I have had participants rate themselves as highly competent and highly confident. Then, I'll ask them if they've ever commanded a structure fire before. Almost every one of them has not. I'll ask if they've been trained in incident command. Most will acknowledge they have (often as an Internet-based training program). Remember, this person I am quizzing is the SENIOR member of the department on the scene. Clearly, these individuals are suffering from the "illusion of superiority".

The Gambler in Corporate Life

Todd Kashdan,[114] an associate professor at George Mason University, reviewed the work of two Stanford Researchers[115] who had analysed 29,663 conference calls by business executives from 2003 to 2007. Kashdan made the following observation:

> Be skeptical when a CEO uses an excessive number of flowery terms to describe the future prospects of the company. Notice the intense positive emotional terms in speeches by Kenneth Lay (CEO of Enron), words such as fantastic, amazing, wonderful, and superb. If a CEO sounds like a hypomanic mother touting the artistic mastery of their two-year-old toddler, there is reason to be afraid, very afraid.

Overconfident CEOs are known to undertake expansion policies that destroy value.[116] Out of a sample of 394 US firms, CEOs who displayed the Gambler bias were 65 percent more likely to pursue a growth strategy through acquisition and were also less likely to draw on external financing. They also firmly believed that the market was under-pricing their stock and thus were much more reluctant to use stock in acquisitions. They were also more likely to acquire just to diversify and the market reaction to their acquisitions was more negative than to acquisitions by cautious CEOs. Take then CEO of Hewlett-Packard, Leo Apotheker's acquisition of Autonomy, a UK soft warehouse. The company took an $8.8 billion write down as a result of this acquisition. Hewlett-Packard lost $30 billion in value and its stock dropped 40 percent during Apotheker's tenure of nearly 10 months. In an interview following his ousting as CEO, Apotheker was still insistent in his belief in Autonomy's market potential as he rated the company's core software expertise as sound.

When CEOs overestimate their own and their company's abilities, they have been shown to neglect their competitors' skills and to underestimate their competitors' strategic countermoves. Netflix is such an example. Netflix is the largest movie-rental-by-mail business in the US but its path to success has not been without its hiccups. Reed Hastings (co-founder and CEO) admits that one of his biggest mistakes came in underestimating the strategy of his competition. "We erroneously concluded that Blockbuster probably wasn't going to launch a competitive effort when they hadn't by 2003. Then, in 2004, they did," says Hastings. "We thought, 'Well, they won't put much money behind it'. But over the past four years they've invested more than $500 million against us." Underestimating the competition in this instance ended in a price war and cost Netflix dearly, with Netflix temporarily having to sacrifice all profits for an all-out growth strategy. In the case of Steve Ballmer of Microsoft, underestimating the competition cost him his reputation. "There's no chance that the iPhone is going to get any significant market share. No chance," said an overconfident Steve Ballmer in 2007. Whereas the iPhone is still going from strength to strength, Steve Ballmer left Microsoft in 2013 after been criticised in the press for a lack of strategic focus and letting Apple and Google take over in mobile technologies.

When competitors operate in the low-cost segment of the market, the Gambler can often create a sense of complacency and arrogance. This produces blind spots within those companies that have traditionally been market leaders. Overconfidence by the market leaders can delay responses to moves in the market and leave incumbents vulnerable. What executive isn't familiar with the case of the low-cost airline Ryanair and its hugely successful entry into the European market at the expense of the traditional carriers? Likewise, the world's leading telecommunications companies were far too confident about their position to recognise the threat from the Chinese low-cost competitor Huawei. Huawei is now a leader in fixed-line networks, mobile-telecommunications networks and Internet switches. And remember Vizio? Vizio was a little-known LCD TV supplier that overtook the premium brands in five years to become the North American market leader in large-format TVs.

The Bigger the Bet, the Stronger our Belief in the Big Win

Contrary to popular belief, CEOs who invest large chunks of their own wealth in the companies they manage are *not* more careful or conservative. The opposite is true. Increasing an entrepreneur's personal liability can actually exacerbate their tendency for optimistic misreporting.[117] The Gambler works like this: because the owner–manager already has a track record of financial success, they believe that being even more decisive and aggressive in the future will inevitably bring even greater returns. The initial success acts to reinforce the Gambler within. When losses occur, they are not seen as indications that mistakes have been made, but are attributed to bad luck or to other people's faults. So owner–managers often pursue a higher-risk strategy and firms managed by those individuals are generally more leveraged.[118]

"Watch, I will be the world's richest. I'm not bragging. It's just a consequence of all the things that we have done. Just look at the assets. By 2015 we will be making $10 billion. Between 2015 and 2020 that will double, or triple. And those are discounted numbers I'm giving you." These are the words of Eike Batista in a now infamous interview with the *Sunday Times* in March 2012 at the height of his fame. He was then Brazil's richest man, the fourth-richest person in the world and on a mission to the top. Yet within two years his empire collapsed and Batista lost much of his personal wealth which had once been valued at $30 billion. He destroyed tens of billions of dollars in shareholder value due to mismanagement and over-optimism of projections in the risky and unpredictable business of drilling oil in deep waters. Clearly "counting his money before the deal was done" he purposefully added the letter 'X' to all his companies' names to signify the coming multiplication of shareholder wealth. Yet the companies did exactly the opposite. His oil company OGX filed for bankruptcy in October 2013 in the largest default in Latin American history after it failed to produce a fraction of the 10.8 billion barrels Batista had promised. A week later shipbuilder OSX, whose fortunes depended on OGX, also went bankrupt. Both OGX and OSX had debts greater than their assets.

In his first post-collapse interview, Batista notoriously blamed the failure of his companies on the oil executives he had recruited himself and who he used to call his 'Dream Team'. According to accounts widely reported by the Brazilian press, Batista's over-optimistic demeanour was widely emulated and replicated by his oil executives at lower levels in his organisations who intentionally inflated the value of drilling projections in order to get higher bonuses. Allegedly the company knew at least one year before the spectacular collapse that their wells were at least 82 percent smaller than levels reported to investors at the time.

How the Gambler Can Turn a CFO into a Felon: The Slippery Slope to Fraud

Even technically qualified executives with interests aligned to the interests of their shareholders can make disastrous decisions as a result of the Gambler at work. In the corporate world, CFOs are generally seen as the level headed and prudent ones. They are not generally known as risk takers and bet makers. According to some fascinating research, this popular view of the CFO is not universally true and CFOs are just as prone to the work of the Gambler as the rest of us.

Researchers surveyed 7,000 CFOs over a six-year period. CFOs were asked to predict a range of one- and ten-year returns of the S&P 500 index and divulge how certain they felt about their predictions. Although most of the CFOs felt very sure of their predictions, they were correct just 38 percent of the time. The level of certainty felt by a CFO about his stock pick, and the frequency of his misjudgements, correlated to his level of confidence. Researchers then looked at the track record of the CFOs. CFOs with the highest levels of confidence regularly applied lower discount rates to value cash flows so they invested more, used more debt and ended up having less money available for dividend pay outs.[119]

"Cocky CFOs often underestimate competitors and the wisdom of the market", says Ben-David who headed up the research. Ben-David maintains that when making financing choices, CFOs might incorrectly price the firm's securities, as they assume the market is undervaluing the company's worth. Based on these erroneous assumptions they might also recommend repurchases of the company's stock. Ben-David also observed that overconfident CFOs can wreak havoc on mergers too, as faith in synergies overshadows real obstacles. "When overconfident CFOs announce mergers, they usually have a negative market announcement return," Ben-David says.

Sadly there is also increasing evidence that the Gambler at work in CFOs might be responsible for fraudulent accounting practices. Schrand, an accounting professor at the University of Pennsylvania, examined patterns of accountancy fraud and came to the conclusion that CFOs' over-optimism can lead to thinking that they can turn their firms around before fraudulent behaviour catches up with them: "The CFO may stretch the rules just a bit or engage in what you might call a 'gray area' of earnings management. But say it turns out that he was wrong and things don't turn around as expected. Then he has to make up for the prior period. That requires continuing fraudulent behaviour and he has to do even more in the current quarter."[120]

The "Don't Mention It" Project: The Gambler at Work in Large Projects

In February 2014, Mark Thompson (the BBC's former Director General) appeared before the House of Commons Public Accounts Committee in order to apologise personally for wasting around £100 million on a failed IT project. When the Digital Media Initiative (DMI) was launched in 2008, BBC management hailed it as their single most important initiative. The project was meant to digitise archives, enabling production teams to access all video and audio material on their computers instead of using tapes. Before a year had elapsed, the project had already run into trouble. The project was widely known within the BBC as the "Don't Mention It" project because the IT firm who had been originally appointed to implement the scheme was fired by the BBC for non-delivery in 2009. The BBC then took the project in-house, but internal resources could not cope with the complexity of the work and subsequently failed to deliver too. Meanwhile, the cost of the project continued to spiral out of control until it was finally killed off in May 2013. So who was at fault? The public spending watchdog investigated and came to the conclusion that it was none other than the Gambler at work. The expected gains had been overstated and the difficulties of delivering the project had been underestimated. In her apology to the public, the CFO, Zarin Patel, said: "I took false optimism from my ability to correct things in the programme, and for that I apologise."

The "Don't Mention It" project is not an isolated case. The work of the Gambler is at the heart of many of the project cost overruns witnessed across the world. Cost overruns can occur in many large projects. For a number of years, the research program on large infrastructure projects at Aalborg University, Denmark, has explored different aspects of the planning and implementation of large infrastructure projects.[121] An extensive study covering 258 projects in 20 nations on five continents included all projects for which data was obtainable. Amongst many interesting findings, the study found that for rail projects average cost overruns were 44.7 percent measured in constant prices, for bridges and tunnels the equivalent figure was 33.8 percent and for roads 20.4 percent. The researchers found that strategic misrepresentation was the overriding explanation for cost overruns. Planners and promoters misrepresent costs, benefits and risks in order to increase the likelihood that it is their project and not the competition's that gets approval and funding. Often, it is not the best projects that are built but the most misrepresented ones – a phenomenon that researchers have termed 'negated Darwinism' and 'survival of the unfittest'.

Are You the Gambler?

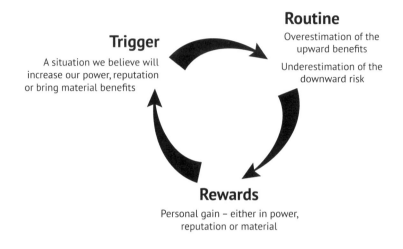

Routine

Overestimation of the
upward benefits

Underestimation of the
downward risk

Trigger

A situation we believe will
increase our power, reputation
or bring material benefits

Rewards

Personal gain – either in power,
reputation or material

Figure 6b: The Habit Loop of the Gambler

The Gambler in us is triggered when we believe we have an
opportunity to increase our power or reputation (both in our
own eyes and in those of others), or to acquire greater material
benefits. Try asking a hairdresser whether you need a haircut, a car
salesman whether he thinks you should change your old model for
a new one or the sales assistant who is on a bonus remuneration
scheme for her opinion on whether you look good in that dress
she is selling. Or maybe you should ask yourself whether you rate
yourself as an above average driver, an above average lover or
above average at your job. The vast majority of people answer
'yes' to these questions – we do not like to think of ourselves as
below average – and we also expect others to look after number
one just as we tend to do. Yet we do not like to admit to ourselves
that we act from self-interest and that the Gambler operates in
all of us, as this would challenge our own self-image. This makes
it very difficult for us to recognise the dangerous Gambler routine
of overestimating the upward benefits and underestimating
downward risks at work in our decision making.

Reflection Point

Can you think of recent examples where the Gambler drove your decision making?

What was the trigger?
Can you describe the routine?
What was your reward?

What We Have Learned in this Chapter

- The Gambler embodies our tendency to see ourselves in a positive light and our propensity to skew our decisions in favour of our own self-interest.
- When we come across an opportunity to increase our power, reputation or material benefits, the Gambler routine is triggered. We tend to count our money when we are sittin' at the table, before the deal is even done. So we are inclined to overestimate upward benefits and downplay the downward risk of our self-serving actions.
- The Gambler affects everyone, even people who are in caring professions such as medicine.
- Referring to self-interested actions in terms of the Gambler at work in us helps us to understand that self-interested behaviour can be risky for ourselves and others. In situations where self-interest is at stake, we need to review our estimates of the upward as well as the downward risks in order to avoid causing damage to ourselves and others.

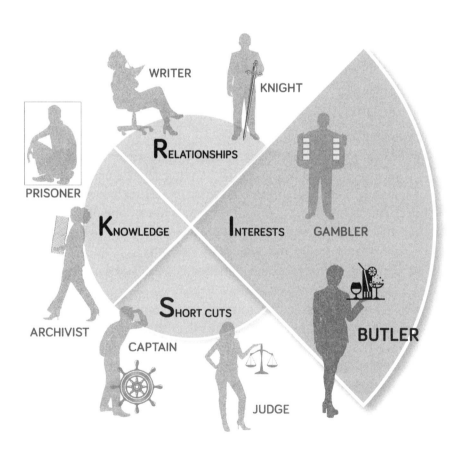

WRITER

KNIGHT

PRISONER

RELATIONSHIPS

KNOWLEDGE

INTERESTS

GAMBLER

ARCHIVIST

SHORT CUTS

CAPTAIN

JUDGE

BUTLER

12

The Butler

"A kite flies against the wind, not with it."

Winston Churchill

The
BUTLER

The Butler's Tale

I am the Butler. I always serve up what people in authority over me want to hear because I live in fear of losing my job or my reputation. I sometimes stay silent. If I speak up, I will rarely challenge those in power. I always try to stay in their good books.

The Butler's Motto: "I aim to please!"

What You Need to Remember about the Butler

The Butler in us is triggered when we interact with people we consider as higher ranking or people who hold power over us.

The Butler:

- ✓ Wants to please those in positions of authority and power
- ✓ Does not reveal a true opinion
- ✓ Will serve up what they think others want to hear.

What Do Smart Deciders Do?

Smart decision makers:

- ✓ Understand the dangers of Butler behaviour
- ✓ Are aware of their authority and power
- ✓ Are mindful that people may not necessarily give them their real opinions and a true view of what is really happening
- ✓ Create a safe place where people feel comfortable expressing their viewpoint.

Fairy tales have a wonderful way of speaking to the depths of the human psyche. They hold up a mirror and allow us to gaze at the mysteries of the human soul. We enter into struggles between good and evil, right and wrong, rescuer and rescued. We encounter the shadows of our own frailties. Fairy tales have an enduring charm because they speak truly about who we are. Remember the famous Hans Christian Andersen story about the emperor's new clothes? It speaks about the vanity and pomposity of power. It is also a beautiful description of the Butler at work.

You will recall that the story tells of an emperor who commissions two tailors to make him a new and fine set of clothes. The tailors set about their task and present to the emperor clothes with magical properties. According to the tailors, these clothes were not only the finest ever made but would enable the emperor to understand who was incompetent or stupid, because such people would be unable to see these fine clothes. So the emperor 'collects' his new outfit and parades about naked rather than admit to being incompetent or stupid. At the same time, he is applauded on all sides by sycophantic courtiers and subjects who pretend to see the beautiful clothes and are also disinclined to reveal their incompetence and stupidity.

"Nobody would confess that he couldn't see anything, for that would prove him either unfit for his position, or a fool". This phrase perfectly sums up the psychology behind the workings of the Butler. As we all know, it took a child to speak truth to power – someone not caught up in the politics and power structures.

The Butler at work in us is, fundamentally, a *fear-based self-protection strategy* we use when faced with power discrepancies. It is widely employed by people in subordinate positions and, if we are honest with ourselves, we are not only able to observe it in our work and social settings, but we have almost certainly let the Butler loose in our own dealings with others.

We were once running a leadership programme for a client of ours. A common complaint made by these senior leaders was that their bosses (members of the executive team) made unreasonable demands of them. They often asked them to meet deadlines they knew they couldn't meet and deliver results they often thought were focused on the wrong things. When I asked them why they didn't challenge or push back against these demands they said that this would not be welcomed by executives and would have a negative impact on their careers. So they said 'yes' and went along with what they were told to do. In this culture, it was considered better to miss a deadline and/or have to do re-work than to try and make a better decision up front.

Our work with another client involved coaching a senior executive. One of the pieces of feedback he had received was that he didn't seem to have enough drive to change the way the business worked. Some colleagues saw him as being rather passive and compliant. When this was discussed he replied that in his role he did enough not to be seen as under-performing and was unlikely to be sacked. If he took more risks and tried to change things, he was likely to upset some people which was more likely to put him in a position where he could lose his job.

This pattern of behaviour and decision making is not unique to these particular clients. We see it all the time. Recent research in the field of neuroscience[122] is helping us to understand why this is the case. This research has found that the same parts of our brain (the rostral midcingulate cortex and caudal perigenual anterior cingulate cortex areas) are activated when positive social outcomes and monetary reward are desired outcomes. This suggests that there is a strong relationship between our desire to protect our reputation and our need to be recognised or rewarded with hard cash. In the light of these findings, it isn't so surprising that we become guarded when we interact with others who are able to dispense the carrots or use the stick and we often take the path of least resistance.

The trigger for the Butler in us occurs when we encounter a situation in which there is a real or perceived power imbalance. Self-preservation and personal advancement are powerful drivers in human behaviour and the Butler in us takes advantage of this survival strategy to distort our assessment of the situation. What we see is the opportunity to protect our personal power or reputation, or to make material gains.

The Habit Loop of the Butler

In Chapter 7 we explained how our thinking habits are formed and how understanding the *habit loop* is our key to unlocking more effective choices. When it comes to the Butler, the habit loop tends to be this:

Trigger
A situation in which there is a real or perceived power differential

Routine
Behaving in ways we believe the more powerful person wants us to behave

Rewards
Conflict avoidance
Protection of reputation
Favour of the superior
Material benefits

Figure 7a: The Habit Loop of the Butler

In this chapter we will particularly focus on how the work of the Butler leads us make choices shaped and informed by perceived or real discrepancies in power and authority. We will explore how the Butler prevents decision makers from getting a better understanding of what is actually happening and encourages subordinates to spend far too much time second guessing what leaders are thinking and want to happen.

The Butler in Corporate Life

The boss returned from lunch in a good mood and called his team into a meeting room to listen to a couple of jokes he had just picked up. Everybody, except one woman, laughed rousingly.

"What is the matter?" the boss barked at her. "Haven't you got a sense of humour?" "I don't have to laugh," she replied. "I am leaving Friday."

Daniel Goleman, a psychologist and author of the books *Emotional Intelligence*[123] and *Primal Leadership*,[124] has observed that subordinates are not only afraid to tell those in positions of authority the truth but they also tune in to subtle signals sent by the boss. Even when a boss doesn't intend to quash dissent, a sour expression or a curt response can send out signals that bad news isn't welcome. The result is a double whammy. On the one hand senior executives are less likely to have an accurate assessment of performance because people hide the truth from them and on the other hand employees spend more time worrying about internal factors – what the boss might think, what management might do – rather than focusing on customers, markets or competitors. As a result, Goleman observes that managers spend much of their time 'managing' their superiors by trying to figure out what they are thinking, so that their actions can match the expectations and beliefs of their bosses. This activity in itself wastes company time and resources but also can lead to decision making based on misleading information.

One of the ways of judging whether people are committed to an idea is whether it survives the person who first suggested it. The evidence isn't good. Extensive research by Shore[125] has shown that projects are significantly more likely to be cancelled when a top executive leaves. This suggests that subordinates have been serving up what the boss ordered until the point at which he or she leaves. There is little deep-seated commitment to the project. Our own experience of observing leadership changes at the top of organisations reflects this evidence. We would only add that acquiescence to the ideas of one leader is often replaced by acquiescence to the ideas of another.

Other research[126] suggests that less able employees are more likely to serve up what the boss wants to hear because of the negative reputational consequences of going against a senior executive's prior beliefs. The researchers highlight a number of significant implications for decision making and suggest that this behaviour may help to explain why some companies make poor investment decisions, pursue bad projects or discard good ideas altogether. One particular consequence highlighted by this research is that the skewed or inaccurate information presented to leaders diminishes the value of delegation and runs counter to efforts to generate multiple assessments of business options. This problem of people serving up what leaders want is compounded when an organisation lacks sufficient resources for project evaluation, thereby creating a bias in favour of projects already supported by senior management.

So where does the problem lie – is it with the leader or the team member? According to this group of academic researchers, the ball stays firmly in the court of leaders who are challenged to call out the Butler at work in their subordinates. They make this point because the Butler flourishes most when leaders are unable to separate their own preconceptions and preferences about the decisions they need to make from their assessments of the abilities of those assigned to evaluate those proposals.

The work of the Butler in our decisions should therefore be seen primarily as a leadership issue in organisations. Leaders can set the tone from the top and have a powerful influence on whether their organisations encourage diversity of opinion or favour yes men. Astute leaders in organisations understand the impact they have on the people who report to them and will want to get feedback and challenge from sources untainted by the Butler.

One such leader was Winston Churchill. During the Second World War, Churchill was concerned that his leadership role and larger than life personality would deter others from giving him honest information about what was really going on the front line and home front. In response to his own insights into the impact he had on others, he set up a separate unit outside of the military command structure dedicated to giving him all the news and especially the bad news. This unit survived the war and is a forerunner of the current Office of National Statistics.

How Widespread is Butler Behaviour?

Sadly, the work of the Butler appears to be widespread as many leaders lack Churchill's wisdom, treating their organisations as personal fiefdoms and their subordinates as mere extensions of themselves. Such leaders compound the effects of the Butler. They create an atmosphere of fear, which feeds their own desire to exercise power. It also silences any expression of independent views.

One such leader was Fred Goodwin (formerly Sir Fred) whose reign as CEO at the Royal Bank of Scotland (RBS) was at one time fêted by the great and the good. RBS was seen as an icon of British banking and its aggressive operational practices had delivered some impressive financial results. However, all was not as well as it seemed. When the lid was lifted on the organisation after the financial crisis of 2008, a highly dysfunctional culture was revealed. Goodwin's leadership style was widely acknowledged as a significant factor in RBS's fall from grace – particularly through his ego-induced takeover bid for Dutch bank ABN Amro in 2007.

Observers[127] say that there were plenty opportunities to question Goodwin's judgement, but these were not taken by those who worked with him. Goodwin's aggressive management style made dissent virtually impossible. In his daily executive meetings (called "morning beatings") he was known to single out at least one of his employees for humiliation. It was commonplace for a regional manager with responsibility for hundreds of branches to be asked very detailed questions, such as how many mortgages one particular outpost had sold the previous week. Not knowing the answer was considered unacceptable. According to insiders, Goodwin had what he called "Fred's black book" for executives who had displeased him. A colleague reported "He liked to say that if your name was written in the book in pencil you were on the borderline. If it was written in ink you were well and truly f*****d." Goodwin would also go on road shows around his offices to explain big changes to the business. Instead of using these as an opportunity to gain valuable feedback from employees at all levels, he was said to note down the name of middle managers who asked an awkward question, then seek ways to get them fired. "Fill in the complaints book on your way out of the door," he told one executive who had been dismissed. For those employees who wanted to stay in the organisation the Butler's outfit was seen as essential survival wear.

Goodwin's dysfunctional management style is extreme, but it is by no means an isolated case. Although there is plenty of anecdotal evidence of bosses suppressing dissent (see Twitter #badbosses if you want to lighten up your day) there are very few systematic studies that explore the risks and consequences of Butler cultures for organisational success. We can only speculate on why not! So we have looked elsewhere for evidence and clues of how the work of the Butler impacts the quality of our choices.

A major research report, produced in 2013 by Cass Business School for Airmic[128] (the Association of Insurance and Risk Managers in Industry and Commerce), offers some deep insights into eighteen major corporate debacles since 2000. The failures which were examined by the report involved substantial, well-known organisations such as Coca-Cola, Firestone, Shell, BP, Airbus, Société Générale, Cadbury Schweppes, Northern Rock, AIG, Independent Insurance, Enron, Arthur Andersen, Railtrack and the UK Passport Agency, as well as some smaller firms. Several of the companies did not survive and most of the rest suffered severe damage. "Poor leadership on ethos and culture and the inability of risk management and internal audit teams to report on risks originating from higher levels of their organisation's hierarchy" were identified as major contributing factors in the calamities which befell these organisations. In plain English, this means that a culture of fear prevailed in these organisations which prevented people working at the lower levels from challenging their superiors and speaking up freely about some of the risky behaviours they saw at the time in their part of the business.

Mayday, Mayday: The Butler on Board

Another effective source that casts light on the work of the Butler in decision making comes from the aviation sector. Here regulators play a critical role in investigating accidents and these thorough investigations help to cast light on the process and circumstances of how decisions were taken. Sadly, in many of these examples, the work of the Butler has led to fatalities.

According to the United States National Transportation and Safety Board (NTSB), 84 percent of the 37 accidents linked to crew error between 1978 and 1990 happened because first officers were reluctant to contradict senior pilots when they made errors or unwise decisions. Here are some of the most shocking examples.

In one situation a co-pilot realised that the plane was coming in too fast and too steep for a safe landing. The pilot was not only his boss but also the owner of the airline. The co-pilot chose not say anything to the pilot even though he was not able to see the runway at all. The co-pilot, who survived the crash, said that he had assumed the problem was with *his* vision rather than with his boss's bungled landing.

In another case, the captain of a cargo plane due to fly out of Anchorage, Alaska, arrived at the airport visibly drunk. He was so drunk that his cab driver noticed and reported it to the airline. Managers in the airline chose not to take any action. What compounds this inaction is that the captain's co-pilots also shared his cab to the airport and they didn't take action either. As soon as the plane had left the parking area, the implications of the captain's lack of sobriety were evident. He steered the plane onto the wrong runway, facing the wrong direction and struggled to work out where he was. Even though his instructions were muddled and confusing, his co-pilots still did not call out his drunkenness, even when he asked directly for open communication and support. When the captain eventually took off his angle of ascent was too steep and the plane crashed. At no point did the co-pilots speak out and challenge the captain, even when obvious errors were made.

An accident in 1978, in which a plane carrying 189 passengers and crew crashed killing 10 people, was the direct result of two experienced crewmembers not speaking up and making the pilot aware that the plane was running dangerously low on fuel. Since 1990, the airline industry worldwide has invested in assertiveness training for crew along with policy and procedural changes.

Despite this investment and procedural change, a recent study by two Swiss academics from ETH Zurich[129] found that crew members at all levels are still very reluctant to speak out on issues relevant to flight safety. The surveyed crewmembers are reported to have remained silent in half of all 'speaking up' opportunities they had experienced. Silence was highest for first officers and pursers, followed by flight attendants. Captains were most likely to speak up. Reasons for silence mainly concerned fears – fear of damaging relationships, fear of punishment or fear of delaying flights when there were severe operational pressures.

The Butler at Work in Hospitals

Another sector in which we are able to get greater visibility of the Butler at work is in health, again through some high-profile organisational failures.

In recent years, the UK has seen a number of very serious scandals within its National Health Service (NHS). The Francis Inquiry[130] into just one hospital in Staffordshire recorded hundreds of needless deaths due to inadequate care. The inquiry criticised the culture of secrecy and bullying in parts of the NHS that "put targets and personal reputations before patient safety". David Prior, chairman of the Care Quality Commission (CQC), the agency responsible for the oversight of hospitals, singled out the work of the Butler as a characteristic behaviour found in senior staff: "If senior doctors are not prepared to put their heads above the parapet when things are going really badly wrong, because the risks are too great or they feel no-one's going to listen to them, then there's nothing we can do" he said. "Everything we do here [at the CQC] will be completely useless if clinicians are not prepared to take strong leadership positions... You the doctors should be going to the Chief Executive and saying 'It's unacceptable. Why don't we do it like this?'... Come up with a solution".[131]

Worryingly, the work of the Butler is even more widespread amongst junior levels in the NHS. A survey of more than 8,000 nurses revealed that about a quarter had been told to keep quiet about incidents in which the safety of patients was put at risk. They said they were worried about victimisation or reprisals, complaining about what the Royal College of Nursing (their trade union) described today as "a culture of fear and intimidation". Not colluding with the Butler can sometimes exact a great price for those who are willing to speak out. Many who did report concerns over patient care said that their employers took no action, making them feel that they had put their careers and reputations on the line for no reason.

The Butler in Politics

A final domain in which we are able to gain greater visibility of the Butler at work is the world of politics. We all know that politicians have to tow their party's line on particular issues. In the UK, a three-line whip basically means that whatever the personal view of a member of parliament, they will be expected to support their party's position on that vote.

When in government, a politician (in the UK at least) is supposed to receive independent advice from their 'politically neutral' civil servants. Sir Sherard Cowper-Coles, in his 2012 book *Ever the Diplomat: Confessions of a Foreign Office Mandarin*, challenges this view and writes that the UK's diplomatic service is all too eager to please its political masters. Far from being independent (and prepared to challenge), he argues that they seldom really mean it when they say "yes minister". He argues that ministers need to be confronted with home truths about the world as it is, rather than as they might wish it to be. Such rare glimpses into the workings of government give us an appreciation of how devastating the work of the Butler can be.

One of the most compelling examples of the Butler at work in the political world came from an Australian member of parliament, Bill Shorten. Shorten had been asked his views on whether the Speaker of the Australian Parliament should return to his role while allegations of sexual harassment were investigated. Shorten replied:

> "I understand that the Prime Minister has addressed this in a press conference in Turkey in the last few hours. I haven't seen what she's said but let me say I support what it is that she said."
> A somewhat surprised the interviewer then said: "Hang on, you haven't seen what she said?"
> Shorten replied: "But I support what my Prime Minister said."
> The interviewer continued: "Well, what's your view?"
> Shorten replied: "My view is what the Prime Minister's view is."
> The interviewer then asked: "Surely you must have your own view on this, Bill Shorten?" Shorten responded: "No, when you ask if I've got my view on this, it's such a general question it invites me to go to lots of places."
> The interview ended with Mr. Shorten insisting:
> "I support what our Prime Minister has said."
> The interviewer replied: "But you don't know what that is?"
> Shorten said: "Well I'm sure she's right."

Needless to say this interview went viral on the Internet and Shorten was ridiculed for supporting the views of someone without even knowing what those views were. Given the dangers associated with the Butler, it is surprising that apart from ridicule there was no greater backlash over such extreme Butler behaviour.

This suggests that the Butler is not just a leadership issue but also a cultural issue.

Whether some national cultures are more prone to the workings of the Butler is open to debate. This issue was widely discussed in the press when the chairman of the commission looking into the Fukushima disaster laid the blame for the 2011 nuclear plant failure on Japan's "reflexive obedience", "our reluctance to question authority", "our devotion to sticking to programme", "our groupism" and "our insularity". In an in-depth article in the *Financial Times* entitled 'Stop blaming Fukushima on Japan's culture' (10th July 2012), Gerald Curtis pointed out that one of the heroes, Tepco's Masao Yoshida, the plant manager, had disobeyed orders not to use saltwater to cool the reactors. Curtis concludes: "If culture explains behavior then no one has to take responsibility... Culture does not explain Fukushima. People have autonomy to choose; at issue are the choices they make, not the cultural context in which they make them."

Nonetheless, what is clear is that when disasters of epic proportion happen, society at large becomes acutely aware of the dangers the Butler presents. It is only then that voices which advocate external, independent assessment are being heard. But disappointingly, external advice is not always the panacea. The Butler can also be found amongst so-called independent advisors.

These include auditors who are reluctant to issue qualified opinions (as in the case of Enron) and/or are reluctant to refuse their clients' requests for improper accounting treatments (as happened in Anglo Irish Bank and Lehman Brothers); investment bankers who advise on mergers and acquisitions or new equity and bond issues; and even expert witnesses. Studies in the US suggest that psychiatrists, psychologists and other health professionals who are called upon to give their expert opinion in court tend to slant their analysis and testimony towards the party who hired them. This is even the case in serious matters such as an insanity defence in criminal cases and child custody cases. The Butler has become so obvious in the US judicial system that many courts and commentators view experts not as objective witnesses but as fully fledged members of the adversarial team of the party on whose behalf they are testifying.

Why Goalkeepers Rarely Stand Still

An evaluation of hundreds of penalty shoot-outs in football[132] (soccer) revealed that players kick one-third of the time to the right, one-third to the left and one-third straight at the middle of the goal. In a penalty situation, the ball takes less than 0.3 of a second to travel from the penalty spot to the goal. The keeper therefore needs to make a choice before the ball is kicked. Although a third of the penalty kicks will come straight at them keepers rarely stand still. They usually dive to the left or the right. The reason for this is that diving looks more impressive than standing still. Fans want to see a desire to save the shot and doing something looks better than doing nothing. Even if the keeper misses and a penalty is scored the appearance of making a gallant, but failed, attempt to save the shot serves up what the fans want to see.

We see this *action bias* in organisations too. The long-hours culture – presenteeism – is often driven by a desire to want to be seen to be busy and committed rather than a genuine requirement of the job. It's serving up what the boss wants to see. A friend who worked in a professional services firm recalls a startling performance review discussion. The review was going well when his manager put on the table a major concern. He said that my friend didn't show enough energy at work. "What do you mean?" asked my friend. "I deliver really good work, you just said so." "I know", replied the manager. "It's just that when you move around the office others don't see a sense of urgency about you. You seem to be taking your time." "But I'm only heading for a coffee, or to the bathroom or to meet someone. What do people expect?" asked my friend. "They expect to see more energy," replied the manager. So my friend responded, "What you are saying is that I need to be seen to walk faster... !"

In the mind of the Butler, serving up what others want also means being seen to be doing something – anything – if it pleases the crowd.

Are You the Butler?

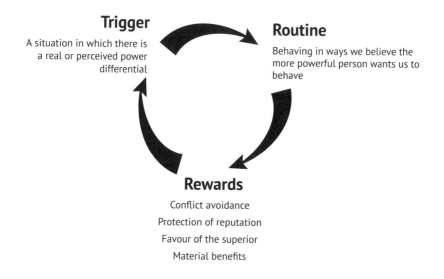

Figure 7b: The Habit Loop of the Butler

The Butler is triggered in situations where there are real or perceived power differences between us and our colleagues. Imagine you are ordered to steal copyrighted materials by your boss for an important presentation due in tomorrow. What would you do? Would you stand up to your boss and tell him that you are very uncomfortable downloading illustrations from the Internet which should be paid for? Will you point out to him that if found out, the company could be sued for thousands of pounds? Or will you just do it, then forget about it, telling yourself that it's not your neck on the line? And that, after all, when your company is sued, you will be long gone!

As we shall see in part three of this book, how you will react is likely to depend on how psychologically safe you feel in the presence of your superiors – whether openness is welcomed and rewarded or whether it is punished.

Reflection Point

Can you think of recent examples when you made a choice which felt uncomfortable but which aimed to please someone who was in authority over you?

What was the trigger?
Can you describe the routine?
Did you observe a reward?

What We Have Learned in this Chapter

- The Butler works in all of us in situations when we are interacting with people we consider as higher ranking or who hold power over us.
- Colluding with the Butler in us can be extremely dangerous and even lead to fatalities in high-risk settings.
- The concept of the Butler invites us to take an objective look at ourselves and our reactions and encourages us to make a conscious effort to speak out.
- Speaking out in some environments demands considerable courage. It is therefore important that leaders in organisations realise that they need to provide an environment in which people can freely speak out to test, challenge and explore proposals or ideas as well as to discuss mistakes openly. Creating such an environment might involve a considerable shift in an organisation's culture, a subject that is addressed in the latter part of the book.

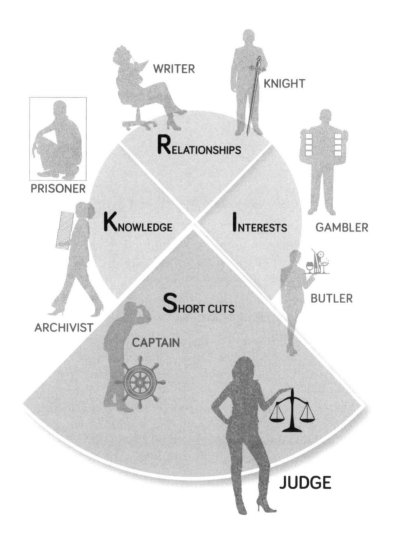

WRITER

KNIGHT

PRISONER

RELATIONSHIPS

GAMBLER

KNOWLEDGE

INTERESTS

BUTLER

ARCHIVIST

SHORT CUTS

CAPTAIN

JUDGE

13

The Judge

"It's not what you say, it's what people hear."

Frank Lutz

The Judge's Tale

I am the Judge – more like a reality show judge than a judge in a courtroom. I make judgements based on **who** is presenting and **how** they present. I'm less interested in the actual content. I value humour and like stories with a coherent beginning, middle and end. I'm impressed by the reputation of the presenter. I value an emotional connection when people communicate with me because I can remember this more easily. In moments of crisis, I will look for someone or something that will fix the problem quickly.

The Judge's Motto: **"Grab my attention and you will get my vote!"**

What You Need to Remember about the Judge

The Judge in us is triggered when our attention is drawn to someone or something.

The Judge:

- ✓ Rates memorable and salient information as more significant
- ✓ Focuses on the qualities of the presenter rather than the content of the presentation.

What Do Smart Deciders Do?

Smart decision makers:

- ✓ Are aware that the most memorable is not necessarily the most significant piece of information
- ✓ Look at the probability of risk rather than his or her own skewed assessment of risk
- ✓ Do not look for quick solutions or recruit a 'saviour' in an emotionally charged crisis situation
- ✓ Put highly regarded operators under as much scrutiny as people whose reputation is less favourable.

She was a frumpy looking 47-year-old who took the world by storm. When Scottish singer Susan Boyle first took to the stage in January 2009 to audition for the TV show *Britain's Got Talent*, the judges and audience sneered. The chances are that you have seen the video of her performance. It went viral on YouTube and has now been viewed over 300 million times. Boyle's awkward initial introduction to the talent show suggested that she would be just another hapless dreamer. She just didn't look like the singing sensation the show was seeking. Your gut and just about every other part of your body screamed out "she's going to flop!"

If you haven't seen the video, watch it.[133] Watch the young women in the audience roll their eyes. Watch the judge Simon Cowell's reaction when Boyle tells him her age. Each time she opens her mouth to speak, the jeering in the audience grows louder and the judges' scepticism grows stronger. The audience is heard laughing loudly when Boyle shares her dream of becoming a successful professional singer like Elaine Paige.

Then she opened her mouth and sang. Her modest stage introduction left everyone completely unprepared for the power and expression of her mezzo-soprano voice. She sang 'I Dreamed a Dream' from the musical *Les Miserables*. Before she had finished the song's opening phrase, the audience rose and gave a standing ovation. A star was indeed born!

The recording of Susan Boyle's performance makes compulsive viewing and it went viral. Within nine days, it was viewed 100 million times. Susan Boyle became an instant global superstar and, five years later, had become one of the most highly paid singers in the world with an estimated net worth of over £275 million.

Ever since that chill January audition, experts have been asking what it was about this unassuming, dowdy-looking woman that caught the imagination of a global audience, propelling her from obscurity to global stardom. She has a great voice, that's clear enough. But as experts at the time acknowledged, there was no shortage of first-class voices. Her voice alone did not get her where she is today.

The answer to that intriguing question is found in the workings of the Judge. The trigger for the Judge in us occurs when someone or something captures our attention. This may be in a positive or negative way, but there is a moment of significance that catches our eye. The Judge in us is much more like the talent show judge than a courtroom judge. The performance is what matters. We therefore need to be alert because the work of the Judge focuses on what captivates us rather than on what is important when framing decisions.

The Habit Loop of the Judge

In Chapter 7, we explained how our thinking habits are formed and how understanding the *habit loop* is our key to unlocking more effective choices. When it comes to the Judge, the habit loop tends to be this:

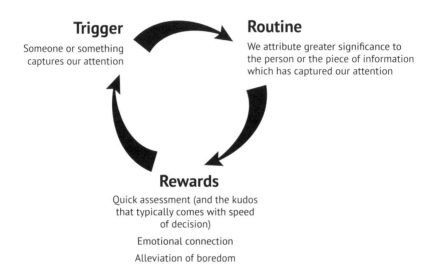

Trigger
Someone or something captures our attention

Routine
We attribute greater significance to the person or the piece of information which has captured our attention

Rewards
Quick assessment (and the kudos that typically comes with speed of decision)

Emotional connection

Alleviation of boredom

Figure 8a: The Habit Loop of the Judge

In this chapter, we will explore how the Judge is captivated by people and situations and how this captivation leads to suboptimal decisions. In Susan Boyle's performance, we can see three aspects of the trigger at work to capture our attention.

The first aspect is what Ben Parr, in his excellent book *Captivology: The Science of Capturing People's Attention*, calls 'disruption'.[134] Disruption is the surprise element. The unexpected thing that makes us sit up and listen. The Susan Boyle performance had two surprises at extremes. Surprise #1 that got our attention was the incongruence between her appearance and demeanour and her dream of stardom. The Judge in us initially shouted "nay!" Surprise #2 was her voice. Wow! We didn't expect that from her. These extremes in Boyle's performance were best expressed by Piers Morgan on the night:

> Without a doubt that was the biggest surprise I have had in three years of this show. When you stood there with that cheeky grin and said "I want to be like Elaine Page", everyone was laughing at you. No one is laughing now. That was stunning! An incredible performance. Amazing! I'm reeling from the shock.

The second aspect to Susan Boyle's performance that night was a strong emotional connection. Parr calls it the *acknowledgement* trigger. This is another powerful way the Judge can be activated. We tend to react most strongly to human-interest stories because they connect with us on an emotional level. Up to the point she stepped out onto the stage of *Britain's Got Talent*, Susan Boyle's story is one of rejection and failure. Branded "The Scottish Virgin" by the UK's tabloid press, Boyle is a village girl from Scotland who grew up being told she had a learning disability. She had been bullied in school, was a loner and long-term unemployed. She lived with her parents and devoted her adult life to caring for her ageing mother. When her mother passed away, Boyle mustered the courage to audition for *Britain's Got Talent* as a way to honour her mum who had always predicted that one day she would be a star. Her story is a feel-good story. In Susan Boyle, we acknowledge the underdog and connect her with our own challenges in life. So, anyone who is a wallflower, insecure, bullied, a minority, too heavy, too thin, too tall, too short, too old, too young – whatever the difference – we all can relate to Susan Boyle.

Finally, Susan Boyle's performance was in perfect harmony with the zeitgeist (the defining spirit or mood of our times). Being in tune with our zeitgeist is another sure way to catch people's attention. This tuning in is also referred to as *framing*, which is our attention to information that reinforces the way we make sense of the world. The song Boyle sang was all about a shattered dream and was performed at a time when the world was facing serious economic problems due to the fallout from the 2008 financial crisis. The lyrics of the song include the words:

> I had a dream my life would be
> So different from this hell that I am living,
> So different now from what it seemed,
> Now life has killed the dream I dreamed.

These words reflected perfectly many people's experiences at the time. No wonder Boyle's performance found such worldwide resonance.

Disruption, acknowledgement and framing are all ways in which people or situations capture our attention. But there is also another aspect of this trigger to the Judge's routine – *reputation*. Although reputation did not initially play a role in making Susan famous, it has certainly played a role in keeping Boyle in business since 2009.

Businesses use reputation to capture our attention and set the Judge's routine in us into motion, with the aim of selling their products and services. Experienced marketers use expert and celebrity endorsements and testimonials because they know that they work. Experts, particularly doctors in white coats, are widely listened to when they endorse particular food, hygiene or medication products. Celebrities with a strong appeal and reputation (like Susan Boyle) can be equally as effective in connecting with us on an emotional level. In Boyle's case, she was signed up to take centre stage in an advertising campaign for Miracle Whip, an American "mayonnaise alternative". This campaign also saw her perform with Lance Bass (a member of 1990s boyband N'Sync), former Guns 'N' Roses guitarist Gilby Clarke and 1980s pop star Tiffany. She recorded a spoof song, called 'Open Mouth' which was a plea to customers to try the alternative dressing rather than unfairly prejudging it. Kraft Foods, which owns Miracle Whip, said it wanted Susan involved because she was an artist who had been underestimated – just like its white salad dressing.

When celebrities endorse a product, the Judge in us feels safe and thinks that they do not need to scrutinise the product quite so thoroughly. We feel we can simply trust the product because we trust the celebrity or expert.

Louis Vuitton is a case in point. Louis Vuitton launched a highly successful advert featuring Mikhail S. Gorbachev (the leader of the Soviet Union who oversaw its ending). The advert captures Gorbachev sitting in a limousine as it passes the remaining part of the Berlin Wall. Beside him on the seat rests a Louis Vuitton road bag. The ad campaign, which also included tennis stars Andre Agassi and Steffi Graf and actress Catherine Deneuve, was intended to make the connection between celebrities, personal journeys and, of course, the high-end luxury product that is the LV bag.

On the flip side, the Judge at work in us can also have the opposite effect on a company's product. The Judge associates a celebrity with a product and when a celebrity falls from grace this also has an impact on the products they endorse. One example is Hertz rental cars. For many years Hertz was closely associated with the American football star O.J. Simpson. Yet the company suffered a setback in their public reputation during and shortly after the stars' high-profile trial for murder.

If there is even a sniff of a scandal, celebrities are likely to lose their endorsement deals. Lance Armstrong, Tiger Woods, Michael Phelps and Kate Moss are just a few famous names who have been dropped by brands because of controversial headlines. These are downsides. The upsides remain. As a result of the work of the Judge in us, celebrities continue to appear in 15 percent of US adverts and companies are estimated to invest some $50 billion each year on corporate sponsorships and endorsements. The popularity of celebrity endorsement can be explained by the very fact that celebrity endorsement significantly improves ad recall.[135] Given that the Judge routinely confuses memorable information with significant information, it is hardly surprising that companies find celebrity endorsement so effective as these endorsements help their adverts to stand out from the surrounding clutter.[136]

An even more powerful cocktail can be mixed when celebrity endorsement is combined with sex. For adults, erotic content scores very highly in terms of salience, which explains why advertisers like to use a little titillation in order to seduce people into buying their products. In 2013, an advert by H&M was voted the sexiest advert on European TV screens. H&M teamed up with David Beckham in order to advertise the 'Beckham Bodywear' range. The ad shows Beckham losing his robe, being locked out, running, swimming and playing soccer, all in his slippers and undies, and with plenty of gratuitous butt shots. Once seen, never forgotten. An advertisers dream!

There is something, however, that trumps even celebrity and sex. The highest salience level is reserved for information surrounding death and injury. Death and injury evoke strong emotions and are the most powerful in terms of memory retention. Researchers call this *mortality salience* and it underlines our deep anxieties and fears about our mortality. The work of the Judge misleads us in many areas, but this is where the Judge is strongest because death and injury evoke a fear response in us. Even as early as 1973, Nobel Prize winner Daniel Kahneman and his colleague Amos Tversky found that when participants in their research had personally witnessed a road accident they subsequently overestimated the risk of road accidents happening to them. This led them to conclude: "It is a common experience that the subjective probability of traffic accidents rises temporarily when one sees a car overturned by the side of the road."[137]

Subsequent studies have validated this research, providing evidence that the Judge in us assesses emotive information inaccurately.[138] In the face of salient and emotive information, the Judge loses all sense of perspective and offers us probability estimates that are grossly inflated. For example, people are more likely to believe that they will be murdered than die from stomach cancer. The evidence tells a different story. Statistics suggest we are five times more likely to die from stomach cancer than murder (and that is with low odds of getting stomach cancer in the first place). Another example concerns the fear of a shark attack.

People who visit seas frequented by sharks have an astonishingly high overestimation of the probability of a shark attack.[139] In reality, shark attacks are a rare occurrence, but when they occasionally happen they are widely reported in the media across the globe. The screaming headlines and highly salient media stories influence the way we see things.

In the UK, we now tend to keep our children from playing outside because of fear of child abduction, even though there is a higher probability of being struck by lightning than having our child abducted. The sad story of Sarah Payne, an eight-year-old from West Sussex in England who was raped and murdered by a convicted paedophile in July 2000 after a day out on the beach, sparked national outrage. Demonstrations against paedophiles occurred across the UK and occasionally spiralled into violence. Fuelled by fear and fury and armed with lists of supposed sex offenders, neighbours turned into vigilante groups with the express aim of carrying out their own form of justice in the name of the innocent schoolgirl. Families were driven from their homes and innocent men became the target for poisonous pen letters when they were mistaken for known sex offenders. A paediatrician (a doctor who specialises in the treatment of children) was even targeted because a mob was confused by the similarity of her job title to the word 'paedophile'.[140]

Researchers[141] have argued that the events of 9/11 left a pervasive sense of mortality salience throughout America. In the USA, there were an additional 1,200 driving fatalities in the weeks following the terrorist attacks of 11th September 2001 (nearly half the number again of those who died in the 9/11 attack). These fatalities were attributed to people choosing to drive rather than fly. With the vivid images of 9/11 fresh in people's minds, people wrongly judged that they were safer travelling by road than by air. Businesses also responded to 9/11 with a widespread ban on business air travel, which hurt the economy badly at the time and put some airlines out of business.

The Judge in us Wants to Mitigate our Fears

There is evidence[142] that the trauma of 9/11 played a significant role in George W. Bush's re-election. The Judge in us leads us to select a strong and charismatic leader when we feel under threat. During the 2004 presidential election, the American public consistently rated George W. Bush higher than his opponent John Kerry on the measures of charisma and strong leadership (Kerry was seen as a relationship-oriented leader who encouraged people to assume responsibility for political outcomes). This suggests that our voting behaviour is driven less by rational choices based on an informed understanding of the relevant issues and more by unconscious forces linked to our existential fears.

According to other researchers,[143] the Judge biases might also explain why Hitler and Mussolini were elected during a time of great economic hardship in both Germany and Italy. These leaders not only exuded great charisma but also openly marketed themselves as saviours of their particular tribe.

The same unconscious processes which lead us to cry out for a saviour figure in a crisis also lead us to demand immediate action in the face of threat. In democratic societies, governments try to respond to public concerns and will often focus on quick fixes and rushed legislation to appease the public's mood. Examples include the State of Florida outlawing 'shark feeding' in response to people's fear of being eaten by a shark while swimming off Florida's coast and the Dangerous Dogs Act in the UK – legislation enacted following fatal dog attacks on infants.

These knee-jerk reactions in response to the Judge at work in us can lead to considerable waste of public money, particularly when solutions on offer have not been scrutinised sufficiently. One such example was the stockpiling of Tamiflu by governments during the swine flu epidemic of 2009. Worldwide, this stockpiling cost the taxpayer billions. In the UK alone, the National Health Service spent £500 million on the drug without a proper assessment of its effectiveness. In the UK, a Cochrane Review reported in April 2014 that while Tamiflu could shorten flu symptoms by around half a day, there was no good evidence behind claims that the drug cut hospital admissions or lessened complications from the disease. The drug also had adverse side effects, which were not considered at the time.

We have learnt so far that the Judge is triggered when a person or situation grabs our attention. This may be because something happens that disrupts what we were expecting; makes an emotional connection with us; captures the mood of the times; builds on the reputation of the person trying to influence us and plays to our fears of death and injury. These are all very compelling triggers. There are other triggers we need to be mindful of. In his book *Captivology*, Parr also adds mystery (we all like a good cliff hanger) and reward (we also like to focus on things that might benefit us). The reality is that there isn't an exhaustive list. Researchers have found a number of very strong drivers behind the working of the Judge, but what grabs *our* attention will change depending upon context, what's on our mind at any particular time and our past experiences.

For many of us, stories and humour are also important triggers that grab our attention. These triggers are very context specific. Rudyard Kipling once wrote that "if history was told in the form of stories it would never be forgotten". Journalists make a living out of packaging information. The objective of a journalist is to package information in a way that grabs our attention. Journalists want us to read the article, listen to or watch a report, subscribe to a publication, a blog, channel or radio show. Journalists tell stories because the Judge in us remembers stories far better than random facts and statistics. Every story has to have an angle. If the journalist does not have an angle there is no story.

The Judge in us particularly focuses on the beginning of the story. To grab immediate attention, a good headline is of utmost importance. As one commentator put it, "writing headlines is like creating bouillon cubes from chicken soup: all of the flavor, none of the filler. Being able to distill a complex story into a five- or six-word heading gives clarity and focus. It's an invaluable skill in advertising and catalog copywriting – for any writing, for that matter."[144]

The British tabloid newspaper the *Sun* is well known for its memorable headlines. The *Sun* uses a range of techniques to grab our attention:

> **Rhyming – "Up Yours Delors"** (This was the *Sun*'s verdict on proposals being made by the then President of the European Union.)

> **Alliteration – "Boris Becker Bonking Ban"** (The *Sun*'s take on Boris Becker's preparations for the Wimbledon tennis championship.)

> **Puns – "Drip Drip Hurray"** (Reflecting how one-million people stood in torrential rain to watch celebrations marking Queen Elizabeth II's Diamond Jubilee – hip hip hurray!)

> **Sensationalism – "Freddie Starr ate my Hamster"** (Who knows what that story was really about.)

> **Humour – "Britain is Paralysed by Hot Air"** (This combined a story about volcanic ash paralysing air travel and a televised UK election debate between the leaders of the three main parties.)

> **Sexual innuendo – "Paddy Pantsdown'** (This referred to an affair the then leader of the UK Liberal Democrat Party – Paddy Ashdown – was having.)

Whether you are a fan of the *Sun* or not, its journalists have an excellent understanding of what makes for a salient, stand-out headline and what sells newspapers. It is salience that the Judge in us focuses on, remembers and recalls as significant at a later date.

The Judge can be Misled by Humour: The Rise of the Comedian–Politician

We all love humour. We want people to make us laugh. Humour entertains us and we remember it. The Judge in us will certainly remember people, situations and information that made us laugh. The Judge will stop us scrutinising people too closely if they made us laugh. This offers us some insight into why those politicians who entertain are often held in great affection irrespective of their personal failings. In Italy, Silvio Berlusconi (the country's former prime minister) charmed the Italian public for many years. Italians kept on voting for him whilst the rest of Europe wondered why and considered his misdemeanours to be beyond the pale. In France, former President Nicolas Sarkozy cut a ludicrous figure but still had considerable public support; and in America, Bill Clinton remained one of the most popular US presidents of all times although his presidency was marred by a number of serious scandals.

In the UK we have Boris Johnson, the popular mayor of London who likes to play the clown. Despite numerous personal scandals, at the time of writing Johnson is still a rising star and tipped to become a future leader of the Conservative Party. Johnson is highly entertaining. A former journalist who clearly understands the power of salience, he has enthralled the British public with bon mots such as "Voting Tory will cause your wife to have bigger breasts and increase your chances of owning a BMW M3" and "I think I was once given cocaine but I sneezed so it didn't go up my nose. In fact, it may have been icing sugar." Our youngest daughter has remarked that any politician who rides on a zip wire is good enough for her!

Corporations: The Search for the Charismatic Leader

Research into the selection of CEOs has highlighted *reputation* as a key influencer of decision makers. When a company is in crisis, the Judge in us is more likely to select a charismatic CEO. This decision-making process echoes our choice of national leaders as discussed earlier. In his book *Searching for a Corporate Savior: The Irrational Quest for Charismatic CEOs*, Rakesh Khurana[145] describes the biases that play out in the selection process for a new CEO. Khurana offers AT&T as a good example of how these thinking errors play out.

In 1997, AT&T was in trouble and needed a new leader. As one of the blue-chip icons of corporate America, the company was operating in a deregulated industry and faced declining profit margins in its core business – long-distance telephony services. After a three-month search, the board made its decision. It passed over a well-regarded insider, John Zeglis, who was intimately familiar with the complexities of the deregulated business environment and instead hired C. Michael Armstrong as CEO. After a 31-year career with IBM, Armstrong had headed Hughes Electronics, a defence contractor with interests in satellite television, with great success for four years. Business magazines pictured him astride his Harley Davidson motorcycle, a knight on an iron steed riding in to save the telecommunications giant.

"The selection of a celebrity CEO can drive up the market value of a company's stock," Khurana notes and indeed, the day Armstrong was selected, the market value of AT&T stock went up $4 billion. The AT&T board also lavished money on Armstrong. In 2000, Armstrong's compensation was reportedly a mere $21.8 million and perks included a $10-million guaranteed price on a block of his restricted stock. As part of his vision to reinvent AT&T as an omni-Internet corporation, Armstrong embarked on an aggressive program of acquisition in cable TV, cellular telephony and Internet delivery systems.

That strategy failed spectacularly. AT&T had to sell those acquisitions at huge losses. AT&T stock, which peaked at about $64 per share in 1999, sank to $10 within a few years. Khurana reflected that the company had actually changed little from when Mike Armstrong walked in – a former regulated company with declining margins in its core long-distance telephone business – except for two things. A $6.7 billion debt had risen to $67 billion and one of the healthiest balance sheets had turned into one of the worst.

Compare Khurana's findings with those described in Jim Collins' excellent book *Good to Great*. Collins researched companies that outperformed their competitors by significant orders of magnitude. According to Collins, the CEOs of these spectacularly performing companies were recruited from within. They were definitely not chosen because they were charismatic leaders but selected for their capabilities. There was no expectation that they would perform miracles or provide instant cures. Collins' and Khurana's findings, taken together, have serious implications for the way boards select business leaders.

This need to resist the Judge's call to opt for quick fixes offered by charismatic leaders also applies to proposals offered by people working in the lower echelons of business. Research published in 2006 by Frank Lefley[146] concluded that a manager's reputation amongst colleagues had a crucial influence on project selection. The Judge in us will make a connection between the person who is presenting and supporting a particular proposal, and the details of the proposal itself. The research found that if someone is highly regarded, we do not scrutinise the proposal as thoroughly as we do for those who don't come with an established reputation. It is a quick and lazy way to make decisions but we all have probably fallen foul of it at some point or another.

This thinking error is backed up by the findings of a McKinsey & Co. global survey of major corporates.[147] McKinsey found that managers reported that they deferred more than is warranted to the person making or supporting an investment proposal than to the merits of the proposal itself. This corresponds to findings of other studies[148] which maintain that many CEOs are prone to over-rely on the judgment of a trusted subordinate, even if the subordinate's bias is obvious. This lack of scrutiny at senior levels will result in suboptimal decision making. At its worst, it can also lead to the covering up of grave errors.

Highly regarded and experienced traders have all been behind the high-profile trading scandals that have hit the headlines in recent years. Nick Leeson, who in 1995 made derivatives-trading losses of US$1.3 billion and thus brought down Barings Bank, is perhaps a classic example. At just 28 years old, Leeson was considered a star trader and Barings' management kept him on a very loose leash. When things started to go wrong, Leeson hid losses in a special account numbered 88888 – a lucky number in Chinese. But hiding could only cover up the losses for so long: eventually Barings collapsed and Leeson was sentenced to six and a half years in jail. (Leeson later recalled that throughout his three years at Barings, he was never challenged or scrutinised. The only time someone did a position check and asked him to explain his trading activities was 23rd February 1995, the day he was found out. It was the Judge's narrow focus on his star status which stopped senior management from asking more searching questions earlier.)

Our Obsession with Fads and Fashions

When researching this book we were struck by how little research existed into the actual processes of organisational decision making – how stakeholders set agendas, what information gets noticed, how other information is ruled out. Given the importance of the work of the Judge in determining our choices, this is a knowledge gap we hope will be closed in coming years. Having worked in business for over thirty years, one thing we have been mindful of, and which casts an interesting light on decision making, is the rise and fall of management fads and fashions. Business leaders can allocate huge amounts of cash and many hours of time into mobilising their organisation behind the latest fad.

We are great fans of the *Financial Times* journalist Lucy Kellaway who has, over many years, poked fun at the various management fads that have found favour in organisations. Her most recent top 10 fads[149] include: management by walking about, emotional intelligence, six sigma, business process re-engineering and there is no 'I' in team. The habit loop of the Judge gives us important insights into why these fads gain traction. Leonard Ponzi and Michael Koenig argue[150] that a key determinant of whether any management idea is a 'management fad' is the number and timing of published articles on the idea. The authors reckon there is a three-to-five-year window on management fads after which fewer articles appear and the fad slowly fizzles out. Danny Miller and John Hartwick have constructed a table that summarises eight common properties of management fads:[151]

1. Simple, straightforward
A fad's ideas are easy to communicate, comprehend and reduce to a small number of factors, dimensions or characteristics. Clear-cut distinctions, perfect contrasts and ideal types are proposed. Simple solutions are suggested.

2. Promising results
Fads promise results such as greater control and efficiency, more motivated and productive workers, more satisfied customers or some other valued result.

3. Universal
Fads propose solutions for everyone. Imparted truths are said to apply to almost all organisations, functions, tasks, individuals or cultures. Fads claim enormous generality and universal relevance.

4. Step-down capability
Fads have the capacity to be implemented in ritualistic and superficial ways. Recommendations can be implemented quickly and easily, often without having much effect on organisational practices.

5. In tune with zeitgeist

Fads resonate with the major trends or business problems of the day. They respond to challenges that are broadly felt and openly discussed. These might result from deficiencies in current administrative practices, technology changes, or shifts in economic or social conditions. Solutions are in tune with prevailing values.

6. Novel, not radical

Fads are novel, not radical. They question existing assumptions, criticise widespread practices and point to fresh new ways of doing things. However, this novelty is not so much a new discovery as a rediscovery and repackaging of older ideas, values and approaches

7. Legitimacy via gurus and star examples

Fads are supported by tales of excellent companies, the status and prestige of gurus, not by solid empirical evidence. Stories of corporate heroes and organisational successes provide role models and suggest prestigious adherents, lending an aura of legitimacy to the ideas being espoused.

8. Lively, entertaining

Fads are almost always presented in a way that can be described as concrete, articulate, bold, memorable and upbeat. Interesting anecdotes and corporate war stories abound. Descriptions are vivid and extreme, making fads fun to read about and listen to.

Figure 9: Eight Common Properties of Fads

These eight characteristics of fads operate along the lines of the Judge's habit loop. The triggers that capture our attention are: these fads are in tune with the *zeitgeist* (which is our framing cue), promote *legitimacy* (via gurus, akin to celebrity endorsement) and are communicated in an *entertaining* way. The Judge's routine is activated as attention turns to understanding and then to implementation. The *simplicity of the concepts* makes them easy to grasp and, when combined with the *over-promising of results* and *dramatic examples*, seduce leaders into action. The reward for adoption of a fad is the quick fix, but this comes at a price and often at the expense of lasting change.

Fads often fail to do justice to the challenges they are trying to address. Organisations are complex and often there are no single or easy answers. In many ways, fad surfing is a worrying trait for a leader, manager or consultant – particularly when the latest fad is promoted because it seems an easier way out than persevering with a previous idea that may not have delivered as fast or as fully as expected. Ultimately, fad hopping creates a tremendous amount of confusion and cynicism as the organisation moves from fad to fad.

Outsourcing: A Case Study in the Work of the Judge

In 2002, the Hewlett Packard Company (HP) made the following announcement: "HP today announced it is planning additional outsourcing of its PC manufacturing facilities worldwide, in keeping with its longstanding strategy to decrease operations costs and improve profitability. This move will allow HP to take advantage of the flexibility and cost benefits associated with using non-dedicated factories..."

Outsourcing (the transfer of in-house activities to third parties) offers the carrot of significant cost savings to organisations. HP's strategy to outsource to low-cost countries was a common strategy for manufacturers in the prosperous noughties. In 2002, HP's leadership was in tune with the zeitgeist. Outsourcing was *the* buzzword at the time (the framing trigger) and every self-respecting business leader had an outsourcing strategy. At first the strategy worked a treat. Costs were indeed slashed and the business press lauded HP's management. HP's greatest competitor, Dell, followed suit by carrying out an extreme outsourcing strategy. In 2006, massive R&D and customer contact facilities were built in India.

However, new information was emerging at the time suggesting that outsourcing could lead to a fragmentation and even disintegration of the supply chain, inviting new competitors into the industry and undermining pricing power and long-term profitability. Yet this was ignored as the management of both HP and Dell fell prey to the Judge. The end result was that through outsourcing both HP and Dell slowly gave away their competitive advantage. Both HP and Dell are now paying the price with erosion of profit margins, revenue and profit growth, as they cope with new entrants to the market. This is in sharp contrast to other consumer electronics companies like Apple and Google who took a broader perspective and limited outsourcing. They retained product design, branding, marketing and after-sales services in house and consequently kept hold of their intellectual capital as well as their customer base.

The Obsession with Benchmarking

Benchmarking is the process of comparing one organisation's business processes and performance metrics to those of other organisations. The belief is that you are comparing like with like and that, through benchmarking, you can identify how well you stack up and where you can get better. There are certainly implicit and often explicit notions of 'best' and 'best practices' across organisations. On the face of it, benchmarking seems beneficial for organisations. After all, an understanding of how others work in your sector or function must surely give insights into how things could be improved. We are also attracted by the idea of measurement and the security a number gives us. Academics have, however, started to point to the serious, even fatal, pitfalls associated with benchmarking which have often been overlooked in the frantic pursuit to measure and compare.

One such academic is Jeffrey Pfeffer, Professor of Organisational Behavior at Stanford University's Graduate School of Business. Pfeffer has been cautioning managers on how to avoid the pitfalls of benchmarking for some time. In his book *Hard Facts, Dangerous Half-Truths, and Total Nonsense: Profiting from Evidence-Based*

Management, he describes the widespread practice of 'casual' or 'mindless' benchmarking. These are instances where organisations try to copy what others are doing without first asking basic questions, such as: Why might this practice enhance performance? Is it the right thing to do for us? Would we see the same results?

According to Pfeffer, organisations often choose to copy the most *visible* and superficial aspects of another organisation's management approach. In other words, the Judge in us selects those aspects of another organisation's practices that have caught the attention of management and then assumes that, because one organisation has used a particular practice successfully, it both provides the reason for that organisation's success and is something that can indeed be copied. Pfeffer suggests that such thinking ignores the reality that management practices work in systems and that you can't just cherry pick individual practices – you have to look at the system as a whole.

One tale of the mindless benchmarking Pfeffer refers to involved United Airlines and its decision to try to compete with Southwest Airlines in the California market. United tried to copy Southwest's legendary practices: quick turnarounds; increased frequency of flights to and from California; reducing the scheduled time United planes would be on the ground; dressing staff and flight attendants in casual clothes; and scrapping in-flight meals for passengers. None of these copied practices produced the intended results as Southwest ended up with an even higher market share in California after United entered the market. The Judge in the United management had selected the most visible aspects of Southwest strategies to imitate without considering the less visible components of the Southwest success story – the company's culture and management philosophy and the priority it placed on looking after its employees, making it an employer of choice in California.

Are You the Judge?

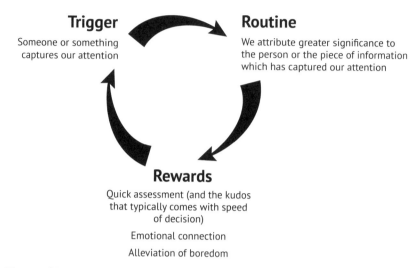

Figure 8b: The Habit Loop of the Judge

The Judge in us is triggered when someone or something captures our attention. Imagine you are in a crowded room with people you do not know. You hear someone calling your name. You immediately look around and try to find out who is calling you. While trying to find out who has called your name, you ignore other important information – like your phone vibrating in your pocket. You miss an important phone call and, as you walk towards where the sound of your name being called came from, you do not see that someone has spilled a drink on the floor. You slip on the wet floor. This is work of the Judge in an everyday situation. We are captivated and sidetracked by instances that capture our attention, to the exclusion of other important things.

Reflection Point

Can you think of recent examples where the Judge in you has led to you ignoring important information?

What was the trigger?
Can you describe the routine?
Did you observe a reward?

What We Have Learned in this Chapter

- The Judge encapsulates our tendency to focus and attend to narrow and more salient information. This captures our attention at the expense of other relevant data which otherwise might have given us a more complete picture of the situation.
- Information that grabs our attention triggers the Judge's habit loop in us. Although what grabs our attention changes depending upon context, the most common triggers for the Judge are emotional connection, framing, reward, reputation, humour and a story.
- The Judge considers the most salient piece of information to be the most significant piece of information on which to base a decision.
- In the corporate context, the Judge's routine plays itself out in many different ways. In the chapter, we highlighted the Judge's contribution in common practices such as management boards trying to find a corporate 'saviour', project selections on the basis of a project champion's reputation, lack of scrutiny and accountability for people with a good reputation, adoption of quick fixes and management fads as well as mindless benchmarking.
- Seeing our decisions through the lens of the Judge invites us to ask ourselves consciously: "What information has grabbed my attention and what information has not been attended to?" By refocusing our attention on information that hasn't grabbed our attention we might be able to get a fuller picture and avoid the pitfalls of the Judge.

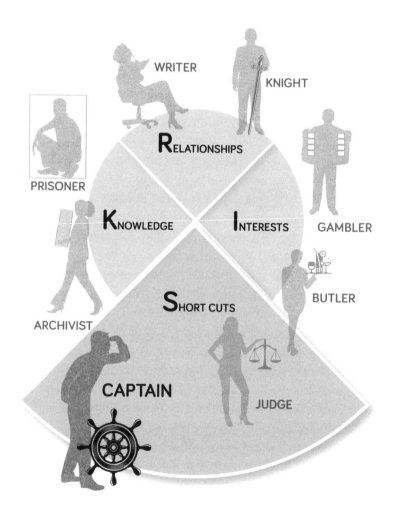

PRISONER

WRITER

KNIGHT

RELATIONSHIPS

GAMBLER

KNOWLEDGE **I**NTERESTS

GAMBLER

ARCHIVIST

BUTLER

SHORT CUTS

CAPTAIN

JUDGE

14

The Captain

The
CAPTAIN

"The human understanding when it has once adopted an opinion (either being the received opinion or as being agreeable to itself) draws all things else to support and agree with it."

Francis Bacon

The Captain's Tale

I am the Captain. My two most essential tools are the anchor and the steering wheel. When I fix on an idea or viewpoint, I anchor it. Even when circumstances change or different information emerges I will stick to my guns and not change my opinion. I also use the wheel to steer a course in a predetermined direction, taking into account only information that confirms the direction of travel I have already decided to take.

The Captain's Motto: "Nothing will divert me from my course or move me from my anchorage."

What You Need to Remember about the Captain

The Captain in us is triggered when a piece of information, an idea or belief system predetermines and anchors a decision.

The Captain:

- ✓ Uses information from the past to make up his mind
- ✓ Has made up his mind
- ✓ Looks for confirming evidence.

What Do Smart Deciders Do?

Smart decision makers:

- ✓ Are aware that pieces of information from the past can anchor the decision
- ✓ Look actively for disconfirming evidence
- ✓ Consider alternative destinations and look for confirming evidence for those alternatives
- ✓ Welcome the devil's advocate.

Whenever you're called on to make up your mind,
and you're hampered by not having any,
the best way to solve the dilemma, you'll find,
is simply by spinning a penny.
No – not so that chance shall decide the affair
while you're passively standing there moping;
but the moment the penny is up in the air,
you suddenly know what you're hoping.

This little poem is called 'A Psychological Tip' and was written by the Danish poet Piet Hein. You may have never heard of him. Yet Piet Hein (1905–96) was an extraordinary man who made an outstanding contribution in a whole range of spheres. As a scientist he invented the Soma cube (a solid dissection puzzle) and, as a mathematician, he developed a mathematical formula to create a new geometrical form – the 'super-ellipse'. In the 1950s and '60s, as an artist and constructor, Piet Hein gave form to beautiful pieces of furniture and he contributed to making 'Scandinavian design' an international success story. Above all else, however, Piet Hein was a popular poet. Millions of his countrymen knew him as 'Kumbel', the pen name he used for his poetry. He invented his own genre of poetry, which he called *the grook*. These are delightful little poems like the one above and sum up human experiences.

The power of grooks is partly their amusing tone and entertaining turn of phrase, but most of all what invites our attention is the truth embodied in each poem. We comprehend and recognise something of ourselves in them. In the poem that opens this chapter, we recognise and experience yet again that intuitive knowing of the answer to a question before a decision is 'officially' made. These unconscious forces that steer our thinking in a particular direction are associated with the work of the Captain. In eight poetic lines, Piet Hein has masterfully managed to reduce the work of the Captain to its very essence.

The Habit Loop of the Captain

In Chapter 7, we explained how our thinking habits are formed and how understanding the *habit loop* is our key to unlocking more effective choices. When it comes to the Captain, the habit loop tends to be this:

Figure 10a: The Habit Loop of the Captain

In this chapter, we will particularly focus on how the work of the Captain impacts typical areas of decision making through what psychologists call anchoring and then steering. The Captain takes a piece of information, an idea or a belief that has lodged itself into our subconscious and suggests a predetermined outcome – 'something we are hoping for'. We then seek other information that validates this anchored choice and steer our thinking in that direction. We can't be sure when anchoring happens, but this personal story illustrates how it *can* happen a long time before we actually have to make a decision.

How Miss Piri Scuppered the Chance of a Windfall Profit for Japanese Housewives

London, November 1989

"Anna-San, how likely is German Reunification?" Twenty-three pairs of dark brown eyes belonging to some of the most senior Japanese asset managers look expectantly at me. Together they manage a whopping $3 billion worth of investments – in 1989 this was the equivalent of the GNP of a small country – and these funds are the cumulative savings of the penny-pinching Japanese housewife.

In 1989, the world is captivated by the television footage coming out of Eastern Europe. There is a rising tide of euphoria throughout Europe and the German stock market is on an upward move. My colleagues want to know whether they should be fully invested in Germany and they look to me for an answer. I am their German market specialist and I need to make a call.

I have not come unprepared for this discussion and I immediately launch into a detailed analysis of the post-war geopolitical landscape. It is peppered with facts and figures and opinion. No-one in the room questions the thoroughness of this short presentation and, given the fear of world leaders of the re-emergence of a strong united Germany, it concludes with the prediction that German unification indeed is very unlikely.

I observe the disappointment on my Japanese colleagues faces. They had hoped for a far more positive assessment. After some debate, the asset allocation committee follows my advice and decides to exercise caution.

Germany 1972

I am a pupil at the local Gymnasium (secondary Grammar school) in Saarburg, a small town in the Rhineland–Palatinate region of Germany. I am in Miss Piri's geography class and in front of us is a big map of Germany. All our eyes are focused on an offensive-looking thick red line in the middle of our country which snakes itself from north to south. Miss Piri is standing next to the map. She is tracing the red line with a thin bamboo stick. Her high soprano voice is laced with emotion and the large horn-rimmed glasses that normally sit flush on the bridge of her nose have inexplicably moved to the tip. I can see them wobbling as she exclaims:

"There is one thing we, as Germans, have to come to terms with.

Our country will always be divided. There will be no German reunification. Ever. This is the price Germans have to pay for the atrocities committed in the war."

Almost immediately the reality of that statement hits home. A sombre atmosphere descends on the class. Everybody is deadly silent. Many of my classmates have families in the East, including Beate, my best friend who sits next to me. I can see she is holding back tears. Her Oma (grandma) lives in the East. She has only ever seen her once. I feel sorry for Beate and her Oma and I also feel guilty. Eventually the shrill sound of the bell puts an end to the geography lesson and the classroom empties at the speed of light.

If I tell you that, in 1972, Miss Piri scuppered the chance of Mrs Suzuki in Nagano Prefecture, Japan, making a quick buck on the back of German reunification in 1989, you might consider it too far-fetched. On the face of it, the musings of a middle-aged geography teacher in an obscure provincial town in Germany should be of little consequence to global capital market flows 20 years later. But on closer inspection, Germany 1972 and London 1989 might be inextricably linked through the work of the Captain.

We know that the brain is constantly bombarded with information and needs to sift through it in order to make sense of the world. The sifting process happens automatically, operating outside our awareness, and is guided by what already exists in our mind: what we know, what we have experienced and what stands out. Miss Piri's emotive speech all those years ago had a big impact on me. What remained was a trace in my memory that anchored my thinking to an idea that German reunification was just a pipe dream that could never be realised. Sadly at that time, because of that call, the Japanese housewife did not benefit from what was later known as the reunification bonus that pushed the German stock market towards stratospheric levels in the weeks following the collapse of the Berlin Wall.

Many of our life experiences are the result of early anchoring. Family therapists and relationship counsellors have long understood this. They have coined a phrase, 'the unconscious couple fit', to describe the early imprinting we all receive from our birth families that shapes our idea of the ideal partner for us. If, for example, a heterosexual man in his twenties is wondering why all his previous girlfriends and his current partner are shy, reticent and needy women, the likelihood is that his mother was a quiet, reserved and dependent woman. Our parents model to us what it is to be a man or a woman and subsequently people will revert back to this early anchor and unconsciously choose a partner who embodies some of the most salient features or behaviours of their parent(s).

Once relationships are formed, the Captain also plays a crucial role in how the relationship is conducted. Let's take the thorny issue of who does what around the house. This is one of the most divisive issues in many relationships. If a husband is doing ten times more housework than his dad ever did, he may feel that his wife should acknowledge and appreciate his contribution to the smooth running of the household. His wife, coming from a background where her dad routinely did as much as her mum around the house, might feel that her husband is not doing enough and should not make such a fuss about the little he does. Early anchoring is very powerful, but more recent anchors also trigger the Captain's routine.

Over the years, psychologists have had much fun demonstrating the power of anchoring on our choices.[152] In 2006, an experiment was run at the prestigious MIT,[153] which involved a very bizarre auction. Students were asked to bid on a number of random items such as a textbook, a computer mouse or a bottle of wine. The researchers would hold up the items and describe them in glorious detail. Then each student had to write down the two last digits of their social security number as if it were the price of the item. If the last two digits were 22, then an item was priced at $22 and if the two numbers happened to be 55 the item was priced at $55 and so on. After the students wrote down the pretend price they then bid for these items in an auction. What the researchers found was quite astonishing. The bidding reflected the anchors – the last two digits of the social security numbers – which had been dropped. Students with high social security numbers bid up to three and a half times more for the items than those with low numbers. It does not matter what type of anchors are used: the impact of anchoring delivers the same result. Kahnemann and Tversky, for example, used a wheel of fortune to anchor a number. Others have used dates of births, average annual temperature and even ping-pong balls drawn out of a bag with random numbers on them. Any number will do to create the same effect, because the Captain keeps referring back to that initial number anchored in our mind.

What this means is that, when given estimates or information before the real data is presented, we will often adjust our expectations to align with the estimates. Negotiations are good examples of anchoring. The opening gambit often becomes the anchor around which negotiations take place. We notice two behaviours. The first is that once an anchor is set, other judgments are made in response to that initial anchor. The second is that there is a bias toward interpreting other information in relation to the initial anchor. If we translate this into the everyday, the initial price asked for a car, a house or any other major purchase we negotiate tends to have ramifications throughout the process of coming to an agreement. The subconscious work of the Captain in us keeps referring back to that initial number.

The Captain's Anchor in Business

Understanding the work of the Captain is important in any type of negotiation. Let's consider salary negotiations. Studies have shown[154] that when the initial anchor figure is set high, the final negotiated amount will also be high. This holds true even for unrealistically high demands. These are not dismissed as pipedreams by the employer, but lead instead, according to this research, to higher salary offers. We will let you draw your own conclusions about the strategy to deploy during your next salary review.

Another example in corporate life is the use of list prices. In many cases these prices are far from a real offer that a selling party would accept. They act, however, as an anchor, convincing a buyer that they have a bargain when getting some level of discount. Anchoring is also at play in a number of common business processes such as budgeting. Typically the current budget or spending level is the anchor and adjustments are often smaller percentage adjustments away from that anchor. The use of zero-based budgeting in some businesses has been adopted in response to this distortion in decision making, although it would be interesting to see if the agreed budgets are still close to the anchor point.

Anchors can even be used to enhance the customer experience. A recent study by the California Institute of Technology and Stanford Business School[155] found that the more expensive consumers think a wine is, the more pleasure they take in drinking it. When the same wine was tasted twice, and where two different prices were stated for that wine, participants in the study preferred the one they thought was more expensive. When designing a menu, restaurants will often place a very high-priced dish next to a medium-priced dish even when both dishes broadly contain the same ingredients. Often these ingredients are gourmet products such as caviar or expensive seafood or truffle. The restaurant wants the customer to choose the medium-priced dish and uses the higher-priced dish as an anchor that suggests to the customer that they are getting a luxury product at a bargain prices.

J.C. Penney, a chain of over 1,000 department stores in the US, is an excellent example of a company that chose to ignore the Captain's anchor, with devastating consequences. On 1st February 2012 under the leadership of their new CEO, Ron Johnson, J.C. Penney announced a new pricing approach, 'Everyday Low Prices'. Traditionally, J.C. Penney customers were used to getting discounts. 'Everyday Low Prices' was a complete flop with the core customer group because it showed only one price (which may have been very good value) instead of showing two prices – the recommended retail price (RRP) and the J.C. Penney discounted price. The impact on customers was to remove the anchor price (the RRP) that signalled what people could be paying elsewhere and also the associated sense of elation that came when getting a bargain. Consequently, sales dropped dramatically by 30 percent within 12 months and management reversed its pricing strategy.

The Captain's Anchor in the Justice System

A study published in 2006[156] showed that both experienced and novice fingerprint examiners are swayed by the work of the Captain through anchoring. In one experiment, the researchers presented six examiners with fingerprint marks that, unbeknown to them, they had analysed before. This time, the examiners were furnished with additional information about the case, for example that the suspect had confessed to the crime or that the suspect was in police custody at the time the crime was committed. In nearly a fifth of their examinations, they changed their decision in the direction suggested by this additional information.

After hearing about this research on the impact of the Captain, Kevin Kershaw (Head of Forensic Identification Services at Greater Manchester Police – one of Britain's largest police forces) decided to buffer his examiners from external factors that could bias their judgements. He therefore prevented investigating officers from coming on-site to wait for results and potentially talking to the examiners about the case. In this case, this was made easier because the forensic division works at arm's length to the Manchester police force (as happens in many British police forces). In the USA, no such separation exists.

A now famous study by Englich and Mussweiler in 2001[157] showed that even judges with more than 15 years of experience were influenced by sentencing demands, even when these demands were made by people who weren't experts. The research showed that when someone set an expectation for a sentence, the result was a prison sentence a third longer for the same crime than when no demand was made.

How the Captain Steers Our Decisions

A 2009 meta-analysis of research into steering biases found that people are almost twice as likely to select information that aligns with their pre-existing attitudes, beliefs and behaviours.[158] Other studies have demonstrated that even the most rigorous, logical thinkers are not immune from the Captain's steering. Software designers are very familiar with the way the Captain steers decisions. During all stages of software testing, extensive testing strategies are employed to fail the code in order to reduce what they call "software defect density".[159] People other than those who designed the software always carry out these extensive tests because the Captain's steering stops designers who originally designed the software from discovering their own mistakes.

We also see the work of the Captain in the field of science. Scientists who evaluate studies by others routinely give better ratings to those that confirm their pre-existing beliefs than to studies that do not. The Ig Nobel Prize[160] for 2012 was awarded to Craig Bennett, Abigail Baird, Michael Miller and George Wolford (US). These researchers found that, by using complicated instruments and simple statistics, brain researchers can see meaningful brain activity anywhere – even in a dead salmon! (No kidding. If you don't believe us, look up the reference!)[161]

There are many other amusing tales of scientists falling prey of the Captain's steering. In 1903, shortly after the discovery of X-rays, the famous French physicist René Blondlot announced the discovery of N-rays (a new form of radiation).[162] Blondlot found instant celebrity status in France and, very shortly afterwards, researchers from around the world confirmed that they too had seen N-rays. You see, at the time, the scientific community was extremely excited about radiation. X-rays, vacuum ultraviolet radiation and cathode rays had been discovered less than a decade earlier and the discovery of radio waves and gamma rays soon followed. So scientists were looking for the new and very much wanted to discover yet another 'ray' – the N-ray! Despite the early euphoria, attempts by other renowned scientists to replicate the experiment failed. In 1905, the American physicist Robert W. Wood even visited Blondlot's laboratory in France to use the actual equipment Blondlot had used. Having substituted a block of wood for the all-important prism through which N-rays could be observed, Wood found that he could still observe the so-called ephemeral light that was supposed to be exhibited by the N-rays. Wood concluded that N-rays were a purely subjective phenomenon, with the scientists involved having recorded data that matched their expectations. These conclusions were the nail in the coffin for N-rays.

In the UK, the discovery of Piltdown Man in 1912 stunned British archaeology.[163] The find was a prehistoric skull believed to be the missing evolutionary link between apes and humans. This belief persisted well into the 1950s. It was then discovered to be the biggest archaeological hoax in history. Yet despite this, scientific research focused for four decades on confirming the original belief rather than disproving it. Even when considering the limited technology and techniques available at the time of Piltdown Man's discovery, this case remains embarrassing for archaeologists and serves as a cautionary tale of the dangers of the Captain's steering.

If the world's most rigorous thinkers can easily succumb to the Captain's routine, those of us who are less rigorous in our thinking should pay particular attention to this steering. This is particularly true when high emotions are involved. Consider the 'objective' assessments of sports fans. Fans, unless they are party to inside knowledge, will base their judgements on what they see in front of them. The Captain in them will pick out events that support their conclusions and rely on fellow fans who share their opinion to confirm what they already know. As a passionate Welsh rugby fan, Mark knows this all too well. Players who are out of favour with the general public find themselves under a microscope and all their errors are scrutinised to a point where they can do no right. The conclusion – we are right and the coach is wrong.

This pattern of thinking is the foundation for *groupthink* where the Captain at work in each group member focuses on salient information, forms an opinion and mobilises the group consensus behind that opinion. Sport is one arena where groupthink reigns supreme. Politics is another.

Politicians will generally seek out information that confirms their existing viewpoint. It takes a special politician to engage actively with opinion that disconfirms opinion and this makes bipartisanship both infrequent and precious when it happens. When in government, the Captain's steering will often guide politicians. Even when presented with evidence that suggests that their preferred policy option is less than optimal, politicians stick with the original policy. Take the US decision to go to war in Iraq in 2003. Tyler Drumheller (a senior CIA operative in Europe during the run up to the war) disclosed in a CBS program[164] that the US administration had met Naji Sabri (the Iraqi Foreign Minister) who told the White House that Iraq did not have weapons of mass destruction. After meeting with this high-ranking source, the White House lost interest in him. According to Drumheller, they didn't want any additional data from Sabri because "the policy was set. The war in Iraq was coming and they were looking for intelligence to fit into the policy".

Armchair politicians are also steered by the Captain. If we think about where we get our information and opinion from, the chances are that we tend to use the same sources and that those sources generally reflect our existing political preferences. For example in the UK, people who identify themselves as readers of the *Guardian* newspaper will tend to be politically liberal and socialist, whilst *Daily Telegraph* readers will tend to be conservative and traditionalist. There isn't much crossover of readership and readers of one newspaper can have quite strong (and stereotypical) opinions about those of the other. What this means for readers is that the primary purpose of taking their favourite newspaper is not to be informed objectively but to confirm their existing views.

When it comes to election time, the Captain also focuses on information that we want to believe. During the 2008 US presidential election, Valdis Krebs at orgnet.com analysed purchasing trends on Amazon. People who already supported Obama were the same people buying books that painted him in a positive light. People who already disliked Obama were the ones buying books painting him in a negative light. Krebs has researched over a long period of time purchasing trends on Amazon and the clustering habits of people on social networks. His research shows that the Captain in us wants to be right about how he sees the world and seeks out information that confirms beliefs and avoids or dismisses contradictory evidence and opinions.

There is also strong evidence that in the US people will choose their TV viewing along partisan lines. As with the written word, TV packages the news in the way its audience wants to hear it. It may come as no surprise that Fox News is predominately watched by Republicans. An interesting narrative unfolded on the day of the 2012 US Presidential election. When it was confirmed that President Obama had been re-elected, many commentators on the Fox channel still maintained that the result could not be true and guaranteed viewers that Republican candidate Mitt Romney would win. Karl Rove, a Fox commentator and long-time Republican strategist, continued denying that Obama had won while on air. The opinion was so out of kilter with the evidence that another newscaster had to take him to one side and confront him with the evidence that Obama had won a decisive victory. That an experienced political strategist like Karl Rove continued to believe the Captain's steering, rather than evidence in front of his face, is an excellent example of how the persistence of the Captain's steering can blow off course even the most experienced people.[165]

The Captain's Steering in Investment

In investment, the Captain's steering can cost us a lot of money. Once an investor starts to like a particular investment idea, let's say a particular stock, the Captain in him may dismiss negative information as irrelevant or inaccurate. Investors often stick with a declining stock far longer than they should simply because they interpret news about the company in a favourable light and even seek out information that justifies their original purchasing decision. The result is that the Captain's steering skews an investor's frame of reference and leaves them with an incomplete picture of the situation.

Warren Buffet, one of the world's most successful investors, has long been aware of the Captain's steering. Long before our knowledge of thinking errors emerged from the corridors of academia, Warren Buffet wrote in *Fortune* magazine: "Charles Darwin used to say that whenever he ran into something that contradicted a conclusion he cherished, he was obliged to write the new finding down within 30 minutes. Otherwise his mind would work to reject the discordant information, much as the body rejects transplants. Man's natural inclination is to cling to his beliefs, particularly if they are reinforced by recent experience – a flaw in our makeup that bears on what happens during bull markets and extended periods of stagnation".[166] Perhaps it was Buffet's early awareness of the Captain at work in investment decision making that gave him an edge over others and contributed to his supreme success as an investor.

In Business, the Captain's Steering is Ubiquitous

The Captain's steering can creep into every area of decision making in business – the list is long and includes decisions affecting strategy, people, products and services, investment, and business model change. There are some high-profile examples out there. Take the US beer manufacturer Joseph Schlitz. Joseph Schlitz was once the third-largest brewer in the US. In the early 1970s, the company introduced a cheaper brewing process, based on the belief that customers were not discerning beer drinkers and could not tell beers apart. It turned out that this wasn't the case. The new beer did not go down well with customers and they told the company so. The evidence was there but senior management chose to ignore customer discontent and stuck with the low cost strategy. Unsurprisingly, Joseph Schlitz went into decline and was later acquired by a competitor.

Unilever is another example. In the '90s, Unilever launched a new laundry detergent. Although this product was tested on new clothes, management failed to accept disconfirming evidence that suggested it would damage older clothing or would react negatively with older clothing dyes. Nevertheless, the product was launched. Unilever eventually withdrew the new product once a large number of customers complained about running dyes and ruined clothes.

Executives at Polaroid and Kodak had built very successful business models around selling and developing physical camera film. They believed that physical film would never be supplanted by digital cameras and therefore failed to adjust their business model to adapt to new technologies. The world's most successful mini-computer firm, DEC, believed that personal computers would never catch on. Leaders in DEC also therefore failed to adapt in the face of change. In all these businesses, smart managers were listening to information that only confirmed their existing strategy and ignored information that suggested the current course would steer them to disaster.

The same holds true for transatlantic cruise-line industry. Between 1900 and 1950, transatlantic cruise ships transported millions of people between Europe and the US. It was great business, but they failed to notice the growth in the airline industry. In the 1960s, they were eclipsed by transatlantic flights. What the leadership of these companies failed to see was both the rise of the airplane and the advent of the holiday cruise. Management was locked into a way of thinking and believed that the old business would continue. It was finally left to a fresh set of entrepreneurs to buy and refit the ships and use them for holiday cruises.

CEOs and other senior executives are particularly vulnerable to such erroneous assumptions. Research suggests[167] that people in positions of power are more likely than others to search for evidence that confirms their beliefs instead of trying to explore contradictory or disconfirming information.

A very public and high-profile illustration of the Captain at work is seen in a conversation Enron's former CEO, Jeff Skilling, had with his legal team. This conversation came out during a trial that eventually led to Skilling's conviction for insider trading and security fraud relating to the collapse of Enron. Skilling's testimony at his trial revealed that he increasingly sought and listened to information that validated what he wanted to believe about the business and shut out information that cast a light on the problems in the business.

The conversation ran as follows. In June 2001, Skilling sought assurances from his legal counsel that everything happening in California's newly deregulated electricity market was above board. Enron has to be "absolutely pure as the driven snow" Skilling told Richard Sanders, then an Enron lawyer. Then he stated, "So one more time, we're pure as the driven snow, right?" When Sanders then told Skilling about the strategies that traders had used, many of which were later found to have contributed to manipulating the market, Skilling was not at all concerned. On the contrary, he chose to focus on the fact that Sanders had now given him assurances that the tactics stopped as soon as they were discovered. Skilling concluded the conversation with the statement "so we're as pure as the driven snow" even though he had just heard evidence to the contrary.

The vast body of academic research[168] shows that most mergers either add no value or actually reduce shareholder value for the acquiring firm. Given the failure of so many mergers, the question of why mergers continue to occur in large numbers remains. A 2009 study by two researchers from Cornell University[169] suggests that the Captain's steering is to blame. Senior executives tend to discard disconfirming evidence. They routinely underestimate merger integration costs and cultural misalignment and overestimate cost savings and speed of returns of investments resulting from the merger.

Are You the Captain?

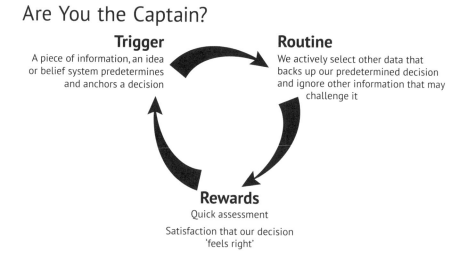

Trigger
A piece of information, an idea or belief system predetermines and anchors a decision

Routine
We actively select other data that backs up our predetermined decision and ignore other information that may challenge it

Rewards
Quick assessment
Satisfaction that our decision 'feels right'

Figure 10b: The Habit Loop of the Captain

The Captain in us is triggered when information, an idea or belief system predetermines and anchors a decision. Imagine you are asked to rate the performance and effectiveness of your colleagues. More often than not, people who are asked this question will have a set view already of an individual's performance. Let's say you do not think very highly of a colleague called Sam. Next time you see Sam being unable to answer a technical question or falling behind on a project, your existing views are reinforced whereas when you see the reverse scenario, such as Sam demonstrating technical depth or timeliness, you will not give this information the same weight as the negative information which confirms your view. If you want to discuss Sam's performance with other colleagues, you might listen to more negative voices than to positives because they reinforce your views and a sense that your judgement about Sam is right.

Reflection Point

Can you think of recent examples where the Captain has predetermined the direction of a decision?

What was the trigger which anchored your decision?
Can you describe the routine?
Did you observe a reward?

What We Have Learned in this Chapter

- The Captain steers our choices through using anchors that have been formed in our past and which are already in our minds.
- The Captain's anchor brings into sharp focus the need to look out for information already in our minds that will steer our decision. It is important to identify and raise the anchor before we start the decision-making process. This is more easily achieved when an anchor has been dropped recently. For example, in negotiations where an awareness of the anchoring effect of the opening offer might help us get a better deal.
- For many decisions, the anchor is less visible as it resides deep in the recesses of our own personal history. Therefore, becoming aware of the Captain's routine of steering is another strategy to help us make better choices.

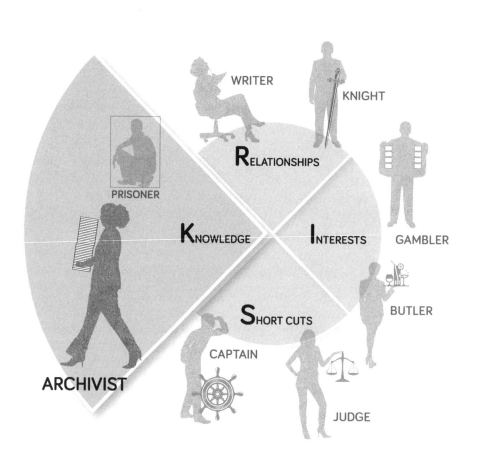

WRITER

KNIGHT

RELATIONSHIPS

PRISONER

GAMBLER

KNOWLEDGE   **I**NTERESTS

BUTLER

SHORT CUTS

CAPTAIN

ARCHIVIST

JUDGE

15

The Archivist

The
ARCHIVIST

"Insanity is doing the same thing
over and again while expecting
different results."

Attributed to Albert Einstein

The Archivist's Tale

I am the Archivist. All learning from my life experiences is stored
in a large archive in my head. I solve new problems by going first
to my archive and recalling learning from past experiences. I solve
new problems with reference to these past experiences, even if
that experience does not strictly apply.

The Archivist's Mottos: "Business as usual."

"There's nothing new under the sun."

What You Need to Remember about the Archivist

The Archivist in us is triggered when a problem reminds us of a situation we have encountered in the past.

The Archivist:

- ✓ Assumes that because a current problem looks similar to a past problem, the same solution applies
- ✓ Will not be aware of what is going on around her
- ✓ Will not be aware that success of past solutions will reinforce her desire to apply the same solution again.

What Do Smart Deciders Do?

Smart decision makers:

- ✓ Are aware that applying past experience is not the only way to solve a problem
- ✓ Don't automatically assume that just because a problem looks similar to one encountered in the past, the solution is also the same
- ✓ Develop situational awareness, particularly when faced with an emergency
- ✓ Explore different options.

A magician was working on a cruise ship in the Caribbean. As the audience was different each week, the magician performed the same routine over and over again. There was only one problem: the captain's parrot was ever-present and saw the same tricks again and again. After a few weeks, the parrot got the hang of the routine and started shouting in the middle of the show: "Look, it's not the same hat"; "Look, he is hiding the flowers under the table" and "Why are all the cards the Ace of spades?" The magician was furious, but was powerless to do anything – after all, it was the captain's parrot.

One day the ship had an accident and sank. The magician found himself clinging to a piece of wood in the middle of the ocean when along came the parrot and perched beside him. For a few days, they were floating on the water and the parrot didn't say a thing. After a week the parrot finally spoke up: "Ok, I give up. You've got me this time," he said. "Where is the boat?"

The Habit Loop of the Archivist

In Chapter 7, we explained how our thinking habits are formed and how understanding the *habit loop* is our key to unlocking more effective choices. When it comes to the Archivist, the habit loop tends to be this:

Trigger
A problem reminds us of a situation we encountered in the past

Routine
Extrapolation of past experiences
Application of old solutions

Rewards
Quick, effortless decision making
Pride and satisfaction in applying past learning – my experience counts for something!

Figure 11a: The Habit Loop of the Archivist

In this chapter, we will particularly focus on how the work of the Archivist misleads us by erroneously connecting memories that seem similar to the situation we are currently facing. The Archivist in us then narrowly applies our past experience to the new situation. Ironically, the larger the Archivist's archive, the more easily we are misled by the Archivist directing us to use old solutions for new problems.

The Archivist operates on two key faulty assumptions. First, the Archivist views two problems as similar and, second, automatically assumes that their solution is also similar. This misapplication of past learning is most prevalent when we are faced with the following:

- During emergencies where speed of reaction is of the essence, and/or
- Where the decision is rooted in either a complex situation, and/or
- In an adjacent situation (i.e. where a situation seems similar but in reality is quite different from previous experiences).

The Archivist During Emergencies

A line from the movie *Titanic* illustrates the work of the Archivist beautifully. Captain Smith's role in the sinking of the ocean liner *Titanic* is summed up in the film as "26 years of experience working against him". Both British and American inquiries into the tragedy found that a steering error was to blame for the iconic sinking. Although Captain Smith was one of the most experienced captains at the time, he had never steered a ship as large as the *Titanic* before (few had) and did not factor this into his thinking when he faced the emergency. He gave his orders to keep on sailing even after the *Titanic* hit the iceberg. Such a manoeuvre would have worked well with a smaller vessel, but with a vessel the size of the *Titanic*, it spelt doom. Enough water was driven into the engine room to overwhelm the pumps and consequently, the fire-damaged bulkhead gave way and the ocean poured into the boiler room like a tsunami. The rest of the story is, of course, history. Smith had to think fast and fell back on his experience. In doing so he succumbed to the workings of the Archivist. Of course he had to think fast, but had he just taken time to step back and analyse the situation more thoroughly, other options would have become apparent and this tragedy would not have happened.

It is this stepping back to understand the circumstances of a new situation that goes awry when the Archivist is at work. The term used by psychologists to describe this ability to know what is going on around you is *situational awareness* and it is this that the Archivist seriously compromises.[170] Situational awareness demands a conscious, dynamic reflection on the situation, which considers past experience but within the context of the uniqueness of the present situation. Sadly, the Archivist can easily take over and situational awareness goes out of the window as we exclusively concentrate on past experience.

In aviation, autopilot has been developed based on the cumulative knowledge of pilots. The more flying hours pilots clock up, the more their flying is performed in an automated manner.[171] This works well most of the time, until the pilot encounters an unusual situation. Such an occasion occurred when an Airbus 330 plunged into the Atlantic during a storm in 2009. The report into this disaster, which killed 228 people, laid the blame firmly at the door of the Archivist at work in the pilots. "The pilots stuck to what they do usually... When you lose awareness of the situation you hang on to what you're used to doing," said Alain Bouillard, who headed up the inquiry into the crash.

The black box, recovered from the Atlantic two years after the accident, shed light on what happened in this tragic incident. It appears that the co-pilot who was flying the aircraft at the time it hit the storm resorted to a routine take-off manoeuvre following the malfunction of the aircraft speed sensors and subsequent loss of height. This was a classic case of the Archivist at work. The loss of height misled the pilot into believing that this situation was akin to a take-off, when height could only be gained by pointing the nose of the plane upwards and applying thrust. Sadly this take-off manoeuvre did exactly the opposite of what was intended and caused aerodynamic stall. This meant that the aircraft literally fell from the sky.

The concept of situational awareness is now taught and used extensively in aviation in order to counteract the work of the Archivist. Increasingly, situational awareness is also seen as a relevant approach to decision making in other fields like anaesthesiology. In a special edition of the journal *Human Factors* devoted to situational awareness, an article by Gaba and Howard[172] highlighted situational awareness as an equally important factor in the complex, dynamic and risky field of anaesthesiology. As a result of this cross-disciplinary thinking, situational awareness is considered to be one of the most essential non-technical skills for the achievement of safe anaesthesia practice.[173]

The following story is taken from an NHS training manual:

> Elaine Bromiley was a fit and healthy young woman who was admitted to hospital for routine sinus surgery. During the anaesthetic she experienced breathing problems and the anaesthetist was unable to insert a device to secure her airway. After 10 minutes it was a situation of 'can't intubate, can't ventilate'; a recognised anaesthetic emergency for which guidelines exist.

> For a further 15 minutes, three highly experienced consultants made numerous unsuccessful attempts to secure Elaine's airway and she suffered prolonged periods with dangerously low levels of oxygen in her bloodstream. Early on nurses informed the team that they had brought emergency equipment to the room and booked a bed in intensive care but neither were utilised.

> 35 minutes after the start of the anaesthetic it was decided that Elaine should be allowed to wake up naturally and was

transferred to the recovery unit. When she failed to wake up she was then transferred to the intensive care unit. Elaine never regained consciousness and after 13 days the decision was made to withdraw the ventilation support that was sustaining her life.[174]

It is important to note that every member of the team treating Elaine was an experienced and technically competent medic. Yet the series of events and actions that ensued resulted in her death. The main reason was that these highly skilled people basing their decisions on their experience and didn't take the reality of this rare event into account. Because of our automatic recourse to learned responses and experiences, underestimating the likelihood of a rare event is one of the main dangers presented by the Archivist at work in us.

The Archivist in Corporate Life

Whilst the work of the Archivist may well have deadly consequences in the arena of medical operations, generally speaking the Archivist has less deadly consequences in the corporate boardroom. Here, organisation-threatening rather than life-threatening decisions can be made if the Archivist is allowed to run riot.

In his book *Beyond the Core*, Chris Zook[175] examines the outcomes of companies that adopted adjacent market strategies. An adjacent market strategy is where a company decides to move into a market that is similar to the one they have been successful in, but isn't quite the same. Finding adjacent market spaces is an attractive way to grow. Adjacent markets are not too far away from the core business in terms of channels, technology, price point, brand and such like. So on the face of it, adjacencies seem more achievable than far out, white space opportunities. However, on closer inspection this is not as straightforward as it seems.

Zook studied 1,850 companies that had followed adjacent market strategies and found that such moves usually failed. A staggering 75 percent of the companies reported outright failure and, of the 25 percent remaining, only 13 percent believed that they had achieved what the study called a "moderate level of sustained and profitable growth". Adjacency moves are riskier than organic growth. Between 1997 and 2005, three-quarters of the 25 most highly publicised (non-tech) stock devaluations involved failed adjacency expansions.

Many business leaders fail to understand the substantial risks associated with even small adjacency moves as the Archivist leads them to believe that the new market they have entered is just like the old market in which they have successfully operated for years. Consequently, they overestimate the strength and importance existing core business capabilities are likely to have in the new market.

Some high-profile deals that didn't work because of the work of the Archivist in misleading senior management include:

- K-mart's merger with Sears: the differences in format and brand were too great to allow for synergies
- Sara Lee's failure to get a lift out of its acquisition of EarthGrains, the fresh bread business: EarthGrains just didn't fit with Sara Lee's frozen baked goods lines, let alone other lines like personal care
- eBay's acquisition of Skype Technologies: eBay had hoped that this would allow it to use the latter's voice technology to let customers close deals faster; but the capabilities didn't match and eBay sold Skype at a US$1 billion loss.

Other notorious acquisition failures include Quaker Oats' failed acquisition of Snapple and the disastrous AOL acquisition of Time Warner.

The Archivist can also cause havoc for new venture activities within organisations, even those that are the result of organic growth. According to research by Sykes and Block,[176] the application of mature company practices to the management of new corporate ventures is not only inappropriate, but breeds failure. Taking a management approach that follows the Archivist's lead and tries to replicate existing operational practices in a new venture is likely to disappoint. To succeed with new ventures, executives must understand the inherent differences in the way the business is managed. According to the authors of the research, some of the adverse effects of using the same management practices for both the mature business and the new venture includes stifling innovation, lengthening of 'go to market' lead times, loss of entrepreneurship, lack of agility, fluctuating venture strategies, misread markets, reduced motivation and incentives to take considered risks and loss of key employees. It's quite a long and impressive list and it ought to make any corporate decision maker think again before allowing the Archivist a dominant voice in strategic moves.

Past success can also reinforce the work of the Archivist as there is an added incentive to apply strategies that worked well in the past to other areas. The Indian airline Kingfisher (KFA), which went bankrupt in 2013, is a case in point. Mr Mallya, a highly successful Indian businessman in the liquor industry, launched KFA as a premium business-class airline. It seemed like a great idea, but he did not fully comprehend the difference in customer preferences between the two industries. Customers may buy expensive alcohol but they aren't equally inclined to buy expensive airline tickets. He discovered that price elasticity is quite different with air travel as airline tickets are extremely price sensitive. The Archivist in Mallya misled him to adopt an incorrect strategy right from the start, believing he could apply the same strategy that made him a success in the liquor market to air travel. Sadly, the business faltered and left him and his shareholders out of pocket.

RBS's disastrous acquisition of the bank ABN AMRO can also be seen through the lens of the Archivist. Alarm bells should have started ringing as RBS was unable to do due diligence with ABN AMRO because it was a hostile takeover. However, Fred Goodwin, then CEO of RBS, was not at all concerned that he could not make a proper assessment of what his bank was buying. As far as he was concerned, he already had an excellent track record because a few years earlier he had bought the NatWest bank in similar circumstances – a hostile takeover in which proper due diligence wasn't possible. In the case of NatWest, there were surprises but fortunately for Goodwin they were all good ones. The Archivist led Goodwin to believe that the same would be true with ABN AMRO bank. The reality was quite different. First time round, he had been lucky. Second time round, he wasn't; and yet both times he bought a cat in a bag!

The Archivist as Forecaster

An American trucker was driving north on the Montreal highway in Vermont. He saw an average of three petrol stations per mile and concluded that there must be plenty of petrol stations all the way to Alaska.

Forecasting is a tricky business and we need to be mindful of the Archivist focusing too much on past experience and simply extrapolating into the future. In his entertaining book *Future Babble: Why Expert Predictions Fail and Why We Believe them Anyway,* Dan Gardner reviews expert predictions about future developments. There are many to choose from but here are a few notable misses:

- In 2008, when the price of oil rose to above $140 a barrel, experts predicted that the price would soon hit $200; a few months later, it had plunged to $30
- In 1967, experts predicted that the USSR would be the world's fastest-growing economy by the year 2000; but by 2000, the USSR had ceased to exist
- In 1908, experts predicted there would be no more wars in Europe!

Gardner concludes that expert judgments generally extrapolate from past events and experiences. As a result they predict that we should expect much of the same, with the result that they are often spectacularly wrong. Gardner draws heavily on the work of Professor Philip Tetlock whose research concluded that pundits are as likely to be wrong as they are right.

Even the best of us gets it wrong. Just listen to Alan Greenspan (former Chairman of the US Federal Reserve and a man not known for eating humble pie) when he reported to Congress about the 2007–8 financial crisis:

> I made a mistake in presuming that the self-interest of organisations, specifically banks, is such that they were best capable of protecting shareholders and equity in the firms... I discovered a flaw in the model that I perceived is the critical functioning structure that defines how the world works. I had been going for 40 years with considerable evidence that it was working exceptionally well.

The Archivist served Greenspan well for a long period of his career, but then came a time when past experience just stopped working – just like the trucker, who got stranded somewhere in Manitoba.

Are You the Archivist?

Trigger
A problem reminds us of a
situation we encountered in
the past

Routine
Extrapolation of past experiences
Application of old solutions

Rewards
Quick, effortless decision making
Pride and satisfaction in applying past
learning – my experience counts for
something!

Figure 11b: The Habit Loop of the Archivist

The Archivist in us is triggered when a problem we come across reminds us of a situation we have encountered in the past.

Consider how you might deal with an invasion of fruit flies in your kitchen. What would you do? If we are more experienced in dealing with houseflies or mosquitos, the Archivist in us will recognise this problem as one of adjacency and this will trigger the Archivist's routine. In this case, what we are likely to recall is how we have dealt with 'flies' in the past. We may then start a hunt for fly spray or mosquito repellent, thinking that this solution, which has worked in the past and might bring relief from these elusive little pests. Yet sadly fruit flies are not the same as mosquitos because, irrespective of how much we spray, fruit flies will always be back with a vengeance. A little situational awareness is likely to solve the problem permanently. Where does the problem come from? What are we observing? In this instance we may observe that the fruit bowl is filled with a few overripe fruit and that the fruit flies are attracted to this. Simply emptying the fruit bowl outside into the food-waste bin is, in this instance, the solution we need.

Reflection Point

Can you think of a recent example where the Archivist in you has misapplied past learning to a business situation?

Can you recognise the adjacency that was a trigger for the Archivist routine in you?
What are the specifics of the routine?
Did you recognise a reward?

What We Have Learned in this Chapter

- The Archivist encapsulates our tendency to apply old solutions to new problems.
- The image of the Archivist is a visual reminder of the internal processes of sifting through our filing cabinet of past experiences.
- Adjacency triggers the Archivist's routine. This routine is to extrapolate past experience and to apply a solution which worked in the past.
- Examples from the corporate world have shown that we are particularly prone to the Archivist if we have had success with a particular solution or strategy in the past.
- In emergencies, the rigid and inflexible application of past learning can lead to disaster.

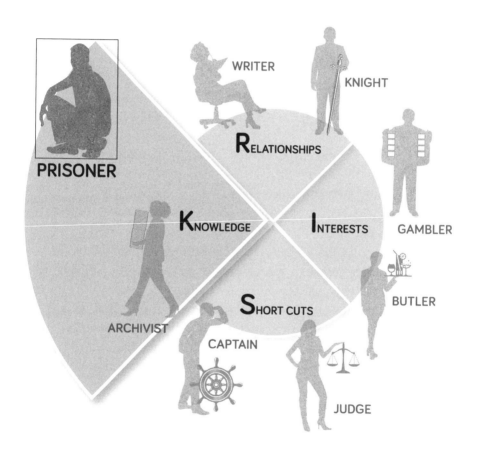

PRISONER

WRITER

KNIGHT

RELATIONSHIPS

GAMBLER

KNOWLEDGE

INTERESTS

ARCHIVIST

SHORT CUTS

BUTLER

CAPTAIN

JUDGE

16

The Prisoner

The **PRISONER**

"If your only tool is a hammer, all your problems will be nails."

Mark Twain

The Prisoner's Tale

I am the Prisoner. I like to address decisions through the window of my own expertise. I know a lot about some things and some might say I know too much at times. I find it difficult to see problems from the perspective of other people's expertise and this often stops me from detecting contradictions in my own paradigm or spot when my thinking is out of sync with reality. As I tend to occupy a narrower world of my own area of expertise, I find it challenging at times to harness my own creativity and I am often hampered in my ability to see innovative ideas in others.

The Prisoner's Motto: "I like it in here."

What You Need to Remember about the Prisoner

The Prisoner in us is triggered when we are faced with a situation that evokes a particular and familiar way of understanding the world.

The Prisoner:

- ✓ Thinks within the confines of his particular paradigm
- ✓ Loses touch with reality
- ✓ Is unable to spot contradictions within his approach
- ✓ Dismisses alternative ways of looking at a problem.

What Do Smart Deciders Do?

Smart decision makers:

- ✓ Have courage to step outside their expert box
- ✓ Use a multi-model approach to shed new light on a particular problem.

> A physicist, a chemist and an economist are stranded on a desert island with nothing to eat. A can of soup washes ashore. The physicist says, "Let's use the power of gravity and smash the can open with a rock." The chemist suggests, "Let's use the power of chemical reaction and build a fire and heat the can." The economist says, "Let's assume that we have a can opener..."

Apart from poking fun at Economists, this story illustrates the dangers of being imprisoned by one's own professional worldview. When our expertise is detached from what it is really going on in the world and becomes our primary way of making sense of situations then, at best, this expertise is rendered useless and, at worst, can seriously mislead others who depend on experts for guidance.

The Prisoner's routine is triggered when a particular way of understanding the world has been deeply embedded in a person's psyche. This often happens when years of training creates a particular way of looking at the world, the problems we face and the choices we need to make. Often this worldview is further reinforced by a particular professional culture, which leads to further isolation from other perspectives. When a problem occurs, solutions are framed within narrow points of reference.

The Habit Loop of the Prisoner

In Chapter 7 we explained how our thinking habits are formed and how understanding the *habit loop* is our key to unlocking more effective decisions. When it comes to the Prisoner, the habit loop tends to be this:

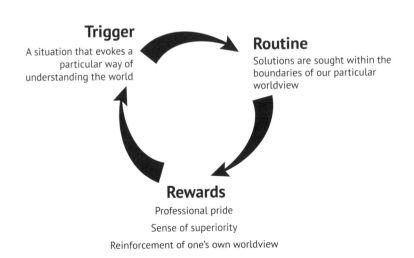

Trigger
A situation that evokes a particular way of understanding the world

Routine
Solutions are sought within the boundaries of our particular worldview

Rewards
Professional pride
Sense of superiority
Reinforcement of one's own worldview

Figure 12a: The Habit Loop of the Prisoner

In this chapter, we will particularly focus on how the work of the Prisoner misleads us by locking us into a way of thinking which is not appropriate to new situations. The Prisoner in us looks for solutions within the confines of our particular familiar paradigm. Ironically, it is often in organisational cultures where there is much pride in professional excellence that the Prisoner thrives and prospers as such an environment can easily stop us from 'thinking outside the box' of our professional training.

Abolishing Boom and Bust

"And I said before, Mr. Deputy Speaker, no return to boom and bust."

Gordon Brown, UK Budget Statement, 7th March 2001

"No return to boom and bust". During his 10 years as the UK's Chancellor of the Exchequer, Gordon Brown was so proud of that boast that he repeated the phrase more than a 100 times in the House of Commons. On average, this amounted to a monthly reminder that the good times were here to stay. When those good times were in full swing, Gordon Brown went one step further, confidently declaring: "we abolished boom and bust".

Gordon Brown was Britain's longest-serving Chancellor of the Exchequer, having been in office for 10 years. Prior to taking up this role in 1997, he was the opposition spokesperson who 'shadowed' the incumbent Chancellor. Brown was steeped in the world of government finance and had certainly developed deep expertise. To have abolished economic boom and bust was, however, a bold claim; when the financial crisis unfolded shortly after he became British Prime Minister in 1997, it sounded rather hollow.

Publically and politically, Brown wanted people to believe that the abolition of boom and bust was linked to his own prudent management of the economy. In his early years, as Chancellor he did indeed keep a tight rein on government expenditure, but after 2002 he allowed a massive expansion in public spending to improve public services. The consequence was huge public-sector debt prior to the 2008 financial and economic crisis. He also abandoned his promise to stop a housing bubble and under his watch, house prices trebled between 1997 and 2007.

The year 2002 was a turning point for Brown as he took the brakes off the economy while still insisting that there was no return to boom and bust. It raises a question why a man like Gordon Brown, who was not prone to risk his political reputation by making fanciful statements, came to believe that he could transcend the laws of economics. After all, just as sunshine follows rain, economic cycles have long been understood to be part of the natural economic order, hard wired into the free market economy.

Those close to Brown suggest that he actually believed what he said – that it wasn't simply political posturing. Viewing the world through a lens of expertise narrowed his focus and increased his confidence. He saw what he wanted to see, using data to confirm his way of thinking.

The Brave New Banking World

The Prisoner can be seen to have been at work during the 2007 financial crisis. During the noughties, banks started to shed credit risk. Credit risk is where the borrower is not able to pay back the amount to the bank that lent the money. Banks shed credit risk in a very cunning way through loan sales and securitisation techniques. Securitisation is the practice of bundling together a group of loans and selling them off in the form of an 'asset'. The best metaphor for this sort of practice is the children's party game pass the parcel, where a parcel filled with candy is passed from child to child and when the music stops the child who holds the parcel opens it and gets the benefit of the candy. Only in this case, the parcel was obtained by payment and the holder had no clear idea whether the holding contained loans which were going to be honoured or not, although rating agencies at the time rated these 'assets' in order to give investors some guidance.

Sadly, as it turned out, many of these ratings were incorrect as bad debt was parcelled up with good debt and rated nevertheless by the rating agencies as triple AAA debt. In addition, in order to make the market in these so-called assets work more efficiently, banks such as JPMorgan, Bankers Trust and Credit Suisse introduced new financial instruments called 'credit derivatives'. A derivative is a contract between two parties whose value is determined by changes in the underlying asset, or in this case the loan parcel. It is essentially a side bet. The result was a multi-billion-dollar global market in these newly invented financial products. These new innovative financial products were understood not only to make markets far more efficient as investors could quickly move in and out of the market by selling or buying those derivative products. With greater efficiency the experts maintained, came even more significant benefits for the wider world – a much safer financial system which could absorb shocks so much better.

According to Gillian Tett[177], who researched the credit derivatives market as a financial journalist at the time, the creation of this multi-billion-dollar market in credit derivatives was pivotal as it ushered in "a Brave New Banking World".[178] Bankers sold off their bad debt so that investors could buy those securities according to their preferred risk profile, thereby diversifying risk across markets. So instead of the banks holding the parcels with bad debt, there were thousands if not millions of investors worldwide holding debt. This was seen as much safer than having risks concentrated in individual large banks.

In other words, financial innovation had saved the world from boom and bust as risks could be dispersed across markets globally. History suggests they were half-right. Risks were indeed dispersed across the globe, but this just meant that the playing field was extended – the whole world went boom and then bust instead of individual countries or banks.

At the height of the credit derivative frenzy, Gillian Tett observed that investment bankers displayed an almost "evangelical zeal" when they defended the benefits of these innovations, repeating to all who were prepared to hear what Gillian Tett called the "good news of risk dispersal" creed.[179]. She wrote that:

> The credit derivatives community was unified in an unquestioning assumption that the triumvirate of financial innovation, globalisation and free-market forces was a very positive thing; since credit derivatives appeared to represent "progress", they were assumed to be good.[180]

Unbeknown to these self-styled 'saviours of the world', they had just fallen prey to the workings of the Prisoner. The excessive focus on their own expertise and worldview made them ignore important information that could have alerted them to evidence that all was not well in this brave new banking world.

Consequently, they were unable to spot that the very same techniques supposed to promote risk dispersal were, in themselves, introducing new risks to the financial system. Far from promoting transparency and efficient markets, the increasing complexity of many of these new financial instruments meant that investors could not adequately monitor what they were taking onto their books as investments. Regulators, rating agencies and even the bankers found it equally difficult to track the credit quality or monitor where risks were situated in the system. Additionally, many market participants did not use the financial instruments for their original intended purpose of risk reduction but instead speculated with them. That changed the nature of the market fundamentally – the tools that were supposed to reduce risks in the system as a whole now fuelled greater risk taking.

Signs of the coming debt tsunami set to hit the markets in 2008 were already evident by 2005. Yet bankers had become so captive to their own ways of thinking that no-one sounded alarm bells. In fact, the situation was quite the opposite. The 'good news of risk dispersal' had become the prevailing wisdom and informed the decisions of many Western policy makers. In its 2006 report, the International Monetary Fund lauded "the dispersion of credit risk by banks to a diverse and broad set of investors" and stated that this approach "has helped make the banking and financial system more resilient." The Prisoner had been unleashed!

One Lone Voice Crying out of the Tajik Wilderness

Sadly, at the time very few people flagged up concerns about what was really going on in the credit derivatives market. Few understood the full implications for global financial stability besides one lone voice in the wilderness. This was the voice of Gillian Tett who, through her Lex column in the *Financial Times*, repeatedly warned her readers of the impeding catastrophe. At the time, Tett was seen as a bit of a maverick. Her warnings were considered interesting tittle-tattle but largely fell on deaf ears. So how did Tett manage to see what others failed to spot?

The answer is found in her background. Tett had not become imprisoned by the bankers' way of thinking. Unlike most of her colleagues in the field of financial journalism, she had no formal training in finance or economics. Instead, she brought a completely different way of thinking to the table. Prior to venturing into financial journalism, Tett had led a very exciting life working as a social anthropologist. For her PhD fieldwork in anthropology, Tett studied marriage rituals in the wilds of Tajikistan.

At face value, a remote hill tribe in a far-flung corner of the former Soviet Union is not exactly an ideal training ground for understanding complex financial products. Yet it was. Tett saw the world of credit derivative banking through the eyes of an anthropologist. Seeing bankers as just another tribe, she gained sufficient emotional distance from her research subjects to be able to see beyond their persuasive rhetoric. Alarm bells started ringing when she became aware that the bankers had lost the connection between their actions and the real economy. She noted that bankers had developed their innovations based on the assumption that the world of finance was built on rationality and detached from normal human functioning "like a silo that was semi-detached from the rest of society." No other journalist, financial analyst or even regulator spotted this all-important disconnect because they were also either imprisoned in the 'silo thinking' of the time or, due to the complexity of the credit derivatives market, had bowed to the bankers' superior expertise.

It should also be noted that Tett, as a financial journalist, was not a direct beneficiary of the extremely lucrative credit derivatives markets. Most other experts were and benefitted richly from not challenging the prevailing wisdom. After all, it is so much more difficult to break out of a gilded prison, as the following example shows.

The Bug that Did not Bite

Most people who remember New Year's Eve 2000 will recall being glued to their television set, anxiously anticipating some sort of calamity. All major networks, including the BBC, had stationed journalists around the globe ready to report the impact of the millennium bug on computer systems worldwide. It was a nervous time. Nobody knew the fate that would befall mankind. Speculations were rife, fuelling scenarios as wide apart as 'the end of civilisation as we know it', at one end of the spectrum, to 'just some localised systems failures', at the other. Some headlines from the UK national press at the time read:

> "Riots, terrorism and a health crisis could follow a millennium bug meltdown"
>
> *Sunday Mirror*

"Banks could collapse if they fail to eradicate the millennium bug from their computer systems"

Guardian

"All trace of pension contributions could be wiped out in businesses failing to cope with the millennium bug"

Independent

It appeared that all depended on whether computer systems were adjusted to the new date of 2000. The bug, according to the people in the know, was a programming error. Until the 1990s, many programs (especially those written in the early days of computers) were designed to abbreviate four-digit years to two digits in order to save memory space. Computer specialists feared that when the clocks struck midnight on 1st January 2000, many affected computers would be using an incorrect date and thus fail to operate properly. The problem had first been flagged up by Peter de Jager, a well-respected writer on IT issues in a 1993 article, 'Doomsday 2000',[181] published in the widely read *ComputerWorld* magazine. The article was written in a most sensationalist fashion: "Have you ever been in a car accident? ... The information systems community is heading toward an event more devastating than a car crash... we're accelerating toward disaster".

Following that first article, De Jager's argument was further elaborated in follow-on articles. His views were widely endorsed by other experts: "No-one who examined the problem in those early days doubted its reality. No-one asserted that there was no risk and that action was unnecessary".[182] Momentum was gathering and by 1996 the US government was beginning to take the problem seriously with a number of senate inquiries.

In 1997, a book published by Edward Yourdon, an American software engineer and IT consultant, *Time Bomb 2000*,[183] brought the problem to a wider audience. His book turned into a *New York Times* bestseller and became required reading for many managers across America.

The race to adjust computer systems was on. In the end, it is estimated that western economies spent some $300 billion to correct the millennium bug. On 31st December 1999 the world held its breath – and nothing happened. The 1st January 2000 was just like any other day. There were no major failures to report anywhere. Tellingly, those countries known to have failed to adjust their systems, notably Italy, Russia and Korea, suffered no ill-effect.

How could the experts get it so wrong? When the sociologist David Knights[184] investigated this question, he came to the conclusion that dissenting voices were simply shouted down by those with the dominant 'version of the truth'. Any deviation from this dominant narrative was considered a heresy. This was certainly the experience of Ross Anderson, Professor of Security Engineering of Cambridge University. In a recent BBC interview with Steven Fry,[185] he recalls that in early 1999 he tried to draw attention to his evidence-based findings that suggested that any millennium-related problems with the computer systems could easily be rectified by simply rebooting. In his opinion, the millennium bug was going to be the non-event it turned out to be. Interest in Anderson's research was virtually non-existent both amongst his fellow experts and the wider media. It should also be noted that the experts profited handsomely in terms of consultancy contracts from the dominant narrative, decreasing their incentive to consider alternative views.

These examples of the financial crisis and the millennium bug illustrate that the Prisoner at work can have a global impact. Gillian Tett warns: "One bizarre paradox of the modern age is that while technology is integrating the world in some senses (say, via the Internet), it is simultaneously creating fragmentation too (with people in one mental silo tending to only talk to each other, even on the Internet). As innovation speeds up, this is creating a plethora of activities that are only understood by 'experts' who tend to only function in their silos, whether in finance or numerous other fields."[186]

Strong professional ties can of course be hugely beneficial. They deepen and broaden professional knowledge and expertise. When harnessed appropriately they will allow for strong peer challenge. A strong professional community can be very powerful in sharpening the sum of human knowledge. Yet within these close-knit expert communities there is also a dark side – negative emotions as expressed in negative groupthink can derail the process of evaluation and implementation of new ideas.

The following examples show how the Prisoner jeopardised product development in two different geographical areas. They also show how impetus for change came from outsiders who brought a new perspective to the table.

When the Swiss Failed to Tell the Times[187]

In 1968, the Swiss dominated the world watch industry. At that time, the Swiss themselves invented the electronic watch movement at their own research institute in Neuchatel, Switzerland. This was a major innovation, but an innovation that was rejected by every Swiss watch manufacturer.

The Swiss were world-renowned experts in watchmaking. They were therefore hesitant to trade their tradition of mechanical watchmaking and 'dumb down' for this new electronic technology. They had a traditional, well-organised, close-knit industry with a strong sense of identity. They knew what watchmaking was about and it wasn't electronics! Their attachment to traditional watchmaking led them to one conclusion only – the electronic watch couldn't possibly be the watch of the future.

Executives of Seiko, a Japanese company with a history in clock making but none in watches, took one look at the electronic watch Swiss manufacturers had rejected at the World Watch Congress of that year and embraced it. They soon dominated the world watch market.

These quartz watches were less expensive, more accurate and lighter to wear than mechanical watches. Watch prices sank, allowing anyone to be able to afford one. The Swiss watch industry watched helplessly as its sales fell. By 1978, the world had moved to quartz movement and the Swiss watchmaking industry was in deep trouble with global market share of 15 percent, down from a comfortable 50 percent. Only a handful of prestigious brands, such as Rolex, Patek Philippe or Jaeger-LeCoultre, were able to hold their own at the luxury end of the market.

The Saviour with the Lebanese Passport

Salvation for the Swiss watchmakers came unexpectedly and in its darkest hour – not through a Swiss watchmaker but through an unlikely industry outsider, the Lebanese-born entrepreneur, Nicolas G. Hayek.

Hayek knew little about watchmaking and originally headed an engineering consulting firm in Zurich. He was brought in by the banks who had taken control of the two leading watch groups. He merged these two businesses into a new group called SMH. This was a last-ditch attempt at saving the industry and Hayek was appointed because of his proven business acumen. Hayek, not imprisoned by the traditions of the Swiss watchmakers, immediately empowered his newly appointed head of the watch division to come up with something completely new. The only stipulation for the new watch was that it had to be contemporary and fashionable in style and it had to be cheap to manufacture.

This brief in itself went against all that traditional Swiss watchmaking stood for – history, craft and strong associations with luxury. Unperturbed, a focused team of engineers set to work and in 1983 came up with the Swatch watch. The Swatch watch incorporated all the modern technology of the day under an analogue clock face and used that face as an opportunity to display fashionable and stylish designs. Swatch quickly became a huge success for SMH as it established itself as the dominant lower-end brand.

Interestingly, many commentators have credited Swatch with the salvation of traditional Swiss watchmaking. As Swatch took over a global mass-market audience, mechanical watchmakers used its success to reinvent themselves as luxury status symbols celebrating craft and tradition. Although the Swiss watchmaking story ended in success, it was at the point of complete desperation – when an outsider arrived and turned the dominant view of the experts on its head – that the Prisoner was set free.

The Prisoner in us is reinforced through our tendency to group together and exchange information and insights with people who share our particular specialism – through professional associations, specialist conferences, Internet groups and so forth. In the Swiss case, this was particularly pronounced due to the long tradition of the Swiss watchmakers.

Cheese Making – Japanese Style[188]

In the centuries-old art of hand-made cheese making, the call to 'cut the curd' has always been key in determining the quantity and quality of cheese. Cutting the curd requires skill and expertise from the cheese maker. A judgement is made through observation over open vats of curdling milk and the timing of this decision is all important. Cutting the curd too early impacts the quantity of cheese produced. Cutting it too late adversely affects the taste of the product.

In April 1980, this all changed when Tomoshige Hori, a young researcher at the Japanese dairy, Snow Brand, went to a symposium in Tokyo on the thermo-physical properties of materials. Because it was part of the conference programme, he happened to attend a lecture by a professor from Keio University. The lecture was about a new way to assess the thermal conductivity of liquids using a 'hot wire' with an electrical current passing through it. The ideas discussed in the lecture fascinated the young researcher although there was no obvious connection with his work.

At Snow Brand, Hori had nothing to do with cheese production. He had been tasked to discover ways to make dairy products more nutritious and better tasting, such as improving the acidity in yogurt or the texture of ice cream. Although thermal conductivity was totally unrelated to his day job, Hori loved experimenting in his lab, so he replicated the experiment he had seen at the conference, only this time with milk instead of water. Hori began to measure its thermal conductivity.

One afternoon, Hori left the lab and forgot to turn off the electric current to the thin platinum 'hot wire' and accidentally left the heat on for several hours. On his return, the milk had curdled. In examining the data, he noticed that at one point there had been a large temperature change in the 'hot wire'. Hori came to the conclusion that this rapid jump in temperature had occurred at the moment when the milk curdled.

At that point in time, Hori was still quite ignorant about the cheese-making process. He just knew it involved curdled milk. So he wandered over to talk to his colleagues in the cheese division for some informal chats. Here he found out that being able to monitor the amount of curdling in milk is crucial to making good cheese and the penny dropped. He began to realise the potential of his accidental discovery – that curdling could be spotted by monitoring temperature changes in the platinum 'hot wire'. This, in turn, could lead to a highly accurate and possibly automated process for making cheese.

Hori got very excited about his findings and approached the senior management of his company, only to receive a severe dressing down. He was told to get back into his 'box', dedicate himself to his assigned task of improving the taste of yoghurt and ice creams and never to meddle in things which were unrelated to his day job.

But Hori did not give up so easily and in his spare time he wrote up his findings. The paper was accepted in the *International Journal of Food Science*. When it was published, it generated considerable professional interest worldwide. He even won a prestigious technology award on the back of this research. Encouraged, Hori once again approached Snow Brand senior management and presented them with the response to his ground-breaking discovery. It was this international attention and coverage that forced the cheese professionals in Snow Brand to acknowledge that Hori might be onto something.

Three years after Hori attended the lecture that sparked his interest in heat conductivity, the management of Snow Brand Milk gave their support to a pilot project resulting eventually in the full automation of cheese production in 1988. Today, hundreds of thousands of tons of cheese are produced each year worldwide using the 'hot-wire' process developed by Hori.

It is home-grown tunnel vision that hinders companies from developing breakthrough products. Companies are often constrained by their own technologists, engineers and designers. As the following example demonstrates, the more success the home team has had with its approach to a solution, the harder it is for its members to imagine a different one.

The Snowboarding PC

Business used to be enormously profitable at Microsoft. Microsoft built the personal computer industry and by the year 2000 was, by far, the most successful software company in the world. In terms of market capitalisation, Microsoft dwarfed all other tech companies. However, the picture looks very different today. Compared to Microsoft, Apple is ahead, Google is about to overtake and Oracle is catching up quickly.

So what happened? How did Microsoft manage to lose the top spot?

Back in 2007, Microsoft's leadership team did not see a seismic shift in the market. Mobile personal computing, smartphones and tablets were about to displace conventional PCs, desktops and laptops. When Steve Jobs stepped onto the stage at MacWorld in January 2007 and presented the iPhone to the public for the first time there were plenty of smartphones on the market – Windows Mobile, Palm Treo, Nokia and Blackberry. What Jobs introduced to the world was about to change everything. Apple's iPhone was an entirely different type of smartphone. It contained a personal computer with a modern operating system. It incorporated a touch screen and kick started a whole new industry of apps development.

Steve Ballmer, Microsoft's CEO, failed to see this as a wake-up call. Instead, he famously scoffed at the iPhone.[189] He questioned its appeal to business people because it did not have a keyboard "making it not a very good e-mail machine". Even when Android phones quickly followed suit and the Smartphone 2.0 race ensued, Microsoft's leadership did not cotton on to the fact that there had been a shift in the market. The Microsoft leadership team confidently predicted in 2008 that, by 2012, Windows Mobile would enjoy a 40 percent market share.[190] This optimism was wide of the mark. Riding on the iPhone's success, the iPad was introduced, with Android-powered tablets not far behind. These new, mobile personal computers caused customers to re-examine their allegiance to the PC. Despite all this, Microsoft's leadership stubbornly remained imprisoned in its own view of the world. Only two years ago Frank Shaw, Microsoft's VP of Communications, still maintained:

> So while it's fun for the digerati to pronounce things dead, and declare we're post-PC, we think it's far more accurate to say that the 30-year-old PC isn't even middle aged yet, and is about to take up snowboarding.[191]

Contrary to this wishful thinking, the PC has never taken up snowboarding. After a change in senior management, Microsoft now sings from quite a different hymn sheet. There is an acknowledgement within Microsoft that we are in a post-PC era and the company's business strategy has changed as a result. But Microsoft is playing catch up. In an interview, Bill Gates, Microsoft founder, made some surprisingly candid statements[192] about the company he used to run. He admitted that Microsoft hadn't been innovative enough and that it had made errors with regards to mobile technology.

What Can Be Done – Handing the Prisoner the 'Get out of Jail Card'

Charlie Munger, Warren Buffett's business partner and possibly one of the most successful investors of all times, has summed up the dangers of the lack of flexibility, tunnel vision and silo thinking that so characterises the Prisoner in decision making:

> That's a perfectly disastrous way to think and a perfectly disastrous way to operate in the world. So you've got to have multiple models. And the models have to come from multiple disciplines – because all the wisdom of the world is not to be found in one little academic department.[193]

Munger uses multiple models from disciplines as diverse as physics and psychology and applies these ideas in order to select his investments. Over a lifetime he has achieved fantastic returns on his investments by thinking differently and defying the machinations of the Prisoner in him and in others.

Corporates in general have been very slow in applying multiple models to decision making. However, there is one business area where such an approach is increasingly popular. This is the area of product innovation. Here we find that a number of forward-thinking companies are beginning to use a multi-model approach. Also known as *'open innovation'*, this approach has yielded many positive results for those companies who have pursued this strategy. Success stories are reported from all industry sectors. Some of the early adopters of open innovation have come from possibly an unexpected place – food companies and particularly crisp manufacturers. (Or 'chip manufacturers' if you're American – we use 'chip' and 'crisp' interchangeably depending on the story.)

The Search for the Perfect Crisp

US corporate PepsiCo wanted to discover a way to reduce the amount of sodium in its potato chips without reducing the salty flavour that customers love. Its search, despite looking across the entire food industry, had not come up with any ideas. Having hit a brick wall, a brief was written and marketed to expert groups from many different disciplines. As a result, ideas came in from a large and varied number of industries and organisation types.

The winning entry came from an unexpected source: the orthopaedics team of a global research lab. The scientists there had developed a way to create nanoparticles of salt needed to conduct advanced research on brittle bone disease. For PepsiCo, this search yielded a valuable new partner and a perspective that helped the company to come up with an innovative solution. The success of this venture was widely publicised, with articles appearing in the *Harvard Business Review*.[194]

'Do us a Flavour'

In the UK, Walkers, a snack food manufacturer owned by PepsiCo, used a different tack to tackle the problem of flagging sales in the crisps market. They launched a nationwide campaign called 'Do us a Flavour' as a way to revive the brand. The general public was asked to invent a unique flavour of crisp. The British public didn't disappoint and around 1.2 million flavour entries were received. In July 2008, the website that hosted the contest became the fastest growing in the UK.[195] As a result of this activity, crisps with new flavours, such as crispy duck and hoi sin, Cajun squirrel, and fish and chips, were brought to market. Year-on-year sales also rose a staggering 14 percent. The Walkers story demonstrates that sometimes the consumer knows best and, for the Prisoner, "getting out of jail" might be as easy as tapping the general public for its ideas. The rise of social media makes it much easier to involve consumers in product development or in any other creative enterprise. The generous prize money on offer was certainly a powerful incentive for the consumer but for Walkers this was a very small outlay when compared to the extraordinary boost in sales that followed as a direct result of this campaign.

The Tattooed Crisp

Unlike Walkers, Procter & Gamble (P&G) did not initially go outside the company to find innovative solutions, but leveraged internal networks. One such example was in 2002 when the company in North America decided to develop a novel line of Pringles potato crisps with pictures and words (jokes, trivia questions, interesting facts) printed on each crisp. At the time P&G USA did not have the in-house technology to print each crisp with edible dye. The company decided to scout out its global network of individuals and institutions in order to discover if anyone in the world had a ready-made solution. Through the company's European network, a small bakery in Bologna, Italy was found.

It was run by a university professor who had invented an ink-jet method for printing edible images on cakes. His ink-jet method could easily be adapted for crisp printing and the innovation proved to be very lucrative for the North American Pringles business as double-digit growth was achieved following the launch of these tattooed crisps.

Since the launch of the printed crisp, P&G have become industry leaders in terms of open innovation. The company reckons that its radical strategy of sourcing 50 percent of innovations outside the company as well as leveraging internal networks produces more than 35 percent of the companies' innovations and billions of dollars in revenue. P&G reported, "As we studied outside sources of innovation, we estimated that for every Proctor & Gamble researcher there were 200 scientists and engineers elsewhere in the world who were just as good – a total of perhaps 1.5 million people whose talents we could potentially use. But tapping into the creative thinking of inventors and others on the outside world would require massive operational changes. We needed to move the company's attitude from resistance to innovations 'not invented here' to enthusiasm for those 'proudly found elsewhere'".[196]

Coming to a Supermarket Near You: Green Giant Crisps[197]

Green Giant is a popular brand of canned and frozen vegetables. It is owned by General Mills, a company that has been a pioneer in open innovation. General Mills has developed the General Mills Worldwide Innovation Network (G-WIN), dedicated to finding novel external knowledge sources ranging from suppliers to customers and niche companies.

G-WIN has been hugely beneficial to the company with a range of new product lines including the Green Giant snack chips, a new product category launched in the United States in 2012. Collaboration with an external supplier via G-WIN allowed the company's Green Giant brand to develop this product and bring it to market in record time. In January 2012 the company invited snack manufacturer Shearer's Foods to showcase its 'ready-to-launch' ideas at an innovation show at General Mills. Shearer's Foods brought along ten workable concepts for consideration and a number of them stood out, particularly at a time when market research showed an increasing interest in healthy vegetable crisps.

Following the show, General Mills' scientists worked alongside those of Shearer's Foods. To great acclaim by consumers, Green Giant Roasted Veggie Tortilla Chips and Green Giant Multigrain Sweet Potato Chips hit the shelves of selected US supermarkets in June 2012 – a record turnaround in terms of development and launch of a new product line.

Open Innovation as a Business Model

Ning Li, CEO of Made.com,[198] has fully embraced open innovation. His online furniture retailer is one of the few businesses that base their whole business model on open innovation. Made.com carries no inventory and therefore has no need for a warehouse. Instead, its products are designed exclusively by outsiders. Visitors to the company's website are encouraged to submit their furniture designs. Members of the Made.com community vote for the best designs, which are then made available for order. The manufacture of products is performed in China and the furniture ordered is then shipped by container and delivered directly to the consumer.

Applying Multiple Models across Business

As mentioned earlier, multiple perspectives and models are currently almost exclusively used in the field of product innovation through open innovation. This suggests that, as far as the corporate world is concerned, the use of multiple perspectives and models has been neatly siloed into the product development arena. Yet there is evidence that multiple perspectives and models can be helpful in solving a wide range of business issues. Of course, depending on the business problem, it might not be appropriate to harness multiple views from outside the company; but involving internal networks might be equally effective in solving a particular issue, as the following example shows.

An Indian Bus company's fuel consumption was well above calculated expectations. They had 100 old buses and 50 new ones, and 400 drivers. Using the expertise of internal staff in order to solve the problem, management attention was turned to the fact that the drivers were allowed to select both their buses and their routes based on seniority. Naturally, they chose the easier routes (that had fewer stops and shifts) and the newer buses. The relationship that resulted was that the older buses drove the stop-and-go routes on three shifts, thus consuming more fuel due to engine inefficiencies, while the new and efficient buses drove more continuously and were parked at night, obviously resulting in much higher overall fuel consumption than necessary. By creating a new relationship within existing available resources, the bus company was able to reduce overall fuel costs significantly.

Finally... A Good News Story

Imagine this nightmare scenario: your one-month-old son lies dying from *negrotising enterocolitis*, an infection which interferes with milk digestion and causes intestinal tissue to die. Standing in front of his incubator, you are told that there is very little hope and that it is now time to say goodbye. This is exactly the situation two young parents, Jodi Baker and Brian Willett, faced in the summer of 2011 when their son Jake was fighting for his life after his small intestine burst. But a visiting doctor attending another baby on the ward came over to the grief-stricken couple and suggested an impromptu stomach operation. "I have never tried this before", he said. "It will either save his life or end his life quickly". In desperation, Brian Willett gave permission to proceed and the doctor reached into Jake's incubator and made two tiny cuts. Jodi Baker, Jake's mum was too distressed to watch and fled the ward in tears. When she returned, two standard issue surgical gloves extended from Jake's body, keeping the wounds open. The procedure was a success. It drained the infection, which bought time for a transfer to another hospital where Jake underwent a six-hour operation, removing his small intestine. Jake is now a bouncy, healthy toddler. He owes his life to a doctor who had the courage to apply some 'out of the box' thinking. This story was widely reported in the press and there was a campaign in the UK to find the visiting doctor who saved Jake's life. The doctor himself did not want to reveal his identity because he feared that he would be criticised by the hospital authorities for departing from clinical protocol.

Are You the Prisoner?

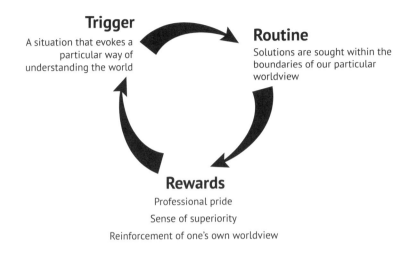

Trigger
A situation that evokes a particular way of understanding the world

Routine
Solutions are sought within the boundaries of our particular worldview

Rewards
Professional pride
Sense of superiority
Reinforcement of one's own worldview

Figure 12b: The Habit Loop of the Prisoner

The Prisoner in us is triggered when we are faced with a problem that evokes a particular familiar way of understanding the world.

Here's a maths question for you. A fishing boat is moored in the harbour. There is a rope ladder hanging over the side with its end touching the water. The rungs of the ladder are one metre apart and the tide is rising at 50cm an hour. At the end of six hours, how many of the rungs will be covered?

The answer to this question is of course *NONE,* as the boat will be rising with the tide.

How did you answer that question? Did you think of the boat rising with the tide or did you come up with the figure 'three'?

If the latter is the case, you have been the victim of the Prisoner. How did that happen? Well, the way the question is framed is tricking you into adopting the view that this is a maths question and demonstrates well how paradigms – ways of thinking – are embedded. In this instance, our way of approaching a question framed as a maths problem triggers our routine for solving maths problems. By sticking to the paradigm, our decision making is effortless and likely to be much quicker than a slower, more creative approach to decision making. You may even have felt quite satisfied with the fact that you could work out simple arithmetic.

This simple puzzle illustrates how easy it is to become a captive of the Prisoner. If the question had started with "Here is a geography question for you", the likelihood is that another paradigm would have been triggered and you would have answered the question differently.

Reflection Point

Can you think of an example where you have been taken captive by the Prisoner through trying to find a solution on the basis of one paradigm as opposed to having a wider perspective?

How did this paradigm/worldview get embedded?
How did you come to a solution?
Can you recall how you felt about the decision at the time?

What We Have Learned in this Chapter

- The Prisoner represents our reluctance to think outside our own professional silos.
- Our particular worldview, which has become embedded through years of training or through living, triggers the Prisoner's routine.
- The Prisoner's routine takes the form of seeking solutions within the confines of their particular paradigm.

- The story of "no more boom or bust" shows that the Prisoner can affect us all, even those of us who work at the most senior levels.
- It is often the outsider who can point out that 'the emperor has no clothes' as they are able to approach a problem from a totally new perspective.
- Sadly, not being heard is a common experience for those who hold the mirror up to the Prisoner. Even for a well-respected insider, coming up with an alternative view to a dominant narrative can be a frustrating experience.
- The Prisoner also blinds us to the true potential of innovative ideas.
- In the area of product innovation, a multi-model approach is gaining increasing acceptance. Open innovation can be a powerful tool in mitigating the creativity-busting effect of the Prisoner.
- At present, a multi-model approach is rarely used outside product innovation. This is regrettable as this approach could enhance major decision making in many areas and guard against the workings of the Prisoner.

Making Better Decisions

"There is nothing in a caterpillar that tells you
it's going to be a butterfly."

R. Buckminster Fuller

However good a decision maker you think you are, the reality is that you are making sub-optimal decisions. For many of our everyday decisions, the consequences of sub-optimal choices aren't that significant. There are times, however, when we need to get the calls right – or at least as close to right as we can.

There is a vast body of evidence accumulated by social psychologists, behavioural economists and neuroscientists that points to why we make sub-optimal decisions. In Chapter 1, we outlined how Nobel laureate Daniel Kahneman highlighted a dichotomy in two modes of thought and discovered an overdependence on System 1 (fast) thinking, even when faced with complex decisions. We have also learnt that effective decision making depends neither on reason nor intuition alone.

The Hidden R-I-S-K™ framework gives us a way of recognising the thinking errors embodied in our eight characters and expressed through our decision-making habit loops. This framework allows us to see our choices more clearly through the eyes of these eight characters and to spot potential biases that may be distorting our line of sight.

We hope that you don't choose to ignore the evidence. While our choices can never be perfect, we believe that they can be better. For the big decisions in life and work, making the right choice at the right time can have a major impact on our health, wealth and happiness.

Part 3 opens up ways to use the Hidden R-I-S-K™ framework.

Chapter 17 is about looking in the mirror and looks at how you can use the Hidden R-I-S-K™ framework for self-reflection and in one-to-one conversations, whether formal coaching meetings or informal conversations with colleagues or friends. We offer you eight calls to action aimed at redefining each of the habit loops linked to our eight characters. These calls to action will help you to make better decisions through breaking entrenched patterns of thinking. As the quality of our thinking is the foundation of the effectiveness of our decisions, we also propose five key conditions that will support generative conversations.

Chapter 18 is about creating a decision-friendly environment and how you can use the Hidden R-I-S-K™ framework to support better decision making in teams and decision-making groups. We look at a case study and offer ten practical tools you can use. We particularly explore the importance of creating workplaces where people can speak out safely and where there is mutual accountability around decisions taken. We give leaders five practical ways they can create environments in which people feel safe to speak up. Finally, we explore how the Hidden R-I-S-K™ framework helps to cast a light on reasons why organisations don't learn.

Chapter 19 sets out next steps and how you can continue to use our Hidden R-I-S-K™ framework to help you unlock unconscious biases and make better decisions.

17

Holding up the Mirror

"The man with insight enough to admit his limitations comes
nearest to perfection."

Johannes Wolfgang von Goethe

A little ole' man was sittin' on a step
And a tear trickled down his cheek.
I said "What's the matter?"
He said "A train just ran over me."
I said "Hmm. How often does this happen?"
He said "Everyday about this time."
I said "Well, why do you just sit out here then?"
He said "Cause I cannot believe that this happened."

Little ole' man was sittin' on the step, same ole' man.
And a tear trickled down his cheek.
I said "What's the matter?"
He said "A herd of elephants just stampeded over me."
I said "Hmm" same "Hmm."
I said "How often does this happen?"
He said "Every day, a half hour after the train runs over me."

> Little ole' man sittin' on a step, same ole' man.
> A tear trickled down his cheek.
> I said "Hey, how ya doin' after that train ran over ya?"
> He said "WHAT train?"
> I said "The train that ran over ya a half hour before the
> elephants stampeded over ya."
> He said "What elephants?"
> I said "Hmm" same "Hmm."
> He says "You're a young boy."
> Says "Ya got a lot to learn."
> He says "Reach out, take my hand, you'll understand."

The Comedian Bill Cosby sang this metaphorical ditty about the 'little ole' man'. The little ole' man knew when the train was coming, but he just couldn't apply that knowledge to get out of the way. In the end, the ole' man is even confused about the nature of what exactly keeps on hitting him. The story seems hauntingly familiar. In the Introduction to this book, we observed that **nobody makes bad decisions out of choice**. Dealing with our own decision-making errors can often feel a bit like that man who is sitting on the railway line. With the help of the Hidden R-I-S-K™ framework, we now know and have a language to talk about the different thinking errors that might hit us at particular points in time. But even with that knowledge, it still takes conscious effort to see them coming and then to act to get off the line.

We also observed in the Introduction that **bad choices often occur when we stop asking questions**. Even with the Hidden R-I-S-K™ framework at our disposal, we need to keep on asking questions. We need to actively seek out the eight characters that hide from our conscious awareness. The whole point about the Hidden R-I-S-K™ framework is to gain insight into our own limitations and those of others. Smarter decision making starts with ourselves, and having the courage to explore our own limitations is the first step in learning to recognise and then mitigate errors in our thinking.

These thinking errors can occur in all areas of our life – public or private, at or outside of work. The more we understand our own limitations, the more we appreciate the limits of our own judgement. When we see thinking errors at work in the choices of others, knowing our own fallibility equips us with the humility to address the thinking errors we see in others in a sensitive and constructive manner. We have already shown that each of the eight characters can be at work in us at any time, depending on the context of the decision. But we should always remember that we never become the characters. **The characters don't define who we are.** They show themselves in certain situations. Understanding which situations might trigger a particular character in us is a significant step in making better decisions. So how do we do this? As the previous chapters illustrate, our thinking errors can be tackled at all three levels of the habit loop: the trigger, the routine and the reward.

In their book *The Knowing–Doing Gap: How Smart Companies Turn Knowledge into Action*, authors Jeffrey Pfeffer and Robert I Sutton observe that "organisations that were better at translating knowledge into action understood the virtue of simple language, simple structures, simple concepts, and the power of common sense, which is remarkably uncommon in its application".[199] With these words of wisdom in mind, this chapter will give you eight easy-to-remember calls to action. These calls to action, when acted upon, will help you break entrenched patterns of thinking. They are the key to making better decisions as they bridge the gap between knowing about thinking errors in decision making and actually doing something about them.

The latter part of the chapter provides information on how the Hidden R-I-S-K™ framework can be used as part of a coaching intervention. We will focus on how to create a thinking environment and the type of questions to ask in a coaching conversation to help the client surface thinking errors and expand their understanding of the choices before them. The whole point of this chapter is to address the final observation we made in our Introduction, that **the quality of what we do depends on the**

thinking we do first. This chapter is aimed at opening up a new vista in our thinking so that we can be more intentional in our choices.

The Eight Calls to Action

The Writer

Call to Action #1: Provide the Writer with Material for a New Script

The Writer's routine is to use the familiar to write a script that fills the gaps created by the unfamiliar. By actively searching material for a new script, we are breaking the routine by expanding the options available to us.

If you recall, this is the habit loop of the Writer:

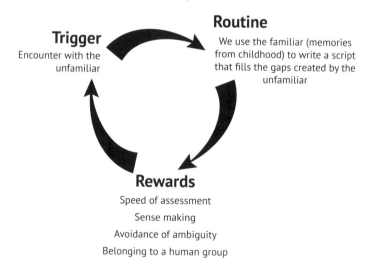

Trigger
Encounter with the unfamiliar

Routine
We use the familiar (memories from childhood) to write a script that fills the gaps created by the unfamiliar

Rewards
Speed of assessment
Sense making
Avoidance of ambiguity
Belonging to a human group

Here are some stories of how providing the Writer with material for a new script changed people's choices.

Toby, Recruitment Consultant

"As a recruiter, you'll soon find out that taking candidates at face value is the biggest rookie mistake ever. Everyone working in the field of recruitment will have a story to tell of how the scripts they have written in their minds have misled them. It is easy to simply trust your 'gut Instinct'. But trusting gut alone is something you should never do when assessing a candidate. Challenge your gut with new material. I have learnt that I make lots of snap judgements even before people walk through the door. I might have already set expectations in my own mind having read their CV. I might have a mental picture of what they will look and sound like. I will often already form a view of my top three candidates before I have even met them. Knowing this, I now focus on getting as much material as I can. I work hard with my clients, helping them to think beyond the 'typical type' that they recruit. We increasingly ask applicants to submit a CV without lots of personal information. This means we reduce the risk of bias when screening. Checking them out on social media gives you another insight into who they really are. Asking another colleague to interview too ensures that there is another perspective. It's our job to fill vacancies with the best candidates so it is important we have as complete a picture of who we are putting forward as possible."

Barbara, Lecturer in Geriatric Nursing

"My experience has been that young nursing students are afraid of old people in any setting. Many students tell me that they don't have anything in common with the elderly and don't really know how to talk to them. The bottom line to me is to get our students to see the elderly as real people and not simply as old people. When they see the person inside that old body they find they have more in common with them than they would imagine. So when students are on placement they are required to do some reflective writing on their experience. They are encouraged to spend time with the people in their care and talk to them about their life history. In most cases, this reflective writing experience allows them to realise that their patients were once young and once had the same hopes and dreams they now have. We also ask them to write a reflective piece on how this experience has impacted their future nursing practice. Throughout the course we challenge their attitudes and show them positive views of aging. By the end of the term views have changed dramatically with the overwhelming majority of students reporting a new-found respect for their elderly patients."

Thomas, Teacher

"We do not like to talk about this as teachers but whether we like it or not, we do write scripts about our students. These scripts are formalised in the School Report. If I'm honest though, we start writing them pretty early on. As mathematics teachers we have had a lot of training around gender and race stereotyping so most of us tend to be quite sensitive around those issues. But we have had no training on how to suspend judgment when it comes to performance. You just can't help but think sometimes 'well that one is not going to win a Nobel prize'. Do we treat those children who we think are brighter differently from those who are just average or below average? We probably do. I always tell myself that I need to bring to mind that these children are not the finished product. A lot can happen between now and age 18 when they move on. Keeping an open mind and seeing that they all develop at different rates is a must if you want to help them reach their potential. It does take mental effort not to judge your students and not to write a script for them. But I have learnt to focus on each child individually and identify how they can each get better at maths."

The Knight

Call to Action #2: Help the Knight to Feel Safe Enough to Disarm

The Knight's routine is the defence of an attachment they don't want to lose. By making it safe for the Knight to disarm, we are tackling the Knight at the reward level. We are taking away the option of loss-avoidance either by taking away this need to avoid the loss in the first place or by not giving the Knight any choice but to disarm. The 'no choice' option involves setting clear boundaries and providing external feedback which encourages the Knight to let go.

If you recall, this is the habit loop of the Knight:

Trigger
Events which impact someone or something we are attached to

Routine
Defence of an attachment by not letting go, and/or increasing investment in the attachment and/or actively attacking forces for change

Rewards
Less avoidance
Enhancement of the attachment
Feelings of loyalty

Here are some stories of how the Knight was able to be disarmed.

Sue, Entrepreneur

"I learned the hard way that the Knight in me can really drag a business down. I'm a really loyal person and want my business to benefit my family and my friends. However, I have learnt that when running a small business you cannot afford to treat family and friends differently and you need to ensure that they can do the job and do it well. A friend of mine had been made redundant and was in a real hole financially. They asked if I could do them a big favour and take them on until they found a more permanent job. I agreed to do so but quickly discovered that they really weren't up to it. I know I should have tackled the situation right away but I let it drift. They were already quite fragile and I thought it would be kicking a friend when they were down if I confronted the problems. The trouble was, their underperformance had an impact on the rest of the team and it wasn't until one of my top people told me either my friend had to go or they would that I was compelled to take action. It wasn't an easy conversation, but do you know what my friend said to me? They said 'why on earth didn't you tell me earlier?' Can you believe it? As it happens, I was able to move them into an area of work they could do for a while and this changed the mood in the team completely. What I have learnt is that I need to contract with people and make it absolutely clear what can be expected by both sides. I also needed to discuss what would happen should the arrangement not work out and how to protect the relationship. It's all in writing now and both sides are clear about where the boundaries are."

Ben, Social Worker (Family Intervention Project)

"I work with families with complex issues like drug and alcohol dependencies, and mental health problems. My job is to build up relationships with them so that they can access the right levels of support when they need it. The truth is these families don't really like you at first but once you break through the hostility and abuse then you often form very strong bonds with people. What I have learnt is that once these strong bonds kick in it's easy to collude with them and their behaviour. The Knight is actually a really good analogy because there is this tendency, this need in you even, to defend them even when they do stuff which harms them. That is why I find supervision so important in my job. Having someone I can talk to about what's going on, who monitors my emotional involvement and gives me feedback really stops me becoming too attached."

Mehmet, Investment Advisor

"You wouldn't believe how attached some investors are to the stocks they buy. In a falling market they just won't sell. So we always set up a stop-loss system in order to preserve the value of their portfolios. Stop-loss systems are a controlled and planned way to sell investments. A stop-loss might work as follows: assume that you have bought shares for 100 pence (£1). If you decide that you wish to set a stop-loss of 20 percent this means that you will automatically sell if the share price fell below 80p. Of course, stop-loss limits should not be adjusted as the shares' prices fall or they will be ineffective. You will also be amazed at how many clients are tempted to adjust their stop-loss limits and are willing to break their own rules in order to avoid the sense of failure associated with sustaining a loss. I think this is a great example of the Knight at work in us. I always tell investors, 'learn from your losses, don't take it personally, it is part of being invested in the stock market'."

Will, Pilot (small commercial aircraft)

"For me, I have to be particularly mindful of the Knight. It takes a lot to abandon a course of action once you decided to go for it. One of the most hairy situations I faced was a descent into Luxembourg Findel Airport. I encountered low-lying fog. It was awful, like pea soup. They really should have just shut the airport. Anyway, visibility was terrible and I couldn't see the runway. It became something of a guessing game. In the end, I did decide to abandon the landing, but it was very last minute. Situational awareness is key. Always monitor what is happening, particularly when you decide on a course of action. Something might emerge that you haven't considered, like the fog. In this instance, I had less than 15 seconds to decide what to do when I saw the runway disappear into a grey haze and was unsure whether it was safe to land. There might also have even been ice on the runway. Anyway, my decision was to discontinue our approach. It was the right decision, although a go around like that is always very unpleasant for the passengers, that is for sure."

The Gambler

Call to Action #3: Show the Gambler the Real Odds

The Gambler's routine is to overestimate the upwards benefits and underestimate the downward risks. By giving the Gambler the real odds, we are breaking his routine and offering a more realistic assessment of outcome.

If you recall, this is the habit loop of the Gambler:

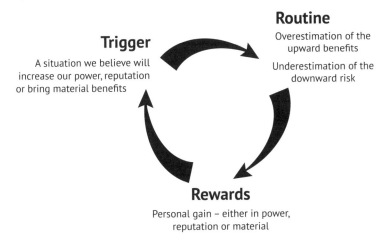

Trigger

A situation we believe will increase our power, reputation or bring material benefits

Routine

Overestimation of the upward benefits

Underestimation of the downward risk

Rewards

Personal gain – either in power, reputation or material

Here are some stories of how the Gambler was shown the real odds.

Giles, Restaurant Owner

"The restaurant business is one of the hardest businesses to get into. A restaurant can run up enormous losses in the first few months, eating up its cash reserves whilst incurring bigger and bigger debts and obligations. New restaurant owners are Gamblers in the truest sense of the word. In my experience restaurants are always undercapitalised. That is inevitable because everything costs twice as much and takes twice as long as you could possibly plan for. If you were to present a realistic budget to begin with that accounts for uncertainty and overruns, very few people would be willing to take the risk. I always advise newcomers to buy an existing failed restaurant off the landlord, redecorate, print some new menus and open a beautiful place for almost nothing. But that is not why people want to get into the business. They want to make their mark. It is all about their own reputation and pride. Of course they are free to delude themselves, but many won't see the signs of failure even when cheques start to bounce and vendors cut you out."

Ruth, Systems Analyst

"In my work I see the Gambler a lot. It's almost like a conspiracy everyone takes part in. You set a date when a system should become operational and then it is always late. You agree a budget and it is always exceeded. You agree a specification and it's always too ambitious. Why? It suits people. Decision makers don't want to hear the reality, what it will really take and cost to deliver what they want. They also like to bury competing interests. Let me give you a typical example. You try to implement an integrated system and then the squabbles start. Different sub-teams argue who should change what and all sorts of fallouts can occur. Over the years I have learnt to become less optimistic in my forecasts and I am beginning to recommend buying software packages and only customizing them where appropriate. It saves a lot of hassle and neutralises the Gambler."

Alex, Vicar

"I bump up against the Gambler all the time and it's nothing to do with not having enough faith. It has more to do with our image as a successful and growing church. We try to do the right things. We have a strategy, we have plans and we set budgets. The truth is that strategic directions and plans need constant recalibration in the light of new information and experience. Despite the best efforts of any leadership team, circumstances change and this means that strategic plans require on-going review. Nothing reveals the Gambler's overconfidence or over-optimism more than the cold reality of actual experience and results. For example, we once projected that youth ministry would grow 40 percent over the following twelve months. This assumption led us to recruit a youth pastor. Growth actually turned out to be more like 10 percent. Or take another estimate that is frequently overoptimistic: the increase in the amount of financial giving from the congregation. We often get half way through our fiscal year and discover that the estimate is being missed. This means our Church Council needs to take some action mid-year so that a significant deficit is not incurred at the end of the year."

The Butler

···

Call to Action #4: Give the Butler a Voice

By giving the Butler a voice – the skills to express his or her views in a non-adversarial manner – we are taking away the Butler's fear of conflict with people who are more powerful and fear of losing his or her reputation. The Butler cannot be tackled on the individual level only. In Chapter 18, we will explore how the right environment can be created where people feel valued for speaking out and where there is mutual accountability.

If you recall, this is the habit loop of the Butler:

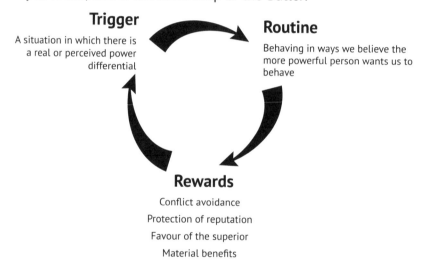

Trigger
A situation in which there is a real or perceived power differential

Routine
Behaving in ways we believe the more powerful person wants us to behave

Rewards
Conflict avoidance
Protection of reputation
Favour of the superior
Material benefits

Here are some stories of how the Butler found a voice.

Sara, HR Business Partner

"I guess HR often has to walk a tightrope between providing a service to the business and making an active contribution to the business by challenging mindsets and current ways of doing things. I have to admit that in my early career I allowed the Butler to surface more than I should have done. The example I can think of was when I worked in a consumer goods business. We had a disciplinary issue with one of our sales people. The guy was totally unreliable and his absence record was appalling, so our case was strong. However, the line manager did not follow proper procedure and had simply dismissed him. No warning or performance plan. He was simply fired. At the time, I was really troubled about the way this was handled, but I was rather timid and did not speak out. The manager was quite a forceful character and rather intimidating. I was just new into the job and trying to find my feet. The upshot was that the salesman got himself a good lawyer and took the company to court. We lost and it cost the business a lot of money. Guess who was left with egg on her face? Well, today I am a bit more outspoken about things. Training in how to give and receive feedback has really helped me in putting my point across without offending anybody. I have found my voice!"

Paul, Marketing Executive

"The Butler is a real dilemma for me. Do you really say what you think or do you tell them what they want to hear? Speaking up might harm your career in the short term. Do you want to take that risk? That is always the question. Well, I recently spoke up at a key meeting. I literally gave myself permission to speak. I thought, if I don't say something now, nothing will ever change round here. It was all about an away day my boss organised. He is new to our company and has a big ego, that's for sure. So he organises this day away from the office with the team. I have no problem with that. At this meeting he starts asking people for ideas, but each time people made a contribution he quickly moved on without taking much notice. It felt a bit like going through the motions rather than being truly consulted. As the session went on, I could see that people were getting more and more disillusioned as they just did not feel heard. Morale was already bad, but the way he went about it on that away day hardly lifted the spirits. If nothing else, the whole thing was quite disempowering. The next day my boss waltzes into my office and declares that the away day was a resounding success. He then asked me what I thought about it. I did not respond immediately and was very measured in my response. I told him first that I thought it was a great idea to take the team away. I then told him that I had the impression that the actual day itself really did not quite hit the button. I told him that I would love to get his permission to talk to people to get some feedback so we can get greater engagement from people next time. I was surprised that he really liked my feedback: maybe it is the way you voice your opinion. I was not confrontational at all, just very factual."

The Judge

Call to Action #5: Let the Judge See Beyond the Performance

The Judge's routine is all about focusing our effort on that which captures our attention – the performance. We break the Judge's routine by letting the Judge consciously look beyond the performance and focus on information that is less visible but often more valuable. If we take the analogy of the performance being on a stage, we need to look behind the curtain and see what else there is that might help us get to a better decision.

If you recall, this is the habit loop of the Judge:

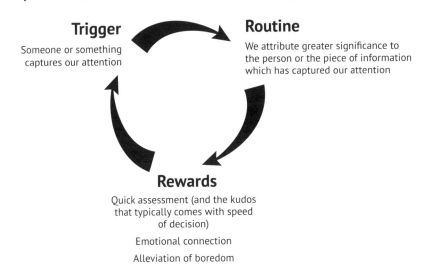

Trigger
Someone or something captures our attention

Routine
We attribute greater significance to the person or the piece of information which has captured our attention

Rewards
Quick assessment (and the kudos that typically comes with speed of decision)
Emotional connection
Alleviation of boredom

Here are some stories of how the Judge has been able to look beyond the performance.

Nathan, Investor

"Many would-be entrepreneurs see passion alone as the ticket to success. Sure, it is good to see passion in an entrepreneur, but don't be fooled. Whether you feel passionate about your business is quite frankly irrelevant to your results a few years out. What matters is preparedness. For me, whether entrepreneurs have fully fleshed out their ideas, gained a deep understanding of their markets and created plans for overcoming obstacles and exploiting contingencies are better indicators of success than passion. Professional investors typically discount founders' passion and pay most attention to preparedness. Entrepreneurs are now increasingly bypassing professional investors and appealing directly to the crowd. Crowd sourcing is in and the crowd loves a passionate founder. They are looking above all for emotional connection. This focus on performance is a really good example of the Judge at work and I would seriously advise future funders not be taken in by the Judge. Look behind the scenes. Look for clear indications of preparedness – signs that the entrepreneur knows how to find and hire the right people and take care of the other details that will be critical to success. Both entrepreneurs and their funders should be aware that without preparedness, passion is worth little."

Donna, Finance Business Partner

"I am in this role because I have got a head for figures and I enjoy it most of the time. One of the most interesting things is that people always think that because you are dealing with figures you are objective. But you know that is not always true. Let's say I have got to make recommendations to reduce costs and increase revenue. How do I go about doing it? It's simple. I pick out those figures that catch my attention. They might be higher than the average or lower than the average. This is the Judge at work. Who is to say that those areas are the right ones to focus on? It is all a bit hit and miss and I now preface any presentation I make to senior management with the warning that headline figures tell a thousand tales and that when I flag up those figures we need to find out what those figures are really telling us before we make any judgement and take any action."

Jean, Investment Banker

"I can see the Judge everywhere in the way we work in investment banking. Our strategic decision making is so driven by fashion. Just to give you an example, I am working in an area in decline. Legislation has eroded much of the attractiveness of investing in offshore tax havens. In the past, that is how my bank used to make a lot of money. Now we try to offset through trading. We have a small number of traders who are treated like royalty. No questions asked. They can pretty much say and do what they want because now they are the rainmakers. I keep asking myself 'but hang on, haven't we been here before?' I think it's only a question of time before their winning streak turns into something else. Maybe there really is nothing new under the sun. Today's heroes are bound to be tomorrow's villains. I'm worried that we aren't looking behind the headline successes and understanding what is really going on and what risks these people are taking on to get such fairy-tale returns."

The Captain

....

Call to Action #6: Direct the Captain to Alternative Destinations

The Captain's routine is all about selecting data that backs up our predetermined decision and ignoring other information that may challenge our predetermined path. By actively considering alternative destinations and searching for disconfirming evidence, we are breaking the Captain's routine. The Captain can, of course, be an individual or a group.

If you recall, this is the habit loop of the Captain:

Trigger
A piece of information, an idea or belief system predetermines and anchors a decision

Routine
We actively select other data that backs up our predetermined decision and ignore other information that may challenge it

Rewards
Quick assessment
Satisfaction that our decision 'feels right'

Here are some stories of how the Captain found alternative destinations.

Roland, Board Member (Large Electronics Company)

....

"Being a Board Member does give you quite an insight into good decision making. We recently had a change in our leadership. A new CEO has come on board and the way he approaches decision making has been a breath of fresh air. He really is dealing with the Captain head on. Before this new CEO arrived, the preparation pack for our board meetings contained all the decisions that were supposedly before us. The problem for me was that these decisions had effectively already been made at all kinds of previous meetings. We could have vetoed them of course. But we rarely did. Our new CEO immediately changed this setup. At his first management meeting he rightly said that a managing board should be a decision-making body where you have a robust discussion around the issues faced by the business. He now makes sure that for every decision, multiple options are presented. He also ensures that for each option we have a devil's advocate. Now we are more thorough in our decision making and it is more enjoyable."

Derek, Global Strategic Portfolio Director (Medical Devices)

"Part of my job is to develop global pricing strategies for various products. Where do you start and how do you value some of these rather specialist medical devices? This can be quite tricky and you always have to be aware of your competitors and market conditions. The issue for me is to dodge the Captain who sets anchors, or markers, that steer our thinking. Reference points, benchmarks and comparisons are everywhere, ready to trip you up at every corner. I am forever reminding my team to think about the uniqueness of our product and about the different market conditions in different countries before setting a price and not to be influenced just by the markers other organisations have placed."

Sylvia, Chest Physician

"As a doctor I am deeply challenged by the Hidden R-I-S-K™ framework. This is a sensitive subject. If you make a mistake as a doctor you have an immediate impact on the wellbeing of another human being. When you make a mistake prescribing the wrong medication, it is easier to say 'I am human, I am fallible' and much harder to admit 'I made a mistake in my thinking'. Making a mistake in your thinking goes right to the heart of who you are as a doctor. We are trained to diagnose and to work through a series of probabilities around the cause of a particular condition. That is why it is hard to admit a thinking error. But we all make mistakes and I'm pleased to say that the profession is starting to recognise that. For me, misdiagnosis is a big issue and is best represented in the Hidden R-I-S-K™ framework by the character of the Captain. The current system of developing a 'working diagnosis' can easily be compromised by the Captain's steering. You see, when a patient is admitted to hospital, a team of doctors formulates a working diagnosis. Although the diagnosis is not certain, the patient is treated as if the working diagnosis is correct. If the patient gets better, the working diagnosis is confirmed. If there is no improvement in a condition we think again and consider whether the working diagnosis is not correct. Hospitals are really busy places and doctors are under tremendous pressure to come up with a working diagnosis. Previous conditions can often act as anchors and the Captain can lead us to look for confirming symptoms and ignore disconfirming symptoms. It is a difficult topic."

The Archivist

Call to Action #7: Focus the Archivist on the Present

The Archivist's routine is all about extrapolation from past experiences and the application of old solutions to new problems. We break the Archivist's routine by firmly focusing on the present and away from the past, actively looking for new solutions to new problems.

If you recall, this is the habit loop of the Archivist:

Trigger
A problem reminds us of a situation we encountered in the past

Routine
Extrapolation of past experiences
Application of old solutions

Rewards
Quick, effortless decision making
Pride and satisfaction in applying past learning – my experience counts for something!

Here are some stories of how the Archivist has come to focus on the present.

Alan, Careers Officer

"Much of my career was spent in one of the most deprived areas in the country. I worked in all of the local comprehensive schools advising youngsters on future career choices. We actually did not have that much to offer the kids and it used to break my heart because these children had such unrealistic ideas about what jobs were around and what it took to become successful. I had kids who wanted to become interpreters but who could barely speak a word in a foreign language, wannabe ballet dancers who could not do the splits and then all those kids who wanted to be pop stars but couldn't sing or play a musical instrument. It was part of my job to introduce some realism into their career choices and I became really good at developing this patter about plan A and Plan B. Plan A was their original plan and I normally did not spend too much time talking about that. But I offered them Plan B, which I suggested should come into operation if Plan A did not work out within a certain timescale. Plan B amounted to the limited number of local apprenticeships I could offer as well as further education courses at the local college. Anyway, one morning I had a group of lads turn up. They were normal working-class kids and, as far as I could tell, there was nothing terribly special about them. Sure enough they told me that they had formed a rock band and that they were going to make it big as pop stars. Needless to say, I immediately launched into my Plan A and Plan B routine and sent them away with information on apprenticeships as motor mechanics. I remember they were none too happy about the advice I had given them and rightly so as it turned out. On this occasion Plan A worked and they became one of the most successful rock groups in the country. You know, the Archivist so misled me. At the time I did not even bother to explore their dream with them. I just did not take them seriously. I should have found out more about them. Unlike the other wannabe pop stars, they were actually quite accomplished musicians. But that information escaped me. I should have encouraged them."

Alan, CEO of a Mobile Phone Company

"So many of our competitors have turned their attention to Asia in the belief that the vast numbers of consumers and their rising spending power can easily translate into rich pickings for their companies. But they have been badly burnt by the thinking of the Archivist. Traditional market strategies, such as establishing a position and securing one's place in the market, do not automatically work where tens of millions of new customers with little brand loyalty enter every year. Take one example, the Indian mobile phone market, where there can be more than ten operators selling the same service at rock bottom prices. If you pursue a strategy that would work in the West, such as chasing the middle of the market, you are chasing fool's gold. Guess what: when it comes to middle-class customers in Asia there is no middle. There is no middle of the road average preference and there is no average brand that consumers want. You have to realise that you are entering a completely different playing field and situational awareness goes a long way. You have to come to understand what drives demand in the local context. Before we enter a market we explore extensively the local and cultural context that drives purchases and consumption. We aim to get a holistic perspective of consumers' wants and needs. Only when we have satisfied ourselves that we have a comprehensive understanding of potential demand opportunities will we develop opportunistic strategies to take full advantage of those opportunities."

The Prisoner

....

Call to Action #8: Release the Prisoner from their Professional Prison

The Prisoner's routine is all about finding solutions within the boundaries of a particular worldview or frame of reference established through our training. By releasing the Prisoner from this prison of the mind, we are actively searching out other ways of seeing the world and breaking the Prisoner's routine.

If you recall, this is the habit loop of the Prisoner:

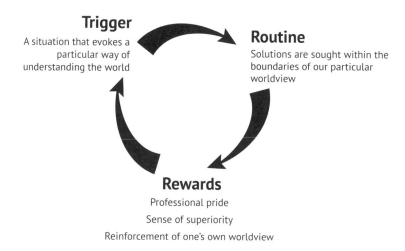

Trigger
A situation that evokes a particular way of understanding the world

Routine
Solutions are sought within the boundaries of our particular worldview

Rewards
Professional pride
Sense of superiority
Reinforcement of one's own worldview

Here are some stories of how the Prisoner has been released from prison.

Rupert, Senior Marketing Executive

....

"Recent developments in marketing are just breath taking. Things are moving so quickly you need to keep your eyes on the ball all the time. It is easy to become complacent and stick with the old view of marketing. If you do, you will miss the boat completely. The Prisoner speaks into the strategic marketing space more than any of these other characters because marketing has undergone a fundamental paradigm shift. We are talking here about a move away from traditional promotions, which in the past have been all about tactics, towards strategic, cross-functional initiatives run by leaders who are really customer focused. The development of networks – by which I mean networks of key relationships with customers, contractors, co-workers and even competitors – is crucial. Harnessing these networks is now a core skill for people who want to make it in marketing. The challenge is to test market choices and your value proposition against the network's capabilities, and that is fundamentally different from running a traditional marketing campaign. Look at some of the most spectacular failings in marketing in recent years. Take Nokia. Nokia got stuck in the old way of doing marketing, running some flashy campaigns. But flashy campaigns don't get you out of jail anymore. Their value proposition was all over the place. It is so easy to fall into that trap and to remain imprisoned in the old ways of doing things."

Gerald, Global Innovation Director (Engineering Company)

"The Prisoner speaks volumes to me. You might have a product that can be used differently in different markets and across different sectors. Yet because of the Prisoner at work, you might just miss an opportunity. You always need to keep your eyes open in order to discover those not so obvious opportunities so that you can get the most out of the investment you have made in developing innovative products. For example, we manufacture very compact air-conditioning units. They are used in offices, hotels and some public buildings in the UK. Elsewhere in the world we sell them in the luxury yacht market and on cruise ships. That is why I send our research guys on tour once a year. Trade shows are good for them. They give them an idea of what other people are doing in the field and they are encouraged to talk to customers, as well as our sales and marketing teams. I want them to be curious about what is going on and to think differently!"

These personal stories show how different people have reflected on their choices and used the calls to action to make better decisions. In summary, the Calls to Action are:

Call to Action #1: Provide the Writer with material for a new script

Call to Action #2: Help the Knight to feel safe enough to disarm

Call to Action #3: Show the Gambler the real odds

Call to Action #4: Give the Butler a voice

Call to Action #5: Let the Judge see beyond the performance

Call to Action #6: Direct the Captain to alternative destinations

Call to Action #7: Focus the Archivist on the present

Call to Action #8: Release the Prisoner from their professional prison.

Space to Think

Exploring these Calls to Action assumes that we are skilled enough to observe patterns in our own behaviour and thinking. There are many traditions that encourage self-reflection and inner examination. You may also be familiar with the practice of mindfulness, which draws on these traditions. Mindfulness is all about paying attention to what is happening in the present moment – on purpose and non-judgementally – with the aim of increasing awareness, clarity and acceptance of what is really going on. Tuning in to what's really happening – the situation, our feelings, mood and emotions, our hopes and desires – gives us a richer context to understand and name the thinking errors that may be in play and the pathways to better choices.

In Chapter 2 we introduced the Johari Window (see Figure 2) as a picture to help us consider the extent to which our thinking and decision-making processes are open or hidden. Self-reflection on each of the characters and the use of our Calls to Action can help us explore our blind spots and the unknown. To self-reflect well, we also need to tune into what Daniel Kahneman called System 2 thinking. We explained System 2 thinking in Chapter 1, but in essence it involves slowing down and creating space to think.

Creating space to think is not a new idea but it is something we don't do often enough and frequently find difficult to do well. We have noted throughout this book that the effectiveness of our decisions often depends on the quality of thinking we do first. Thinking well can be a solo exercise, but is often improved when we are supported by others – either through the conversations we have with another person (whether informally or in more formal coaching/managerial relationships) and through our participation in groups or teams.

In her book *Time to Think: Listening to Ignite the Human Mind*[200], Nancy Kline sets out ten components of a thinking environment.[201] These ten components apply to one-to-one and group conversations. Many thousands of people have found them extremely helpful. Nancy Kline sets out the parameters for effective thinking extremely well in her book and we won't attempt to cover the same ground here.

When we step into the decision-making space and attempt to make the unconscious conscious, we can expect to bump into a number of strongly held beliefs that can derail our thinking and lead to defensive behaviours. These underlying beliefs about ourselves could be:

- I trust my gut and intuition
- I am not prone to thinking errors
- I always use evidence and data
- I am impartial and objective
- I always think things through.

Whatever we believe about ourselves, the chances are that the Gambler will be at work in convincing us that we are far better decision makers than we really are. So our challenge is to make both the unconscious conscious *and* to do so in a way that keeps the conversation in a generative, productive space that encourages deeper thinking and reflection.

To achieve this, we would like to highlight five of the components set out by Nancy Kline that will move conversations about thinking errors into a constructive and purposeful thinking space:

1. Incisive Questions
2. Equality
3. Feelings
4. Information
5. Diversity.

1. Incisive Questions

When someone presents you with a choice they are facing, how do you respond? Do you frame an opinion about that choice quite quickly? Do you spot the flaws in their thinking? Do you just sit back and listen? Whatever you do, the chances are that you will be more adept at seeing the thinking errors of others than you are at seeing your own. The question then is what do you do with these observations?

One course of action is, of course, immediately to stick them on the table and tell it as it is: "You are being just like the Butler here, serving up what they want." "You have already made your mind up haven't you? You just want me to agree with what you want to do." "You are just holding on to what you know. You are just like the Knight. You are defending something that isn't working for you and you can't see how anything could change." Sometimes straight talking is what is needed. But direct statements like these can easily back people into a corner. They frame how the conversation will go. They don't encourage thinking.

Kline observes that incisive questions remove limiting assumptions and free the mind to think afresh. We would agree. Helping others to explore their assumptions through the art of questioning creates an environment in which others are able to think and reflect, drawing conclusions that they own and are more likely to do something about.

The Hidden R-I-S-K™ framework offers a powerful vehicle to frame questions around each of the characters. Here are some example questions:

The Writer	What script are you writing?
	If you could write an alternative script, what would it be?
	What is a fact?
	What is a possible fact?
The Knight	What are you particularly attached to?
	What do you find difficult to let go of?
	What conditions would help you to let go?
	What would happen if you let go?
The Gambler	Why do you believe these outcomes are possible?
	What evidence is there to suggest this is realistic?
	If things didn't work out as you expect, what would happen?
	What could get in the way of this outcome?
	What other outcomes could there be?
The Butler	What assumptions are you making about what others want?
	If you put yourself in their position, what would you want to happen?
	What's the worst thing that could happen if you gave your real opinion?
	What can you do to get your opinion across in a way that engages them?
The Judge	What is it that is appealing about the performance?
	What connected with you emotionally?
	What assumptions are you making about the performer?
	What really matters in this decision?

The Captain	To what extent have you already made up your mind?
	What is staring me in the face that I am not facing?
	What other alternatives are there?
	If this destination isn't an option, where would you go?
The Archivist	In what way is this situation different from those in the past?
	What are the unique characteristics of this particular decision?
	If this situation is nothing like any other you have faced, what further information would you need to gather?
	If you were an outsider looking in on this situation, what would you see?
The Prisoner	What assumptions are you making about this situation?
	If you could stand in the shoes of your colleagues, what would they be seeing?
	If you look at this decision from three different positions (e.g. your boss, a colleague, a customer), what might they choose?
	If your way of seeing this situation isn't an option, what other ways of seeing this situation could there be?

Questions like these will help to break habitual patterns of thinking and they do so in a constructive and non-threatening way. As you question, listen to the answers. Keep testing for facts; possible facts and underlying assumptions or stories we have created to fill the gaps.

2. Equality

We have already highlighted the importance of exploring our decisions in a constructive and generative way. As we ask our incisive questions, it is important to do so from a position of equality rather than superiority. Adopting a parental attitude towards the decision maker will not create this healthy environment. Their decision is not ours to make. Our role is to help a colleague or friend explore their decision in ways to surface and mitigate those unconscious forces that will be in play.

Kline stresses that in a thinking environment it is important to balance contribution with listening. As a helper to someone making a decision, it is even more important to balance listening with contribution and certainly to hold back on dispensing your pearls of wisdom.

In his book *The Empty Raincoat*, Charles Handy once asked "How can I know what I think until I hear myself speak?" Giving people space to talk, to speak out and articulate what's already in their mind provides that springboard for exploration and questioning.

3. Feelings

All our decisions involve feelings and emotions. We have come across people who claim that they don't do emotion. They are the ones who wear the face of objectivity and rational thinking. But they do. We are human beings. We all do emotion and we all have feelings. Even if you don't wear your heart on your sleeve, your emotions and feelings are there even if they are expressed below the surface. However self-contained you may think you are, your feelings and emotions will permeate your thinking and choices as much as those of the next person.

How well are feelings and emotions dealt with in your workplace? If it is anything like the many we have worked with, the answer is not well at all. Many organisations have developed cultures that don't work well with feelings and emotions. Being seen to be in control of your emotions is encouraged. As Nancy Kline put it, "our society is terrified of tears, and of anger and fear". But even if we don't show tears, anger or fear they are still there.

Kline suggests that there is a deeply held belief that thinking stops when we are upset. We would agree and even suggest that many believe thinking stops when we express our feelings and emotions. But feelings are an integral part of our thinking about choices. As Kline goes on to say, "if we express feelings just enough, thinking re-starts".

In addressing unconscious thinking errors, our challenge is to tune in to our feelings – to name them, to understand them, to sift them. Each of the eight characters has an emotional dimension:

- The Writer will write scripts that elicit a full range of emotional responses. We saw this in the research presented in Chapter 9, where there are many examples of these unconscious biases surfacing in criminal prosecutions, recruitment, promotions and development decisions. The Writer is very skilled at tuning our emotions into the wrong things.
- The Knight will fight to avert loss. The Knight in us creates strong emotional attachments and threats to these are strongly resisted.
- The Gambler in us thrives on the adrenalin rush and is characterised by self-belief, over-optimism, a belief that success is down to us and failure down to others. It's a heady cocktail of emotions that obscures our view of the real odds.
- The Butler is paralysed by fear, anxiety and doubt. The Butler embraces limited beliefs and assumptions and plays these out as if fact.

- The Judge is dazzled by the performance. The emotional connections made by the performer go deep and overwhelm other information.
- The Captain in us has already made a choice and screens out conflicting information. Stubbornness, a closed mind, dismissiveness and even bullying are feelings elicited by the Captain.
- The Archivist finds security in the known and the familiar, and is fearful of the unknown.
- The Prisoner also finds security when viewing situations through the lens of their own expertise. It's a daunting prospect to step into someone else's shoes and see that same situation from their perspective.

We need to listen to and listen through our feelings. They are insightful. They are valuable. They reveal much truth about what is really going on in our thinking.

4. Information

We need information to create an accurate picture of what is going on. Information can be facts and figures, opinions, feelings and assumptions, concepts, policies, rules and laws. In tuning in to our unconscious thinking, we are trying to discover what is really going on. Is our sense-making reliable? Have we been able to develop as good an understanding of the situation as we are able to? What are facts, possible facts and simply the assumptions I am making to fill the information gaps?

Note too that providing information and interpreting information are two distinct steps. In working with others, either one-to-one or in groups, if you have information that is relevant to the decision being made then it would be wrong to withhold it. As coaches and group facilitators, we have learnt that how you choose to share information is as important as the information itself. We need to be mindful of our own needs in sharing information – is it because we want to look good or are we really trying to help the person get to the best possible decision? Information should be shared in a way that invites the decision maker to take and explore that information for him or herself.

For example, in a conversation I may notice that someone is getting carried away with an idea: the Gambler in them may be in play and I need to help them test whether their optimism is well-founded. I may well have several pieces of information that could help in this situation. I may have facts and figures that challenge their optimism. I may be able to notice and reflect back how they seem to be feeling. I may know the opinions other stakeholders have about this particular decision. A direct approach – along the lines of "it won't work because so and so won't agree", "you are wrong because of facts X and Y" or "you're just getting carried away and there's no way you are going to be able to do this" – is unlikely to create a constructive thinking environment. Inviting people to consider the reactions of others, or asking people what they think of facts X and Y or encouraging someone to reflect on the feelings you are observing are far better ways of sharing information.

Information offered in a timely and helpful way is key to supporting each of the Calls to Action outlined earlier.

5. Diversity

When we are faced with difficult, complex decisions, no one person can see the full picture and no one person has a monopoly over the truth. We will all see the same situation differently. We will all notice something that others haven't yet seen. This is what diversity is. And we can either feel threatened by it or embrace and value it.

When it comes to thinking and to effective decision making, there is no doubt in our mind that diversity enhances thinking and therefore improves the quality of decisions made. Diversity of opinion also challenges directly the work of each of the eight characters and supports our Calls to Action. Diversity of viewpoint speaks very directly to the work of the Butler because:

- Diversity challenges the view that the dominant group is superior and everyone should think like, agree with and be like them
- Diversity challenges the power inherent in the dominant group; diversity in itself opens up other possibilities; and permission is granted for other viewpoints to prevail.

The importance of bringing diversity of voice into major decisions is clearly a challenge for groups and organisations and we explore this further in the next chapter. When working with individuals it is important to keep asking questions that help them explore situations from different viewpoints and to think about what other information might help them challenge, confirm or simply offer another perspective on the decision in hand.

In this chapter, we have looked at how to use the Hidden R-I-S-K™ framework for self-reflection and in one-to-one conversations, either informally or in more formal coaching and/or line-management situations. Our focus has been on helping you to turn **knowing** about thinking errors in decision making into **doing** something about them. To help you do this we have given you:

- Eight Calls to Action to mitigate the thinking errors embodied in our eight characters
- Five components to help create a generative and constructive thinking environment within which you can surface and address thinking errors.

The next chapter looks at how thinking errors can be addressed in decision-making groups and teams, how organisations can create the right environment for diversity of voice to thrive and the role leaders need to play to support better decision making.

18

Creating a Decision-friendly Environment

"It is not the strongest of the species that survive, nor the most intelligent, but the one most responsive to change."

Charles Darwin

The Corporate Sales team had worked for many months on this proposal. The most optimistic forecast suggested that a significant number of employees in a large corporate could open a retirement savings plan as a result of this deal. It was the biggest deal currently on the books and the financial targets required a successful outcome on this one. When the Proposals Committee approved the deal you could smell the relief in the room. The final hurdle was sign off by the Executive Board and all the indications were good.

There was one itch however and it was being felt by the Director of Risk. The regulator had flagged in a recent report a concern that there wasn't sufficient challenge within the organisation. She was concerned that if this deal was scrutinised by the regulator, it would appear to have been approved without a robust enough critique. Deep down she thought the proposal was sound, but having recently been exposed to unconscious thinking errors in decision making, she wondered whether there were forces at work that hadn't been fully explored. The trouble was, too many people had an interest in this proposal being a success and she thought it would be political suicide to raise a red flag at this stage of the process. Then again, that is what Directors of Risk are paid to do, so she scheduled a meeting with the CEO and raised her concerns.

It wasn't an easy meeting and the CEO was very reluctant to hold up the deal. The Corporate Sales Director was brought into the meeting and the conversation got even hotter. An agreement was reached to hire an external consultant to conduct a human due diligence on the proposal before it was taken to the Executive Board.

A consultant was hired who was skilled in using the Hidden R-I-S-K™ framework and was mindful that in a situation like this many of the characters could be at work and reinforcing one another. After briefing the board and other key people about the process, he then held one-to-one meetings with each member of the team. What he found was that a number of hidden risks were in play.

For the Executive Board, there was a dominant script being written (the Writer). This script was a very positive script with returns at the high end of expectations. There was also an expectation that winning this deal would lead to more work with that client and similar work with other large corporates (the Gambler). Many on the Board saw the deal as a catalyst to opening up a large revenue stream and were already mentally using this script to shape future business plans.

There was another script that was being written by the Customer Services and Technology Directors (the Writer). Their script focused on the potential surge in new customers and the operational capacity to cope well with increased volumes. No additional resources had been factored into securing a successful deal and there was real concern that after-sales service would be poor, damaging reputation and prospects of future revenue growth (the Prisoner). When challenged over why these concerns hadn't been tabled earlier, the response was that it wasn't what colleagues wanted to hear and that so much effort had been put into winning this deal that there was little chance of slowing it down or changing direction (the Butler).

The interview with the CEO also revealed that Alex, the Director of Corporate Sales, was seen as a rising star with a strong reputation as a rainmaker. With this strong reputation, Alex was already the leading internal candidate to succeed the CEO. The CEO trusted Alex completely and thought that the proposal should be passed without too much scrutiny: "Alex is the safest pair of hands we have and if he says there is a big prize to be gained on this deal then I'm with him all the way" (the Judge).

The meeting with Alex highlighted how significant this deal was to him and his career ambitions. He made it absolutely clear that he wasn't going to let it go and that he expected his colleagues to get behind him in delivering it successfully. Alex had personally invested much of his time and effort in recent years building relationships within the client organisation and considered this deal to be the fruit of all that hard work (the Knight).

A meeting with members of the proposal team reinforced the view that resources had been focused exclusively on winning this deal. Some of the team members believed that profitable opportunities with other clients had been downgraded and that some new and innovative product offerings had been put on the backburner because they were seen as distraction from the task in hand. The decision to focus the team on this proposal hadn't gone down too well with everyone. Others had invested a lot of time cultivating other clients and developing new business. They felt that other opportunities were being missed. There was also a suggestion that some critical data had been downplayed because it suggested far lower returns than the projections in the proposal (the Captain). The trouble was, none of the team was prepared to stick their neck out and bring clear evidence to back up that claim or to challenge the amount of time being spent on this single proposal (the Butler).

These meetings gave the consultant much food for thought. Some of the issues raised had a direct impact on the proposal under consideration whilst others highlighted broader issues about how proposals are developed and the culture within the team. There were also some issues that were quite contentious and would need to be handled sensitively.

Reflection Point

How would you use your knowledge of the Hidden R-I-S-K™ framework and the eight calls to action to present your findings and recommendations to the Executive Board?

What issues would you raise separately and with whom?
What actions would you recommend to support future decisions on large proposals?

Through using the Hidden R-I-S-K™ framework and the eight calls to action, the consultant was able to help the Executive Board take decisions to strengthen the current proposal and improve the way future proposals were developed. The consultant was also able to provide one-to-one feedback to the CEO and Director of Corporate Sales to help them understand better the thinking errors that were impacting their choices.

Focusing on the proposal being evaluated, the consultant took the Executive Board through these five steps:

Step 1 helped the Executive Board to understand two substantive problems:

- There was a dominant narrative that may or may not be true but hadn't been fully tested; and alternative narratives hadn't been explored
- Moreover, there was a sub-narrative about the risks associated with implementation that hadn't been discussed and needed to be. The costs of implementation had not

been fully addressed and this omission posed a significant risk to effective after-sales.

Step 2 was to play back to the board the narratives, to test them and to explore possible alternative narratives.

Step 3 was to run a pre-mortem – to imagine future failure and then explain the cause. This highlighted potential problems that could be proactively addressed.

Step 4 was to agree the desired outcome to which all could commit.

Step 5 was to reshape the proposal based on the agreements reached. After the discussion, the board decided to approve the proposal with the following changes:

- Identify other possible outcomes besides the more optimistic and consider broader financial possibilities
- Strengthen actions to maximise take-up in the client organisation
- Address operational implications to ensure effective after-sales.

Focusing on the overall process for proposal development, a number of actions were also taken. These actions responded to the calls to action as a way of surfacing and mitigating thinking errors throughout the proposal process:

- The provision of material to develop multiple scripts – to mitigate the Writer
- Executive sponsorship of significant proposals from outside the sales team – to mitigate the Knight
- Use of at least three scenarios to get a better understanding of the odds – to mitigate the Gambler
- Widening of options early in the process to identify alternatives – to mitigate the Captain in particular

- Involvement of others outside the immediate sales client team – to mitigate the Prisoner.

The one-to-one feedback with the CEO helped him to understand how the Judge at work created a situation where the CEO took at face value proposals from the Director of Corporate Sales without serious scrutiny. There was also a discussion about how a culture had built up that discouraged people from challenging (the Butler). This enabled the CEO to take proposals to the Executive Board to help create an environment where speaking out was highly valued (see later in this chapter).

Finally, the one-to-one feedback with the Director of Corporate Sales helped him to appreciate how the Knight at work had led him to defend this proposal against any perceived threats, including exploring realistic alternative client opportunities and new products. The feedback also helped him understand how the work of the Gambler had seduced him into believing only in his highly optimistic forecasts. The unresolved issue of focusing only on information that justified the position already taken was also discussed in terms of how the Captain in us anchors particular viewpoints and then eliminates information that goes against that viewpoint.

In this case study, the organisation was able to surface and address a number of significant hidden risks in time to make a commercial proposal more robust and successful.

We know that however attentive we are, unconscious thinking errors will creep into our decision making. We also know that decisions are situational and that for any decision one or all eight of the characters in the Hidden R-I-S-K™ framework could be in play. The situation is complicated further when decisions are taken by groups of people. As we saw in the example above, different characters may be more active in different people. The interplay between different characters means that multiple errors may be in play at any one time and the default to System 1 thinking – which lends itself to fast, driven, unreflective decision making – becomes very seductive.

Effective decisions taken by groups on complex issues depend on System 2 thinking, because firstly, these choices are complex and therefore do not lend themselves to quick, System 1 decisions; and secondly, because of the added complexity a group of decision makers brings.

If we are serious about using the robust body of evidence that highlights the thinking errors in our decision making, it is likely to mean that we will need to change current approaches to group decision making and decide to be more intentional and deliberate in surfacing and addressing the hidden risks that seek to distort our thinking. So what can be done?

The good news is that there are tools that can be used within the context of the Hidden R-I-S-K™ framework to assist groups tasked with decision making. The foundational awareness about thinking errors is found in the Hidden R-I-S-K™ framework. The eight characters in the Hidden R-I-S-K™ framework embody all the major thinking errors that are likely to be in play and the Hidden R-I-S-K™ framework gives all those involved in decisions a shared language to discuss these unconscious forces.

A Toolkit to Aid Better Decision Making

The Hidden R-I-S-K™ framework is the most important tool we have. The framework allows us to spot hidden risks as they appear and it gives us a language to challenge thinking errors in self and in others in a way that is positive and leads to action. The tools suggested are informed by the Hidden R-I-S-K™ framework and are intended to support the calls to action aimed at mitigating thinking errors.

The story that introduced this chapter highlighted some of the tools that can be used to support better decision making. Below we say more about those suggested tools, focusing on 10 tools that can be used in conjunction with the Hidden R-I-S-K™ framework to surface and address unconscious thinking errors when working with decision-making groups.

Not all 10 tools need to be used at once. Depending on the decision and which characters are tending to emerge, appropriate tools should be selected as part of the people due diligence around key decisions.

1. Widen Options

Too often our decisions are made within a narrow frame of reference. As we reflect on the eight characters in the Hidden R-I-S-K™ framework we can see how each narrows our options:

- The Writer focuses on a particular script
- The Knight won't consider options that threaten protected relationships
- The Gambler is convinced about their winning strategy
- The Butler is bound by the views of those in power over them
- The Judge will only see the things that grab their attention
- The Captain won't see beyond their pre-determined decision
- The Archivist will validate options against past experience
- The Prisoner will only see what fits with their professional worldview.

Dan and Chip Heath, in their book *Decisive*,[202] propose "widening your options" as a first step in making better decisions. To some extent many of the tools listed below and beyond this list focus on widening your options – helping you to think differently about a decision. We would agree that this widening is a foundational step as it really does speak to the thinking errors embodied in all of the eight characters.

Some ways to widen options not covered in the tools below are:

- *Find people who could help shift your focus of attention.* Talk to people you are trying to help; involve others who can bring a different perspective; ask people who have solved the problem what they did.
- *Thinking about your opportunity costs.* Put simply, this is about identifying what else you could do with the time, money and resources if used in a different way.
- *Think AND, not OR.* We often fall into binary – either/or – thinking. Often we have our cake and eat it. AND is a very permissible word to use when considering options.
- *Combine options.* Look for the best in several options to create new possibilities.
- *Use "what if…":* This is a useful tool to create alternative scenarios.
- *Involve people without a vested interest.* Use colleagues, friends or peers who aren't close to the problem you are trying to solve to offer options.

Here's an example of how these tools helped to shape a decision. In my role as a trustee, the leadership team had been looking at ways to renovate a hall we own. We needed to make some critical repairs because it was old and needed upgrading. But we had been captivated by the idea of a fundamental remodelling of the space to give us a whole new floor for meeting and counselling rooms (the Captain had been steering us on a particular course). As our work with architects progressed, we became more and more locked into this idea, despite estimated costs rising and the negative operational impact this remodelling would have on the work of our organisation for at least one year (the Gambler had been shielding us from the real odds). We also found ourselves starting to tell a story of how wonderful this new space would be despite the costs and 12-month disruption (the Writer had been busy developing this script).

At a recent meeting, the trustees stepped back and intentionally widened our options. We considered what basic renovation work was required to upgrade the current hall. We thought about how we might secure additional meeting space without the major remodelling. We also considered the likely spend on this remodelling and how the money and resources could be used differently. We explored other possibilities that might have an even greater impact on our community than the ones we had considered up to that point. In short, we reacted to the calls to action. We:

- Gave the Writer new material for alternative scripts
- Showed the Gambler the odds, and
- Provided the Captain with alternative destinations.

The upshot was a much better decision: to complete a basic upgrade on the hall, to look for alternative meeting room space and to launch another project that will have a much bigger community impact.

2. Multiple Scripts

In 2015, the professional services firm Deloitte announced that it would be changing the way it hired people with a view to recruiting a more diverse workforce. In an intentional effort to mitigate unconscious biases in recruiting decisions, the firm is using contextualised data in order to develop alternative scripts. An example of this is to put achievements of students leaving secondary education into context. This means that an applicant who scores the highest grades in a school that is situated in a deprived area and where peers commonly achieve much lower grades will be seen as someone who has secured a bigger achievement than an applicant with the same high grades from a school where many peers achieve similar results.

Whether you agree with this approach or not is not the point. What Deloitte is doing is moving away from a single, one-dimensional script based on examination results. Instead, Deloitte is dealing with the work of the Writer head on by creating multiple and richer scripts. These scripts try and understand how difficult it was for someone to achieve the results they did and to open up alternative possibilities that might otherwise have been ignored.

The most obvious challenge is to understand the script we are already creating about a person, situation, idea or object and then to challenge it. A good example comes from our work in supporting internal discussions about senior managers, their performance and potential. If only one person has had exposure to the work of a senior manager, then we only have one script to work with. We strongly encourage leaders to meet, work with and form views of others they might be involved in assessing so that there are multiple scripts on offer.

Other instances where alternative scripts can be helpful include picturing a changed workplace and thinking about how an acquisition or merger might play out, or a key project. We have used many different ways to engage people in creating multiple scripts:

- Writing a story (almost the same as actually creating a script) about the future and what it will look like
- Drawing a picture or creating a collage that describes a future situation
- Acting out a situation as if rolling the film forward.

These are quite creative techniques. They help articulate what we already have in our own mind and discover the thinking of others. At their core is our desire to explore alternative possibilities, whether finding new material that challenges the dominant narrative of the Writer; creating scenarios that show the real odds to the Gambler; identifying alternative destinations for the Captain or releasing the Prisoner from their narrow thinking.

3. Estimating Techniques

Let's say that you are asked by your boss to lead a project. A deadline for delivering this work is required and you, your boss and an outsider have all been given an opportunity to give a view on when that project should be completed by. Who of the three people is likely to give the best estimate?

Track record would suggest that it is the outsider. Your boss will always want it done quicker and you will always want to build in some slack, just in case. The outsider will be able to look in with greater objectivity and balance.

Developed at the beginning of the Cold War as a way of estimating the impact of technology on warfare, an excellent tool that has now become mainstream to improve estimating is called the Delphi Technique. Given a need to estimate something (timescale, budget, quantity) the Delphi Technique has the following three characteristics designed to mitigate unconscious thinking errors, allow free expression of opinion and encourage open critique:

- *Anonymity of participants:* typically, participants remain anonymous so that the influence of power imbalances, reputations or strong personalities are mitigated
- *Structuring of information flow*: opinions from participants are collected usually via a survey or questionnaire and moderated by a facilitator
- *Regular feedback*: participants are able to comment on their own forecasts, the forecasts of others and on the progress of the panel as a whole.

Experience in running the Delphi Technique suggests that this approach creates deeper enquiry and thinking. It also mitigates two behaviours that characterise face-to-face meetings: the tendency for participants to stick to their original opinion (the Knight) and the tendency for any adjustments in opinion to mirror those of the group leader (the Butler).

There are other estimating techniques, of course. Another often used in project management is three-point estimating. The three points are your:

- Best case estimate
- Best guess estimate
- Worst case estimate.

The process aims to mitigate the over-optimism of the Gambler ('this project has few or no real risks') and the padding of estimates indulged in by the Butler (overestimating in order to protect people from blame). The process encourages discussion of 'good' and 'bad' risks by team members and other key stakeholders. The outcomes of these conversations can then be translated into formulas to get to a specific estimate.[203]

Whichever estimating technique you choose to use, in our experience the most important part of the process is the conversation held between those involved in delivering the work and others with an interest in the outcomes of the project. The more open people are, and the more the focus of the conversations is on understanding what is really happening that could impact the outcome of the work, the better the estimate is likely to be.

4. Diversity of Voice

We noted in Chapter 17 that for difficult and complex decisions, no one person has a complete picture of what is really happening or of the information needed to make the best decision. We need to gather diverse opinion to make sense of what is happening. We already have many tools that help us bring diversity of voice into our thinking. These tools include:

- The voice of the customer
- Employee surveys

- Focus groups
- Workshops
- Cross-functional/cross-business/multi-agency teams.

The real challenges come when we bump up against the characters of the Prisoner, who only sees their own view of the world, or the Captain, who has already made their mind up. In these instances we may have captured diversity of voice but our characters persuade us not to make use of it. When cultures are allowed to develop that reflect the images of the Prisoner or the Captain, it becomes very difficult to gather genuine diversity of voice as people tend to give up. They know they won't be heard and they therefore become the Butler, serving up what those in power want to hear. There are deeper actions that need to be taken in creating an environment where people feel safe to speak honestly and constructively. We explore how to do this in the next section in this chapter.

5. The Outside View

Bringing the outside inside is a powerful way of bringing alternative options to the table. Again, a number of tools are already used by organisations to help us to achieve this, such as:

- Research into practices in use and/or comparisons with other organisations
- Visits to other companies
- Use of consultants and other experts who are able to 'cross-fertilise' ideas, offer challenge and contribute alternative perspectives.

In counselling, coaching and the caring professions another tried and tested method is external or group supervision. Supervision creates a space for practitioners to bring client cases for review with others outside of the intervention. It provides opportunity for reflection on the relationship and any unhealthy attachments that may be developing and allows others to notice and challenge what is going on.

In professional services and academia, peer review is often used. When I worked for PwC some time ago we often brought a team of consultants into a room who had no knowledge of a particular project to hear and critique a key report or presentation we might be making to a client.

A good example of how external expertise can be used to moderate internal estimates is the research of Bent Flyvbjerg. Flyvbjerg was requested by Dutch officials to review a massive rail project called the Zuiderzee Line. He was asked to give a realistic costing as a counterpoint to the systematic downward adjustments of cost projections officials had made based on referencing similar projects. Flyvbjerg came to a different view and suggested that officials had underestimated construction costs by $2.5 billion and that there would be a likely cost overrun of 45 percent. As a result the project was cancelled.

The outside view is particularly helpful in counterbalancing internal knowledge and experience (helping to mitigate the Archivist and the Prisoner) and in offering alternative destinations that those inside are unable to see (mitigating the Captain).

6. Checklists

Many of us use checklists. We don't mean your 'to do' list, but lists that either record operating procedures or lists that have been created as a basis for evaluation. Checklists harness expertise and aim to mitigate risk. They record what needs to happen and eliminate the need to rely on memory. Even experienced professionals use checklists. Pilots always go through a checklist of routines at each stage of the flight from before engines are started to after landing. The medical profession uses checklists to ensure that procedures aren't missed. In multi-disciplinary teams these checklists are invaluable as they reduce the risk of procedures being missed.

When we work with clients through organisational re-designs, an early step in the process is to develop a set of design principles. These set out the criteria against which new designs can be evaluated and largely reflect an assessment of what isn't working well with the current operational model and what is needed to be successful in the future. This checklist will be developed through analysis and a set of conversations between decision makers. These conversations enable people to share and explore their understanding of what's not working and why, and their understanding of what's required in the future. The process surfaces our scripts, identifies what we are defending, widens possibilities, guards against over-optimism and harnesses expertise. During evaluation, the checklist keeps the team focused on the outcomes that really matter.

Here are four benefits of checklists[204]:

- They ensure that the necessary minimum gets done
- They free up our minds to focus on what is happening (the unforeseen and emergent stuff) rather than on remembering procedures
- They instil discipline: there is a clear did/didn't do it, yes/no answer to checklist questions
- They save time as they stop reinvention of the wheel and the skipping of basic steps.

The problem with checklists is that they seem boring. They appear to inhibit our creativity and place us in a straightjacket. Good checklists do establish routines, but developed well – through the capturing of good practices (including the simple, stupid stuff); through involving diverse expertise; through the examination of failures and validated through application – they are a powerful tool in mitigating the work of the Judge (setting the evaluation criteria before the performance), the Butler (through giving voice to and capturing good practice even if unpopular) and the Prisoner (by eliminating the reliance on memory, even when someone is experienced).

7. Vanishing Options

This is a simple tool that encourages people to think more broadly. If you believe people are using too narrow a frame of reference in shaping their options, then run the vanishing options test. Just take that option they were considering off the table and ask them "now what are you going to do?"

It is a powerful tool to encourage broader thinking. Anyone who has seen the film *Apollo 13* will have witnessed this technique being used to powerful effect to identify ways of using materials on board the spacecraft in different ways to the ones intended, so that the crew can return to earth safely.

It is a tool that particularly speaks to knowledge and experience thinking errors as it gives permission for the Prisoner to step outside the boundaries of their professional worldview and it focuses the Archivist on the present problem that needs to be solved. Removing options can also have a powerful impact in mitigating the work of the Gambler (showing them the odds and helping them to see other possibilities), the Writer (giving them material for a new script) and the Captain (removing pre-determined courses of action).

8. Pre-mortems

A sad fact is that projects fail to deliver their anticipated benefits at a spectacular rate. A reason often cited is that many people are reluctant to speak up about their reservations or about their real understanding of the situation during the all-important planning phase. The Butler plays a strong role in this.

Pre-mortems[205] were developed to help teams identify a fuller range of risks at the outset of the project (and updated throughout the life of the project). The idea is that imagining that an event has already occurred increases our ability to identify correctly the reasons for this successful outcome. A pre-mortem is a hypothetical opposite to a post-mortem (which in a medical setting allows health professionals to understand the causes of a person's death).

The aim of a pre-mortem is to understand the possible causes of failure so that people can focus and create the conditions that will deliver success. Its focus is therefore on two questions: "what could go wrong?" and "what could we do to put things right?"

So how does a pre-mortem work? Pre-mortems should include all those involved in delivering the project and other people who can affect the outcome of the project. In an ideal world, it is good to have all these people in the same room as this will create a generative conversation. If this can't be done, then a combination of one-to-one meetings supplemented by a workshop involving as many key people as possible can work.

There are three simple steps:

- The leader starts the exercise by announcing that the project has failed spectacularly. Those involved then write down individually every reason they can think of that may have contributed to the failure. A ground rule is that any reason is permissible – even those that may be considered to be politically sensitive (examples we have come across are "because the budget was cut half way through the financial year" and "because the executive team lost interest and found their next new toy").
- Everyone then contributes one idea until all the ideas have

been captured. The discussion held during this stage is purely to clarify and to capture similar points that may have been expressed slightly differently. No idea can be ruled out.

- The list is discussed, risks assigned and plans and/or business case updated. A re-contracting around the project occurs with key stakeholders.

The pre-mortem is extremely good at surfacing what scripts are being written (the Writer); what is being defended (the Knight); understanding the odds (the Gambler); giving voice to the undiscussables (the Butler); and in understanding track record (the Archivist). There is a risk, of course, that the pre-mortem throws up so many issues that the project does not get off the ground. We would suggest that this is a very good risk to take, as it is better to stop a project at this stage than deliver failure at a later stage. The more typical outcome is a much more robust understanding of what needs to happen to deliver a piece of work successfully.

9. Disconfirming Evidence

Once we have decided that a particular decision or course of action is correct, we then tend to interpret additional information as supporting that thinking (the Captain). This tendency is exacerbated once we invest time, money and other resources in a course of action (the Knight). At this point, we also find a need to justify this investment and are more prepared to continue investing even when information suggests that this would be unwise (the Gambler). Taken together, these tendencies mean that decision makers discount contradictory evidence and ignore better alternatives (which can encourage Butler behaviour).

Seeking disconfirming evidence from the outset of a key decision helps to mitigate these thinking errors. What this means in practice is that a decision-making group will intentionally search for evidence that will challenge the prevailing viewpoint. This might mean intentionally taking time to throw tough questions at the emerging decision. For major decisions, it might involve setting up a counter group with the express intention of bringing challenging evidence.

A practice adopted in many professional firms, banks and governance groups is to rotate roles to get fresh perspectives. A different person overseeing a function, a key project or committee often notices things others who have been in situ for a while miss. All these actions are about keeping thinking moving so that we don't settle into complacency in our thinking.

This tool is particularly effective in disarming the Knight, showing the Gambler the real odds, pointing the Judge at evidence that may not have stood out and showing the Captain an alternative course.

10. Blinding

This tool is effectively the 'blind audition' and is particularly helpful in mitigating the Writer and the Judge. The approach is all about intentionally keeping an open mind about people or situations. If you have ever seen the UK singing competition *The Voice*, you will know that in the first round the judges have their chairs turned so that they are looking away from the performer. In this way, they want to convey that their focus is solely on the voice and not other factors such as looks or performance.

The wine industry has for years picked its winners through the process of blind tasting, often giving emerging wine-making countries huge breakthroughs in winning gold medals against long-established wine houses.

In organisations the screening of applications without names and other personal information that may bias choices is increasingly being used. Although this approach to screening has its critics it is at least attempting both to recognise the thinking errors that impact our decisions and do something about them.

Blinding has been used to select contractors by government organisations and is a tool with wider potential. As we refine its use, it is not unimaginable to see blinding more frequently used in procurement, sourcing and promotions as well as appointments.

Blinding is also a technique that can help us think differently about a person or situation. In one of the stories in Chapter 17, Thomas, a maths teacher, practised blinding when he intentionally disregarded a particular script he had written about children who weren't good at maths, replacing it with one that saw the potential in all children. This process of reframing and challenging our assumptions can help us in many situations where we are making decisions about people. For instance, we can challenge the scripts we write about people who resist change or invariably challenge new ideas (the Writer) and we can use blinding to challenge our assumptions about how others might react if their thinking is challenged or they are offered an alternative (the Butler and the Captain).

Each tool will be able to mitigate the work of a number of the characters in the Hidden R-I-S-K™ framework and Figure 13, below, highlights which tool best addresses which character.

	Relationships		Self-Interest		Shortcuts		Knowledge	
	Writer	Knight	Gambler	Butler	Judge	Captain	Archivist	Prisoner
Widen options	✔	✔	✔	✔	✔	✔	✔	✔
Multiple scripts	✔		✔		✔	✔	✔	✔
Estimating techniques	✔		✔	✔		✔	✔	✔
Diversity of voice	✔		✔	✔		✔		✔
Outside view		✔	✔	✔		✔	✔	✔
Checklists					✔	✔		✔
Vanishing options	✔		✔			✔	✔	✔
Pre-mortems	✔	✔	✔	✔			✔	
Disconfirming evidence		✔	✔		✔	✔		
Blinding	✔	✔		✔	✔			

Figure 13: How each Tool Addresses Thinking Errors Embodied in each Character

Creating the Right Environment for Effective Decision Making

An issue that emerged in our story at the start of this chapter, but which hasn't yet been discussed, was that some people did not feel safely able to give their true opinion. Whilst serving up what others want to hear is something the Butler in us encourages, how strong a voice the Butler has in our decision making is often the result of the prevailing organisational or group culture – how things are done around here.

I was working with a management team on one occasion and we had decided to hold the meeting away from the office at a local hotel. During a break, I sat chatting with one of the directors when a call came in. The director excused himself and said he needed to take the call. As it happened, the call was from his boss and I could see that this director was getting more agitated the longer the call went on. When he had signed off from the call he slumped back in the seat next to me and poured out his frustrations. "He wants me to do something I know just won't work", he said. "He has made up his mind, but all of us know it can't be done. When it fails, we will take the blame." So I asked him "Why don't you tell him? Why don't you put an alternative on the table that could work?" "You must be joking", he replied. "He doesn't do feedback. If you challenge what he wants to happen it is a major career-limiting move. So we'll just muddle through and hope for the best."

We hear stories like this a lot in our work and from people at all organisational levels. We saw earlier that the Butler has two faces that are self-serving. The first face is all about ingratiating oneself with those people who hold power and is driven by a desire to find favour in their eyes. The second is even more insidious. It is about avoiding challenge and the expression of alternative opinions because of fear. It is this face of the Butler that creates an environment in which people are simply too afraid to say what they really believe or talk about what's really going on. As a result, cultures are created where people don't talk about what is really happening, how they are really feeling and what customers are really saying, and fail to take accountability for decisions taken. These two areas – safety to speak out and mutual accountability – need to be cultivated if we are to create the right environment for effective decision making.

On another occasion I was talking with a business leader who proudly announced a recent decision to invest in new back-office technology. Then she said the most staggering thing: "We all know, of course, that it won't be delivered on budget or on time and that it won't do all that we are hoping for, but it is a really important step forward for us." I had to pinch myself before asking "so if you all know this, why didn't you set a budget, timescale and functionality that could be achieved?" Her reply was illuminating. "We all knew that wouldn't wash. The board would never sign off a budget and timescale that we really needed and we all knew that whatever budget was agreed now would be cut within the financial year. So the alternatives were, get something or get nothing. We'll cross the other bridges later." This may have been smart organisational politics at work. Yet, if everyone involved in the project knew what the outcome would be, it begged the question why the real situation couldn't be discussed and why decision makers colluded in a game that would inevitably lead to much wasted time and energy further down the line.

At its extreme, this lack of safety to speak out and the absence of mutual accountability can have devastating consequences. In Chapter 12 we gave examples from the aviation, energy, banking and health sectors that illustrated this. You may want to reflect on your own organisation, your own team, even your family and other organisations you are involved in outside work. Can everyone say what's really on their mind? Does everyone get behind a decision once it has been made?

In the field of psychology, an environment in which people can say what's on their mind without fear is said to have psychological safety. In an environment where psychological safety exists, people feel supported by their team members and are able to express opinions freely or make suggestions for improvement. This includes constructively criticising other team members' performance as well as being able to critique their own performance (for example, to admit to mistakes or omissions) without fearing adverse reactions or career-limiting consequences from their colleagues or managers.

There is considerable face validity in the value of a psychologically safe environment. Who would choose to be in an environment where you have to watch your back and keep your mouth shut all the time as opposed to one where we can be ourselves and have our voice heard with the respect it deserves? You may think that the answer to this question is a no brainer. That may be so, but the value of environments where people feel psychologically safe is also borne out by a large body of research. This research, which is extremely robust and spans over 20 years, points to psychological safety as an important factor in team performance.

Professor Ed Schein[206] (MIT Sloan School of Management) first advanced the concept of psychological safety. Schein, a noted clinical psychologist, became the first management theorist to define corporate culture and suggest ways in which culture is *the* dominant force within an organisation. Schein emphasised the need for people to feel psychologically safe if change is to happen. He found through his research that achieving organisational learning and transformation crucially depended upon a feeling of safety and overcoming the negative effects of past incentives and past "punishments".[207]

Professor Amy Edmondson (Harvard University) has recently expanded and operationalised the concept further to encompass teams. She measured team psychological safety through the use of a psychological safety questionnaire and demonstrated that team effectiveness is positively influenced by psychological safety.[208] Although her work in the area of psychological safety over the past decade spans many different industries, it is her work in the health-care sector that is particularly noteworthy as she found a significant correlation between high levels of psychological safety within health-care teams and patient safety.[209] Edmondson's ground-breaking studies have since been replicated in health-care systems across the world and her findings have been borne out in widely divergent health-care settings.

In the airline industry, the importance of all members of the crew feeling able to speak up has long been recognised as key in ensuring the safety of those on board. This understanding followed a number of high-profile air crashes (see Chapter 12), which were attributable to the Butler at work. Within the airline industry, equipping people to speak up is supported by considerable investments in assertiveness training of staff as well as the introduction of supportive policies and procedures. However, a recent study by two Swiss academics from ETH Zurich found that crew members are still very reluctant to speak out on issues relevant to flight safety. The reasons for not speaking up included fear of damaging relationships, fear of punishments and operational pressures. The authors of the research therefore concluded that speaking up in the first place was not a question of assertiveness training but a question of organisational culture.

Edmondson's research points to the systemic nature of psychological safety. Put simply, psychological safety is the result of an accumulation of things that happen in an organisation or group and it either exists or it doesn't. There is no half-way house in psychological safety. You cannot feel half safe with someone. You either feel safe to speak out or you don't. So what can be done to create environments where people feel safe to speak out and are willing to be mutually accountable for decisions?

The answer to this question isn't as difficult as we might think. Thanks to the work of Amy Edmondson, we have a good idea of the questions we go through at a subconscious level in deciding whether to say something or keep quiet. This means that we can test for psychological safety and that testing will help us understand whether people feel safe to speak out and whether the culture is likely to promote honest enquiry into our unconscious thinking errors. Edmondson has discovered that there are a small number of key questions we need to ask in order to determine whether we will speak out or not. These questions relate to four areas: (1) the extent to which people feel supported in a positive way by their colleagues and manager; (2) whether they feel they have permission to speak out about things that concern them; (3) whether they can admit to mistakes without fear and (4) whether they feel able to express a different viewpoint to colleagues without fear. Understanding how individuals in a team or members in an organisation rate each question will enable leaders to direct efforts to create a safe culture.

Amy Edmondson makes a compelling case for psychologically safe organisations. She writes that in psychologically safe environments "people are willing to offer ideas, questions and concerns. They are even willing to fail, and when they do, they learn. The need for psychological safety is based on the premise that no-one can perform perfectly in every situation when knowledge and best practices are in flux".[210] We would add to this that in a world where no one person has the full picture of what is really going on and in which we are all prone to thinking errors in reaching decisions, our ability to speak openly to one another, share insights and learn together is essential to effective decision making.

Edmondson offers seven compelling reasons why psychological safety is necessary:[211]

1. It encourages people to **speak up**. In the context of surfacing and addressing thinking errors in decision making, speaking up helps us to discuss in a generative way how each of the characters may be at work in our thinking and the thinking of our colleagues. It encourages feedback, learning and seeking help from others. Fundamentally, speaking up helps us to reduce risk as potential barriers and pitfalls are discussed openly and constructively.

2. It enables **clarity of thinking**. Research from the field of neuroscience shows that when fear is neurologically activated, our performance deteriorates.[212] We are less able

to analyse, innovate or communicate if we don't feel safe. An inability to think clearly, driven by an environment of fear, will create the right conditions for our thinking errors to thrive.

3. It **supports productive conflict**. Disagreement and conflict within groups is inevitable. The issue is always the nature of that conflict. Healthy conflict is when differences in viewpoints are explored in a respectful and constructive way. Often there is no one 'right' answer, particularly when we are faced with complex decisions. We have already underlined the importance of diversity of voice and viewpoint in helping to mitigate thinking errors. Creating a safe space for people to disagree is actually generative and produces an environment where people can learn and where better decisions are made. In this situation people are able to say what they think and are willing to be proven wrong. As Edmondson writes: "In a psychological safe environment teachers with conflicting beliefs about pedagogical methods will express them; nurses will challenge the use of specific procedures; and members of a project team will express resentment about differing levels of responsibility".

4. It **mitigates failure**. We all make mistakes. Yes, even you do and you will still make mistakes even if you are fully aware of the thinking errors at work in your decision making. In organisations and groups the two issues we bump into most are first, our honesty in admitting even to ourselves that we fell short or failed, and second, our ability to discuss failure openly with others. Recently we were working with a global professional services firm. The internal team decided to partner with a select few external consultants to bring in external expertise and also to build internal capability. One of the really innovative aspects of this work was a regular meeting of internal and external consultants to discuss in a very open and transparent way how work with the firm's partners and their teams was progressing. During these times, very candid conversations were held that explored the reasons why some interventions went very well and why others didn't.

5. It **promotes innovation**. A safe environment is critical to innovation. Innovation requires tangential thinking – an ability to suggest and explore novel, unusual and unorthodox ideas. In this context many of our characters need to be put on mute and in particular the Knight, the Gambler, the Captain, the Archivist and the Prisoner. Many unconscious thinking errors stifle innovative thinking. Fortunately there is much research that casts a light on the link between safe environments and innovation showing that innovation is most fruitful when we bind these characters.[213]

6. It **removes obstacles to performance**. Over the years we have worked with many teams. The foundational requirement for any high-performing team – any performing or effective team even – is trust. Like psychological safety, trust is either present or it isn't. You can't have a bit of trust. Trust disappears when people don't feel respected; when they aren't valued for who they are and what they bring; when important information isn't shared; when other team members exclude them or don't cooperate; when they are let down, or worse, when they feel deliberately undermined. When it comes to decision making, good decisions won't be made if they are taken behind a veil of fog. Apparent, rather than real, agreement will be the typical outcome.

7. It **increases accountability**. My decision not to speak up, to say what someone wants to hear, to share only the information that confirms the decision people want to make or exclude other options because they don't align with my own experience means that I'm not taking responsibility for that decision. If a decision goes wrong I may join with others in pointing the finger at the accountable person. But my omissions are significant and are complicit in allowing a poor decision to be reached. A safe environment encourages the opposite behaviour to the examples above and means that even if the buck stops with one person, all those involved in contributing to that decision share accountability. If the decision goes awry, then (linked to point 4, above) the ability to deal with failure and learn is also something the team can deal with constructively.

When it comes to groups, teams and larger organisational units, environments where convergent thinking is encouraged and alternative perspectives discouraged creates the conditions within which our eight characters can flourish. We hope that we have made the case for organisations to be safe places where people can speak up without fear. Leaders, at whatever level in the organisation, play an important role in creating that safe environment.

Actions for Leaders at all Levels

The self-interest cluster of thinking errors embodied in the characters of the Gambler and the Butler illustrates how attuned we are to power and hierarchy. We can smell power and we often defer to it. As Edmondson writes: "People are well aware of where they fall in the power hierarchies at work... Their position shapes their perceptions of how safe it is to take interpersonal risks within their team or group". She goes on to cite research that shows that the lower down the hierarchy you perceive yourself to sit, the less likely you are to speak out. Fear takes hold and people are less willing to raise tough issues or ask challenging questions. A good litmus test for this is to reflect for a moment on the times senior executives speak at 'town hall meetings' (meetings of large groups of employees) and say "Ask us anything you want to. No holds barred." Do employees ask senior managers about the topics they are really discussing with others? If they do and there aren't recriminations afterwards (if there are, they won't speak up next time), this is a good sign that people feel safe. If they don't, it is unlikely to be shyness. People simply don't trust that the leadership actually mean what they say and are fearful.

Fear of those with status and power in organisational hierarchies is nothing new. Fear has long been a weapon crafted and used to achieve control and exercise authority. If you are a leader intent on requiring the subordination of others to your power, you may want to consider the difference between real performance and box ticking. People will often do just what you ask to get the job done (tick the boxes) and often with great frustration and resentment. This means that what you won't get is a genuinely empowered team or a team that takes the initiative or that proactively brings ideas to the table or sounds early warnings when things aren't going right. What you will get are anxious team members, driven by fear, and content to accept sub-optimal performance.

So what do effective leaders do to create the right environment for decisions and manage this tension between accountability and psychological safety? Here are five practical ways:

1. **Remember that you cast a long shadow as a leader**. We use this image a lot when working with leaders to help them think about the impact they have on their teams and wider organisation. If you are a leader (whether middle ranking or senior) what you do and say will always be under the spotlight. People notice your moods, your tone of voice, how fast you walk, whether you say hello to them or pass them by, whether you seem receptive or closed, and they will write and share their scripts to support their observations. The Writer is a very active player in the coffee machine, corridor and smoking area conversations. The call for leaders to role-model effective behaviours can come across as a cliché, but it is true. Because people notice what you say and do, what and whom you pay attention to and what you put a value on, the tone you set matters. Others will mirror it. Your shadow is cast across your team and beyond. To ensure your shadow creates the right environment for honest conversations and effective decision making, be conscious of your moods, language and tone. Use language that invites others to discuss and share viewpoints. Ask questions rather than make statements. Use straightforward language. Get feedback.

2. **Have an open door and an open mind**. Many leaders will pride themselves on having an open-door policy. They want their team to be able to get help, ask questions and seek

their counsel. They try hard to be accessible. This is good and to be encouraged. The second aspect of the open-door policy, though, is also having an open mind. What happens when a team member steps through your door? However dumb you may think the question is, the one thing your team member doesn't want to feel as they leave the room is stupid. So remember that one of your roles as a leader is to create the right environment for people to think for themselves. We covered some of this ground in Chapter 17. A couple of things to remember are that asking a question is far more powerful than giving an answer and that taking time to build relationships with your team will help you to understand them (and them you). So, invest time in getting to know people and get out of your office or walk away from your desk. Meet your team. Go and sit with them. Talk with, not at, them. Listen to them.

3. **Encourage diversity of voice**. It is really tempting to give the impression that you do have all the answers. We pride ourselves on our expertise and feel we ought to know even if we don't know. If questions are straightforward and the answer isn't too difficult, that is fair enough. However, when we are faced with tough, complex problems it is far better to accept the limits of our knowledge and admit that the issue is tough and welcome the contribution of others. This focus on inquiry rather than holding the pretence of certainty will both make it more likely that others will speak out and take accountability for the quality of the decision made. So ask questions – What's going on? How do you see it? What do you think would make a difference? – and gather the insights others in the team and wider organisation will bring.

4. **No double binds**. Put simply a double bind is when people are put in a no-win position – damned if they do and damned if they don't. Asking people to speak up, then putting them down for speaking up, and then criticising them later for not speaking up (when they have concluded it's a waste of time) is the type of double bind we have seen many times. So if you ask for opinions, tell people where the boundaries are – what

can be influenced and what can't be. At least help people to see where the boundaries lie. Allow them to challenge as even you may have missed options and viewpoints that could be useful. Think about the words you use. Use words that build trust and invite contribution. Follow through on your promises – no politics, no deception! If you leave people thinking they have been set up then you will struggle to get their viewpoints next time.

5. **Hold people accountable for what is theirs**. Being clear on where accountability lies is an important role for the leader. A psychologically safe environment means that even when the buck stops with the leader, others still have a role to play in the quality of that decision. A decision of a team member or colleague to withhold information that might be important to a decision is an act of negligence. There is mutual accountability in bringing information to the table that enables the decision maker or makers to reach the best possible decision. An exercise we often run with teams helps to set the boundaries around what's mine, what's ours and what's yours. We think of it in terms of a contract between a leader and their team. The leader and the team independently list what they need from the other in order to succeed and what they can give to the other to help them succeed. These 'trades' are put alongside each other and we help the leader and team contract around a set of 'needs' and 'gives'. It is important that these matters are discussed openly. If they are left in the world where we make assumptions and think we know where accountabilities lie, accountability remains a rather blurred, hit-and-miss affair.

We are confident that if you take action in these five ways you will go a long way to creating a team environment in which people feel safe to speak up and which, as a consequence, will enable you to surface and mitigate thinking errors in decisions more effectively.

The final area we want to address in this chapter is at the organisational level.

Helping Organisations to Learn

Virtually all leaders believe that to stay competitive, their organisations must learn and improve each day. Often such beliefs remain good intentions and many organisations struggle to become 'learning organisations'. In a 2015 article published in the *Harvard Business Review*, Professors Francesca Gino and Bradley Staats[214] shared their insights from decades of research into why organisations don't learn. They conclude that biases, or thinking errors, which people are barely aware of are to blame for this lack of organisational learning. According to their research it is unconscious thinking errors that derail many of the costly efforts to turn organisational learning into learning organisations. They point to the following four fundamental thinking errors:

1. Organisations inadvertently focus too much on success
2. Organisations take action too quickly
3. Organisations focus too much on ensuring people fit in
4. Organisations depend too much on experts.

By this point in the book, we hope you recognise the characters in the Hidden R-I-S-K™ framework that correspond to these errors. They are the Gambler, the Captain, the Butler and the Prisoner.

1. Organisations inadvertently focus too much on success (the Gambler)

Here, there are four substantive challenges. The first is whether we have an open or a fixed mindset. Research by psychologist Carol Dweck[215] suggests that those with a fixed mindset limit their ability, and the ability of others, to learn because a fixed mindset focuses individuals too much on performing well. A flexible mindset focuses on growth, which seeks challenges and learning opportunities. Failure is therefore not seen as a sign of inadequacy but as a springboard for learning.

The second challenge is the product of the first – a fear of failure. Organisations may pay lip service to the right to fail, but in reality we try to avoid mistakes, don't own up to them, hide them under the carpet and ensure that failure is attributed to others and not ourselves. In our consulting work, the 'review and learn' step is the one least completed and even when a 'lessons learnt' exercise is undertaken, the lessons are rarely learnt. Whether consciously or unconsciously, there is a culture of institutionalised fear of failure.

The third is the flip side of the second challenge – we ascribe success to our own ability and failure to external factors. Our failure to take personal accountability when things go wrong will not lead to learning. The fourth challenge is an over-reliance on past performance. Closely linked to the work of the Archivist, we tend to look back rather than forward. In recruitment and promotion decisions we look at track record rather than potential. We believe that what was successful yesterday must deliver success tomorrow. The reality is that this isn't always the case.

At an organisational level, we can mitigate this focus on success and shift the culture. There are practical actions that can be taken to reframe failure and embrace a growth mindset. The development of psychologically safe cultures creates an environment for honest review and for genuine learning. The use of evidence (whether hard or soft data) enables people to explore outcomes to understand underlying causes. These approaches are valid for all projects – whether perceived as successes, failures or points in between – and are underpinned by a mindset of inquiry.

2. Organisations take action too quickly (the Captain)

We are trained to solve problems. Speed of decision making is a highly valued quality in most leaders. "Come to me with solutions not problems" is a well-rehearsed cliché drummed into most managers. Being seen to do something is more valued, even if we behave like the proverbial headless chicken, than not doing something. Our own experience in working with many business leaders suggests that they are more comfortable in executing tasks than in planning them and often see planning as wasted time and effort.

The biggest challenge that emerges from this preoccupation with action is that many organisations have created cultures in which people find it really difficult to reflect. Taking a step back, researching a problem, finding out more, gathering different perspectives, reflecting on what went well and what could be done differently or better are all seen as an unproductive waste of time. Sadly, two informal measures of productivity we now see at work in organisations are the number of hours spent in meetings each day and the number of emails answered. We need to be seen to be busy.

A second challenge is that of exhaustion. Perpetual action is very tiring. Being tired isn't the best condition for learning and therefore we fall back on the Archivist and keep doing what we know, which is not necessarily what's right.

This focus on action leans heavily on System 1 thinking identified by Daniel Kahneman. We lean towards speed and urgency, and as a result fail to take the time needed when decisions are difficult and complex. Action is used as a façade to convey purpose.

At an organisational level, we need to encourage slow (or at least slower) thinking, particularly when it comes to those difficult and complex decisions. Instead of attending meetings you know are a waste of time just press the 'decline' button and set up a meeting with yourself to think, plan and reflect. We have referred earlier to mindfulness. At a very practical level this could mean taking breaks, using our commutes or journeys between meetings, locations or clients to build in disciplines of reflection. When we facilitate workshops, observe meetings or run learning sessions, we build in time for people to reflect: to notice things; understand what is going on; tune in to what they are learning. In meetings we encourage checking in (for people to say what they are feeling and thinking now and to express their hopes for the meeting) and checking out (how people are feeling and what they are taking away from the meeting). In this way we check the impulses of the Captain in our organisations and create the habits that nurture thinking as well as action.

3. Organisations focus too much on ensuring people fit in

Organisations want people to fit in and be good team members. They want employees to share their organisation's values. They want a high level of alignment between what employees want and what the organisation wants to achieve. These are all important and understandable wants. There are two challenges that need to be met in order to mitigate the work of the Butler and encourage people to be themselves.

The first challenge is to differentiate between fitting in and conforming. We are quite adept as human beings at reading the written and unwritten codes and norms – what works, how I get things done, how I build relationships. We are often mortified when we get things wrong. In my mid-20s, I was fortunate to be invited to join the executive team of the business I was working in. Shortly after, the executive team decided to take time out away from the office. In the past, off-site meetings I had attended had a smart–casual dress code and I therefore turned up smart but casual. My heart sank when I entered the room to discover all of my new executive team colleagues in formal business suits. The drive to conform can take many forms and can set many constraints on what people believe they can do or say.

The second challenge is a failure to work with strengths. When employees serve up what they believe their organisations want, they are less likely to be themselves. How often is feedback seen as a time to hear about what you have done wrong? How much time during performance reviews is spent on highlighting weaknesses and areas for improvement? The Gallup Q12 – which is an instrument to measure employee engagement – highlights that a positive answer to the question "At work, do you have an opportunity to do what you do best every day?" is a significant predictor of engagement and high organisational performance.

There is much to be gained in focusing on strengths. Letting people 'be themselves' was highlighted in research that examined what the best workplace on earth would look like.[216] They pointed to the need for organisations to encourage differences in perspective, habits of mind and assumptions. This often means opposites working and thriving alongside one another. LVMH was an organisation quoted in their research.

We are great fans of StrengthsFinder 2.0[217] and the focus on strengths. Identifying strengths, cultivating strengths, and recognising and appreciating strengths are all positive steps organisations can take to use fully the gifts and talents of the smart people they employ. Another action organisations can take is to look hard at their management practices. In what way are your performance management, appraisal, incentives, career paths, competence models, management by objectives, recruitment and promotion practices actually narrowing the range of acceptable behaviour and encouraging conformity?

Fundamentally (and this is linked to the environment of psychological safety), organisations need to make it safe for difference to flourish and to be used in a generative and creative way. Shared vision and values does not mean a cloning, 'yes-man', compliant, conforming culture.

4. Organisations depend too much on experts

Organisations are full of experts. Expertise is valuable. We work hard to become expert and we work hard to stay expert in our field. In our examination of thinking errors associated with knowledge and experience, we have highlighted the dangers of expertise and won't repeat them here. Suffice it to say that organisations have too easily believed in the idea that experts are the best source of ideas for improvement and learning.

The characters of the Archivist and particularly the Prisoner highlight that we define expertise too narrowly, rely too easily on titles, degrees and experience and hesitate to challenge those considered to be expert. As we have learnt through the work of the Prisoner we can become blinded by expertise, unable to see beyond the walls created by our professional silo. One of the most common issues we face when working with clients is 'silo thinking'. We all know it exists. We all know it hinders creativity, innovation and learning. We all find it difficult to address.

There are some things that can be done at the organisational level. The people experiencing a problem can be given rights to fix it. Employees can be encouraged to acquire different types of expertise, gaining knowledge of how other parts of the organisation work. There can be an intentional focus on multi-disciplinary teams. How handoffs of work occur across organisations (or between organisations and agencies) can be explored by those involved in that process.

The gain in addressing these thinking errors at an organisational level is well summed up by the authors of the *HBR* article: "If leaders institute ways to counter the four biases we have identified they will unleash the power of learning throughout their operations. Only then will their companies truly improve continuously."[218]

In this chapter, we have looked at how to use the Hidden R-I-S-K™ framework when decisions are taken by groups and the way the eight characters shape sub-optimal decision-making cultures in organisations. Our focus has been on helping you to turn *knowing* about thinking errors in decision making into *doing* something about them. To help you do this we have:

- Explored how the Hidden R-I-S-K™ framework is itself a powerful tool in helping teams to recognise and address unconscious thinking errors
- Offered 10 tools to mitigate the work of different characters

- Shown how creating a safe environment for people to speak up is critical to effective decision making
- Set out how leaders can play their part in creating the right culture to support better decision making and
- Shown how unconscious thinking errors stop organisations from learning.

The final chapter summarises the key themes of this book and identifies how you can access further material to unlock unconscious biases to make better decisions.

19

Going Further

"Leadership and learning are indispensable to each other."
John F. Kennedy

In a speech crafted for John F. Kennedy to be delivered by him on that fateful day in Dallas in 1963, we were to be reminded that "leadership and learning are indispensable to each other." That speech was never given, of course, but the point JFK sought to make has endured. The statement highlights the circular relationship between leadership and learning. Leadership casts a spotlight on learning and learning in turn helps to improve our leadership. That is exactly what happens in successful organisations. Leaders in successful organisations empower individuals and teams across all levels to articulate effectively and then work towards their mission, vision and goals. As we have seen in the last chapter, effective leaders also nurture a culture of psychological safety and mutual accountability in which learning can flourish as a foundation for quality, improvement and growth.

Developing awareness of unconscious thinking errors and equipping people with the tools to discuss and mitigate them is crucial for the sustainability of organisations. This necessitates that we become mindful of the work of the unconscious and learn to confront and reflect on our own propensity to fall foul of thinking errors. It also requires heightened skills to hold generative conversations with others, whether in one-to-one conversations or in larger groups, teams and other organisational settings. What we have in the Hidden R-I-S-K™ framework is a powerful window through which we can recognise these characters in ourselves and others, in decision-making groups and in the cultures of organisations.

The ability to make effective decisions is a core requirement of leaders and the Hidden R-I-S-K™ framework facilitates that crucial and indispensable relationship between leadership and learning. This is so exciting.

For the first time ever we are able to take advantage of the vast knowledge which has been accumulated over two decades by cognitive psychologists and neuroscientists in a way which is clearly understood by all. This easy accessibility makes our Hidden R-I-S-K™ framework such a powerful, dynamic and versatile tool. It can be used in all sorts of situations, from complex business decisions to decisions affecting our personal lives. We maintain that nobody makes bad decisions out of choice. Bad choices often occur when we stop asking questions. The Hidden R-I-S-K™ framework helps us to ask the right questions so that we can cover all the bases before we take action. The quality of the decisions we make depends on the thinking we do first. Using the Hidden R-I-S-K™ framework is certain to improve our thinking and break patterns of thinking.

The Hidden R-I-S-K™ framework also gives us a shared language to express thinking errors. It is a language which is easily understood and accessible to all. There is no excuse now not to talk about unconscious thinking errors and no excuse to avoid learning. With our Hidden R-I-S-K™ framework, learning can be put into immediate practice as thinking errors can be explored and mistakes rectified as and when they occur.

This ability to use the Hidden R-I-S-K™ framework in real time is even more important in a world that is increasingly more complex, less predictable, more interdependent and more riddled with problems and issues. When faced with difficult problems no single person, or even small group of people, has all the answers. Don't kid yourself if you think you do. We are all, at best, feeling our way through the fog a step at a time trying to make sense of the world around us. This naturally leads us to ways of communicating that depend on enquiry, dialogue, understanding, reflection and sense making.

Increasingly, good decision makers are also sense makers. They try to gather information about what is going on so that they can make sense of a problem, and we know that unconscious biases creep into this process of sense making.

So how can we keep learning so that we make timely, agile decisions that have been through a robust human due diligence? We encourage you to use the Hidden R-I-S-K™ framework to focus on four areas of learning:

1 **Self:** Be mindful of the decisions you are making and the characters that are in play. Catch yourself in your habits and be courageous enough to consider alternative ways to make sense of what you are presented with. Challenge yourself.

2 **With others:** Find other people you can reflect and do some sense making with. This might be a coach, mentor, trusted adviser, colleague, friend or partner. Reflection with others helps to tune into the characters in play and open up our blind spot.

3 **In groups:** Notice how different characters will be in play in how members of a group approach a decision. Use the Hidden R-I-S-K™ framework to create a common language to explore how these characters are shaping the decision and where the hidden risks lie. Learn and practise how to create an environment where these unconscious forces can be surfaced and discussed in a generative and constructive way.

4 **Organisationally:** Do what you can to create opportunities to discuss, reflect and think with others. Ask questions about what is going on, why people see things the way they

do, what they observe about the way decisions are made, and invite them into the conversation. Pay attention to the patterns in everyday decision making. Notice whether any of the characters are dominant in your organisational culture and what this is telling you about areas to pay particular attention to when making decisions.

Although there is still much to learn, we live in an age that is increasingly unlocking the workings of the human mind and helping us to understand why we do what we do. We are confident that the more you bring the eight characters in the Hidden R-I-S-K™ framework into your day-to-day decision making, the more robust your decisions will be both in your private life and in your professional life. Getting to the end of this book will, we hope, have given you much to think about and lots to take away and use. We hope too that you are inspired to take your learning further and share it with colleagues, family and friends.

Throughout this book we have explored the power of habits, and so we end with a fundamental question: are you prepared to translate your *knowing* about these powerful unconscious biases that distort our thinking into *doing* something about them? We hope you do!

If you would like to continue the conversation, we would be delighted to hear from you. If you have enjoyed this book and found it helpful, please help us to spread the word. This could include:

- Word of mouth recommendations
- Writing a review on Amazon
- Posting your thoughts about the book on LinkedIn, Twitter, Facebook and other social media
- Using it as your book-club book
- Sharing it with colleagues, friends and your team.

Many thanks!

To get in touch contact us via: riskybusinessbook@btinternet.com, www.mightywaters.co.uk@riskybusinessbook

How Thinking Errors Map onto the Hidden R-I-S-K™ Framework

In this appendix, we show how different thinking errors and unconscious biases map onto the four areas of the Hidden R-I-S-K™ framework. Researchers have identified over 100 of these thinking errors. Below we highlight those most relevant.

Relationships

(Thinking errors that apply to the Writer and the Knight)

Thinking Error	Definition
Actor–observer bias or fundamental attribution error	We explain an individual's behaviour by over-emphasising the influence of their personality and under-emphasising the influence of their situation
Defensive attribution hypothesis / 'just world' phenomenon	People's tendency to believe that the world is just or that people get what they deserve; this leads to a tendency to either rationalize away injustice or blame victims for their misfortune

Thinking Error	Definition
In-group bias	The tendency for people to give preferential treatment to others they perceive to be members of their own groups
Outgroup homogeneity bias	Individuals see members of their own group as being relatively more varied than members of other groups
Ultimate attribution error	A tendency to make an attribution to an entire group instead of individuals within a group
Cross-race effect	The tendency for people of one race to have difficulty identifying members of a race other than their own
Stereotypical bias	Memory distorted towards stereotypes, e.g. "black-sounding" names being misremembered as names of criminals
Bias blind spot	The tendency to see oneself as less biased than other people, or to be able to identify more cognitive biases in others than in oneself
Barnum effect or Forer effect	The observation that individuals will give high accuracy ratings to descriptions of their personality that supposedly are tailored specifically for them but are, in fact, vague and general enough to apply to a wide range of people; this effect can provide a partial explanation for the widespread acceptance of practices such as astrology, fortune telling and graphology
Illusion of transparency	People overestimate other's ability to know them, whilst overestimating their ability to know others
Endowment effect	People often demand much more to give up something than they would be willing to pay to acquire it
Loss aversion	People's tendency strongly to prefer the avoidance of losses to the acquisition of gain

Thinking Error	Definition
Pro-innovation bias	The tendency to reflect a personal bias towards an invention/innovation, while often failing to identify limitations and weaknesses or address the possibility of failure
Emotional tagging	An emotion associated with a memory of an event or action
Status quo bias	Prefers the status quo in the absence of pressure to change it

Interest (self)

(Thinking errors that apply to the Gambler and the Butler)

Thinking Error	Definition
Egocentrism	We focus too narrowly on our own perspective to the point that we can't imagine how others will be affected by a policy or strategy; we assume that everyone has access to the same information as we do
Gambler's fallacy or Monte Carlo effect	The belief that the chances of something happening with a fixed probability become higher or lower as the process is repeated; people who commit the gambler's fallacy believe that past events affect the probability of something happening in the future
Hyperbolic discounting	People more often prefer smaller to larger payoffs when smaller payoffs come sooner in time relative to larger payoffs, except when all the payoffs are either distant or proximal in time, in which case they tend to prefer the larger
Irrational escalation	The phenomenon where people justify increased investment in a decision, based on the cumulative prior investment, despite new evidence suggesting that the decision was probably wrong
Pseudo-certainty effect	The tendency to make risk-averse choices if the expected outcome is positive, but make risk-seeking choices to avoid negative outcomes
Egocentric bias in memory	Recalling the past in a self-serving manner e.g. remembering one's exam grades as being better than they were

Thinking Error	Definition
Empathy gap	The tendency to underestimate the influence or strength of feelings, in either oneself or others
Escalation of commitment	We invest additional resources in an apparently losing proposition because of the effort, money and time already invested
Excessive optimism	We are overly optimistic about outcomes, overestimating the likelihood of positive events and underestimating the impact of negative events
False-consensus effect	The tendency of someone to overestimate how much other people agree with them
Groupthink	We strive for consensus at the cost of a realistic appraisal of alternative courses of action
Hindsight bias	Sometimes called the 'I-knew-it-all-along' effect, the tendency to see past events as having been predictable at the time those events happened
Illusion of asymmetric insight	People perceive their knowledge of their peers to surpass their peers' knowledge of them
Illusion of control	The tendency to overestimate one's degree of influence over other external events
Impact bias	The tendency to overestimate the length or the intensity of the impact of future feeling states
Optimism bias	The tendency to be over-optimistic, overestimating favourable and pleasing outcomes
Outcome bias	The tendency to judge a decision by its eventual outcome instead of based on the quality of the decision at the time it was made

Thinking Error	Definition
Overconfidence	We overestimate our skill level relative to the skills of others and consequently overestimate our ability to affect future outcomes; we take credit for past positive outcomes without acknowledging the role of chance
Present bias	We value immediate rewards very highly and undervalue long-term gains
Reactive devaluation	Devaluing proposals that are no longer hypothetical or purportedly originated with an adversary
Social comparison bias	The tendency, when making recruitment decision, to favour potential candidates who don't compete with one's own particular strengths
Self-serving bias	Perceiving oneself as responsible for desirable outcomes but not responsible for undesirable ones
Sunk-cost fallacy	We pay attention to historical costs that are not recoverable when considering future courses of action
Bandwagon effect	The tendency to do (or believe) things because many other people do (or believe) the same; this is related to groupthink and herd behaviour
Choice-supportive bias	The tendency to remember one's choices as better than they actually were
Overconfidence effect	Excessive confidence in one's own answers to questions, for example: for certain types of questions, answers that people rate as "99 percent certain" turn out to be wrong 40 percent of the time
Planning fallacy	The tendency to underestimate task-completion times
Post-purchase rationalisation	The tendency to persuade oneself through rational argument that a purchase was good value

Thinking Error	Definition
Egocentric bias	Occurs when people claim more responsibility for themselves for the results of a joint action than an outside observer would credit them with
Illusory superiority	Overestimating one's desirable qualities, and underestimating undesirable qualities, relative to those of other people
Naïve cynicism	Expecting more egocentric bias in others than in oneself
Projection bias	The tendency to unconsciously assume that others share one's current emotional states, thoughts and values
Trait ascription bias	The tendency for people to view themselves as relatively variable in terms of personality, behaviour and mood while viewing others as much more predictable
Choice supportive bias	Remembering chosen options as having been better than rejected options
Consistency bias	Incorrectly remembering one's past attitudes and behaviour as resembling present attitudes and behaviour
Rosy retrospection	The remembering of the past as having been better than it really was
Self-relevance effect	That memories relation to the self are better recalled than similar information relating to others
Action bias	Feeling compelled to do something, not because action is correct but because it is what others expect

Shortcuts

(Thinking Errors that Apply to the Judge and the Captain)

Thinking Error	Definition
The wrapper bias	We are misled by how information is presented to us – we are dazzled by the packaging
Hostile media effect	The tendency to see a media report as being biased due to one's own strong partisan views
Ambiguity effect	The tendency to avoid options for which missing information makes the probability seem 'unknown'
Base rate neglect or base rate fallacy	The tendency to base judgments on specifics, ignoring general statistical information
Conservatism or regressive bias	Tendency to underestimate high values/ likelihoods/probabilities/frequencies and overestimate low ones
Belief bias	An effect where someone's evaluation of the logical strength of an argument is biased by the believability of the conclusion
Decoy effect	Preferences change when there is a third option that is asymmetrically dominated
Denomination effect	The tendency to spend more money when it is denominated in small amounts rather than large amounts
Distinction bias	The tendency to view two options as more dissimilar when evaluating them simultaneously than when evaluating them separately
Framing	Drawing different conclusions from the same information, depending on how that information is presented
Negativity bias	The tendency to pay more attention and give more weight to negative than positive experiences or other kinds of information

Thinking Error	Definition
Recency bias	A cognitive bias that results from disproportionate salience attributed to recent stimuli or observations – the tendency to give greater weight to recent than to earlier events
Recency illusion	The illusion that a phenomenon, typically a word or language usage, that one has just begun to notice is a recent innovation
Rhyme as reason effect	Rhyming statements are perceived as more truthful; a famous example comes from the O.J Simpson trial, where the defence used the phrase "If the gloves don't fit then you must acquit"
Bizarreness effect	Bizarre or uncommon material is better remembered than common material
Context effect	That cognition and memory are dependent on context, such that out-of-context memories are more difficult to retrieve than in-context memories
Halo effect	Our overall impression of a person (a figurative halo) colours our judgment of that person's character. An example is that if we find someone likeable we may also consider them smart
Generation effect	That self-generated information is remembered best; for example, people are better able to recall memories of statements that they have generated than similar statements generated by others
Google effect	The tendency to forget information that can be easily found online
Humour effect	That humorous items are more easily remembered than non-humorous ones, which might be explained by the distinctiveness of humour, the increased cognitive processing time to understand the humour, or the emotional arousal caused by the humour

Thinking Error	Definition
Mood-congruent memory bias	The improved recall of information congruent with one's current mood
Next-in-line effect	That a person in a group has diminished recall for the words of others who spoke immediately before or after this person
Peak-end rule	That people seem to perceive not the sum of an experience but the average of how it was at its peak and how it ended
Picture superiority effect	That concepts are much more likely to be remembered experientially if they are presented in picture form than if they are presented in word form
Von Restorff effect	That an item that sticks out is more likely to be remembered than other items
Zeigarnik effect	That uncompleted or interrupted tasks are remembered better than completed ones
Backfire effect	When people react to disconfirming evidence by strengthening their beliefs
Anchoring	The tendency to rely too heavily on a past reference or on one trait or piece of information when making decisions (anchors)
Availability heuristic	Estimating what is more likely by what is more available in memory, which is biased toward vivid, unusual or emotionally charged examples
Availability cascade	A self-reinforcing process in which a collective belief gains more and more plausibility through its increasing repetition in public discourse
Clustering illusion	The tendency to under-expect clusters in small samples of random data
Confirmation bias	The tendency to search for or interpret information in a way that confirms one's preconceptions

Thinking Error	Definition
Congruence bias	The tendency to test hypotheses exclusively through direct testing, in contrast to tests of possible alternative hypotheses
Conjunction fallacy	The tendency to assume that specific conditions are more probable than general ones
Exaggerated expectation	Based on the estimates, real-world evidence turns out to be less extreme than our expectations
Expectation bias	The tendency for experimenters to believe, certify and publish data that agree with their expectations for the outcome of an experiment, and to disbelieve, discard or downgrade the corresponding weightings for data that appear to conflict with those expectations
Focalism	The tendency to rely too heavily, or 'anchor', on a past reference or on one trait or piece of information when making decisions
Frequency illusion	The illusion in which a word, a name or other thing that has recently come to one's attention suddenly appears 'everywhere' with an improbable frequency
Illusion of validity	When consistent but predictively weak data leads to confident predictions
Illusion correlation	Inaccurately perceiving a relationship between two unrelated events
Insensitivity to sample size	The tendency to under-expect variation in small samples
Just-world hypothesis	The tendency for people to want to believe that the world is fundamentally just, causing them to rationalise an otherwise inexplicable injustice as having been deserved by the victim(s)
Mere exposure effect	The tendency to express undue liking for things merely because of familiarity with them

Thinking Error	Definition
Neglect of probability	The tendency to disregard probability completely when making a decision under uncertainty
Observer-expectancy effect	When a researcher expects a given result and therefore unconsciously manipulates an experiments or misinterprets data in order to find *i*
Pessimism bias	The tendency for some people to overestimate the likelihood of negative things happening to them
Subjective validation	Perception that something is true if a subject's belief demands it to be true; also assigns perceived connections between coincidences
Texas sharpshooter fallacy	Pieces of information that have no relationship to one another are called out of their similarities, and that similarity is used for claiming the existence of a pattern
Moral luck	The tendency for people to ascribe greater or lesser moral standing based on the outcome of an event rather than the intention
Fading affect bias	A bias in which the emotion associated with unpleasant memories fades more quickly than the emotion associated with positive events
Illusion-of-truth effect	That people are more likely to identify statements they have previously heard as true, regardless of the actual validity of the statement; in other words, a person is more likely to believe a familiar statement than an unfamiliar one
Testing effect	That frequent testing of material that has been committed to memory improves memory recall

Thinking Error	Definition
Tip-of-the-tongue phenomenon	When a subject is able to recall parts of an item, or related information, but is frustratingly unable to recall the whole item; this is thought to be an instance of 'blocking' where multiple similar memories are being recalled and interfere with each other
Vividness bias	We pay attention to vivid information and overlook less flashy data

Knowledge

(Thinking errors that apply to the Archivist and the Prisoner)

Thinking Error	*Definition*
Functional fixedness	Limits a person to using an object only in the way it is traditionally used
Information bias	The tendency to seek information even when it cannot affect action
Lucid fallacy	The misuse of games to model real-life situations
Unit bias	The tendency to want to finish a given unit of a task or an item
Déformation professionelle	The tendency to look at things according to the conventions of one's own profession, forgetting any broader viewpoint
Curse of knowledge	When knowledge of a topic diminishes one's ability to think about it from a less-informed perspective
Normalcy bias	The refusal to plan for, or react to, a disaster which has never happened before
Omission bias	The tendency to judge harmful actions as worse, or less moral, than equally harmful omissions (inactions)
Well-travelled road effect	Underestimation of the duration of frequently travelled routes and overestimation of the duration of less-familiar routes

Acknowledgements

We are both, first and foremost, practitioners and consultants. We don't possess a laboratory in which to conduct experiments to surface cognitive errors, nor do we have a team of researchers we can use to identify appropriate content for this book. We are therefore extremely grateful to all those researchers and academics who have provided such a great service in identifying unconscious biases over many decades. In particular, we are grateful to Daniel Kahneman, Amos Tversky, Naseem Talib, Amy Edmondson, Andrew Campbell, Sydney Finkelstein, Jo Whitehead, Max Bazerman and Charles Duhigg whose research and work has been such an inspiration to us.

This book could not have been written without the support and encouragement of our family, friends, colleagues and clients. We are particularly grateful to our two wonderful daughters, Mireille and Amelia, who have put up with our frequent dinner-table discussions of this topic. Mireille has also read and offered valuable insights on the manuscript, helping us to articulate our ideas more clearly. We are also grateful to Bryan Withers for taking such an interest in our work and for reading and commenting on early drafts.

We would like to thank Dr. Linda Holbeche, Professor Helen Francis and Dr. Martin Reddington for their encouragement at the start of our journey and for including a thought piece in the book *People and Organisational Development* (2012).

A huge 'thank you' to everyone who has tested our emerging thinking and has read and commented on our manuscript. You know who you are and there are too many people to list. You have given your time, insights and wisdom generously. Not only have you helped us shape a better book but your encouragement has sustained us over many months of research and writing.

Our thanks to Paul Jervis, Celia Cozens and the Libri Publishing team. Paul encouraged us to write this book at the inaugural OD Network Europe conference and has been incredibly supportive and patient with us throughout the book writing process.

We also thank Warren Wysocki who leads MyTHRU. Warren is the creative force who brought our eight characters to life in the Hidden R-I-S-K™ framework visuals.

Finally, our thanks to you, the reader. Thank you for taking time to read this book. We hope it will help you make better decisions at work and in your private life.

Notes

1   Kahneman, D., *Thinking Fast and Slow*, New York: Farrar, Straus & Giroux, 2011, p.85

2   Heath, C., and Heath, D., *Decisive: How to make better decisions*, London: Random House, 2014, pp.3–4

3   *Daily Telegraph*, 5th November 2008

4   Besley, T., and Hennesy, P., *Unofficial Command Paper: The global financial crisis – why didn't anyone notice?* Subsequently published in the *British Academy Review*, Issue 14, November 2009

5   For a great, short TED lesson on how optical illusions play tricks on our brains go to: http://ed.ted.com/lessons/how-optical-illusions-trick-your-brain-nathan-s-jacobs

6   Sandro Del-Prete is an artist who paints figures, situations and processes that cannot exist in the real world. He helps us to explore the difference between 'looking' and 'seeing'.

7   Although Kahneman has rightly won many plaudits for this work, he is not without his critics. Gerd Gigerenzer, for example, believes that intuition through the application of heuristics can be effectively applied in situations of high uncertainty. See pp.31, 282 – *Risk Savvy*.

8   For an excellent reconstruction of this short flight go to: https://www.youtube.com/watch?v=E8itHvXd0oM

9   This article points to a number of factors that combined to enable the captain and crew to make a successful emergency landing and a safe exit, and rescue of passengers from the plane. Disciplines honed through training, mutual accountability and a degree of good luck all played their part.

http://money.usnews.com/money/blogs/flowchart/2009/02/03/how-sullenberger-really-saved-us-airways-flight-1549

10 An excellent summary of many of these (ninety-nine in fact) can be found in Rolf Dobelli's book *The Art of Thinking Clearly* (Hodder and Stoughton, 2013).

11 Coulter, K., and Coulter, R., 'Size Does Matter: The Effects of Magnitude Representation Congruency on Price Perceptions and Purchase Likelihood', *Journal of Consumer Psychology*, 15(1), 2005, pp.64–76

12 Thorndike, A., Sonnenberg, L., Riis, J., Barraclough, S., and Levy, D.E., 'A 2-phase labeling and Choice Architecture Intervention to Improve Healthy Food and Beverage Choices', *American Journal of Public Health*, 102(3), 2012, pp.527–33

13 You can watch this excellent video on YouTube: https://www.youtube.com/watch?v=h-8PBx7isoM

14 Quoted on: http://behaviouralinsights.co.uk/publications/east-four-simple-ways-apply-behavioural-insights

15 'Ponzi scheme' is a term coined for 'get rich quick' investment scams which pay returns to investors from their own money, or from money paid in by subsequent investors.

16 Davies, H., *The Beatles: The Authorized Biography*, New York: McGraw-Hill, 2009, p.131

17 The Johari Window model was devised by American psychologists Joseph Luft and Harry Ingham in 1955, while researching group dynamics at the University of California Los Angeles. The model was first published in the *Proceedings of the Western Training Laboratory in Group Development* by UCLA Extension Office in 1955, and was later expanded by Joseph Luft. The Johari Window model is helpful in addressing areas such as behaviour, empathy, cooperation, team development, inter-group development and interpersonal development. The name 'Johari' is an amalgamation of the first names of Joseph Luft and Harry Ingham. You can download a great summary of the Johari Window from www.businessballs.com.

18 Huffington Post, interview with Elizabeth Kuster, 9th September 2012

19 Lambert, D.M., and Cooper, M.C., 'Issues in Supply Chain Management', *Industrial Marketing Management*, 19, 2000, pp.65–83

20 ISO 31000, 2009, p.4

21 Sydney Finkelstein, Andrew Campbell and Jo Whitehead, *Think Again: Why Good Leaders Make Bad Decisions and How to Keep it From Happening to You*, Harvard Business School Press, 2009
    The framework introduced in *Think Again* aims to alert decision makers to four aspects of erroneous decision making, what the authors call the four red-flag conditions:
    • Misleading prejudgments
    • Misleading experience

- Inappropriate self-interest
- Inappropriate attachments.

The authors advise decision makers to *stop and 'think again'* when they observe themselves making decisions on the basis of those four red-flag conditions. The four conditions are very helpful in identifying when we are likely to be tricked into false judgments. The foundations of our Hidden R-I-S-K™ framework elaborate on this thinking.

22 We have looked at all the thinking errors identified through research and have selected those biases that are most relevant to day-to-day choices. Not all cognitive biases discovered by scientists are of equal importance in the day-to-day running of our lives. Some thinking errors that have been discovered are very obscure indeed and are valid within the confines of a particular research paradigm. For example, the *ludic fallacy* refers to the misuse of games to model real-life situations; the IKEA effect is the tendency for people to assign a disproportionately high value to objects that they have partially assembled themselves, such as furniture from IKEA, regardless of the quality of the end result. Cognitive biases such as these have not been reflected in our framework. We have given details on how we clustered the biases in the Appendix.

23 If you would like to read a more comprehensive summary of this story, Finkelstein and colleagues give a compelling account in *Think Again* (op. cit.).

24 A 2008 survey conducted by CPP Inc. across nine countries in Europe and North America found that employees spent an average of two hours a week (or a day a month) dealing with some form of conflict at work. This adds up to a significant amount of unproductive time and points to the disruptive influence that our unconscious thinking processes can play as transference can explain the high frequency of these conflicts, with employees re-enacting sibling rivalries or conflicts in parent–child relationships. See: http://img.en25.com/web/CPP/Conflict-report.pdf

25 Murry, C., 'The use and abuse of dogs on Scott's and Amundsen's South Pole expeditions', *Polar Record*, 44(4), 2008, Cambridge University Press, pp.303–11

26 Finkelstein, S., *Why Smart Executives Fail and What You Can Learn from Their Mistakes*, New York: Portfolio, 2003, p.34

27 Finkelstein and colleagues also tell this story in *Think Again* (op. cit.).

28 Bevan, J., *The Rise and Fall of Marks & Spencer... And How It Rose Again*, London: Profile Books, second edition, 2007, p.81

29 Finkelstein et al., op. cit., p.148

30 Ibid., p.40

31 Smith, A., *The Theory of Moral Sentiments*, London: Millar, Kincaid and Bell, 1759, p.47

32 We like the definition of self-interest used by Finkelstein and colleagues in *Think Again*. They propose two manifestations: (1) where there is a differential impact depending on options selected and (2) where the decision maker's interests are different from those of other key stakeholders.

33 Hastings, M., *Armageddon: The Battle for Germany, 1944–45*, London: Pan Macmillan, 2006, p.66

34 Dixon, N., *On the Psychology of Military Incompetence*, London: Random House, 1994, pp.147, 168

35 Ariely, D., *Predictably Irrational: The Hidden Forces that Shape our Decisions*, London: Harper Collins, 2008

36 Bazerman, M., and Moore, D., *Judgement in Managerial Decision Making*, London: John Wiley & Sons, 2013

37 Finkelstein et al., op. cit., p.110

38 http://en.wikipedia.org/wiki/ReykjavpercentC3percentADk_Summit

39 Finkelstein et al., op. cit., p.112

40 If you really want to learn more, see: http://michaelpollan.com/books/food-rules/.

41 Stewart, A.E., Lazo, J.K., Morss, R.E., and Demuth, J.L., 'The Relationship between Weather Salience with the perceptions and uses of weather information in a nationwide sample of the United States', *Weather, Climate, and Society*, 4, 2012, pp.172–89

42 Justesen, M.K., *Too Poor to Care? The Salience of AIDS in Africa*, Afro-Barometer Working Paper No. 133, 2011

43 http://common-resources.org/2014/salience-attentiveness-and-the-decision-to-have-home-energy-audits

44 Ciuk, D.J., and Yost, B., *Issue Salience, Elite Influence, and Public Opinion in an Informed Electorate*, Paper presented at the 2013 Annual Meeting of the Midwest Political Science Association, 2013

45 Finkelstein et al., op. cit., pp.89–91

46 Tversky, A., and Kahneman, D., *Judgement under Uncertainty: Heuristics and Biases*, *Science* 185, no. 4,157, 1974

47 Finkelstein et al., op. cit., p.97

48 Finkelstein and colleagues describe the circumstances surrounding the Battle of Midway in greater detail in *Think Again* (op. cit., pp.55–9).

49 Proverbs 19:2, New Living Translation

50 http://hbr.org/2006/12/the-curse-of-knowledge/ar/1

51 http://en.wikipedia.org/wiki/Candle_problem

52 http://blogs.hbr.org/2013/04/the-innovator-who-knew-too-muc/

53 http://sloanreview.mit.edu/article/when-too-much-it-knowledge-is-a-dangerous-thing

54 Finkelstein et al., op. cit., pp.75–8

55 The availability heuristic relates the context of an event or situation with the availability of similar information in our memory rather than carefully assessing all the available data. For example, when we discussed the Hidden R-I-S-K™ framework with clients, colleagues and friends during its development, we often elicited responses which focused on either what they knew about cognitive psychology or neuroscience (books they had come across or people they had heard about) or frameworks they were familiar with such as six thinking hats, Belbin's team types, the Myers–Briggs type indicator (MBTI) or enneagram. They were more focused on accessing their knowledge and experience and less focused on understanding what was new and different, and indeed outside of their experience. This changed of course and we are indebted to the many helpful comments we have received, but our starting point was to overcome the availability heuristic.

56 Our thanks to Finkelstein and colleagues (op. cit., pp. 81) for their pithy summary of these three biases.

57 http://blogs.hbr.org/2012/05/overcoming-functional-fixedness

58 Pope, A., *An Essay on Criticism*
(The opening lines are: "A little learning is a dangerous thing, / Drink deep, or taste not the Pierian spring".)

59 Wallace's commencement speech at Kenyon College in 2005 was later turned into a short video which you can view here: https://www.youtube.com/watch?v=IYGaXzJGVAQ – it's very good!

60 Duhigg, C., *The Power of Habit: Why we Do what we Do and How to Change*, London: Random House, 2013, p.xvi

61 Ibid., p.xvii

62 Ibid., pp.xvii and 294 for references

63 You can read an excellent summary of this ground-breaking research in the Charles Duhigg book (ibid., pp.12–21).

64 *What's the Right Diet for You?* was first shown on 12 January 2015 as part of the BBC2 Horizon Programme series.

65 Isaacson, W., *Steve Jobs*, New York: Simon & Schuster, 2011

66 This poem is well known and generally accessible, but if you would like to read it online go to: http://www.wordfocus.com/word-act-blindmen.html

67 Pinker, S., *How the Mind Works*, Norton, 1997, p.50

68 Willis, J., and Todorov, A., 'First Impressions: Making up your mind after 100ms exposure to a face', *Psychological Science*, 17, 2006, pp.592–8

69 Roehling, M.V., 'Extra pounds hurt more than your health', *Business Insight*, January 2001, pp.24–9

70 Bertrand, M., and Mullainathan, S., 'Are Emily and Greg More Employable than Lakisha and Jamal? A Field Experiment on Labor Market Discrimination', *American Economic Review*, 94(4), 2004, pp.991–1,013

71 Abu-Ras, W.M., and Suarez, Z.E., 'Muslim men and women's perception of discrimination, hate crimes, and PTSD symptoms post 9/11', *Traumatology*, 2009, pp.15, 48–63

72 Unkelbach, C., Forgas, J., and Denson, T., 'The Turban Effect: The influence of Muslim headgear and induced affect on aggressive responses in the shooter bias paradigm', *Journal of Experimental Social Psychology*, 44(5), 2008, pp.1,409–13

73 http://www.theguardian.com/news/datablog/2014/dec/15/how-diverse-are-ftse-100-companies-vince-cable

74 http://theabd.org/2012_ABDpercent20Missing_Pieces_Final_8_15_13.pdf; http://www.egonzehnder.com/files/2014_egon_zehnder_european_board_diversity_analysis.pdf

75 *Economist*, 27th September 2014 – Schumpeter column: 'The Look of a Leader'

76 You can read the whole of 'We and They' here: http://www.kipling-society.co.uk/poems_wethey.htm

77 Sinclair, S., Lowery, B.S., and Dunn, E., 'The relationship between parental racial attitudes and children's implicit prejudice', *Journal of Experimental Social Psychology*, 2004

78 Avenanti, A., Sirigu, A., and Aglioti, S.A., 'Racial Bias Reduces Emphatic Sensorimotor Resonance with other Race pain', *Current Biology*, 20, 8th June 2010, pp.1,018–22

79 To take the IAT go to: https://implicit.harvard.edu

80 Swami, V., and Furnham, A., 'Unattractive, promiscuous and heavy drinkers: Perceptions of women with tattoos', *Body Image*, 2007, pp.4, 343–52.

81 Gueguen, N., 'Effects of a Tattoo on Men's Behaviour and Attitudes towards Women: An experimental field study', *Archives of Sexual Behaviour*, Vol.42, Issue 8, November 2013, p.1,517

82 Antonio, M.E., 'Arbitrariness and the death penalty: How the defendant's appearance during trial influences capital jurors' punishment decision', *Behavioural Sciences and the Law*, 2006, pp.24, 215–34

83 Ben-Zeev, A., Dennehy, T.C., Goodrich, R.I., Kolarik, B.S., and Geisler, M.W., *When an 'Educated' Black Man Becomes Lighter in the Mind's Eye*, SAGE Open, 4(1), January 2014

84 Sheppard, L., and Aquino, K., 'Much ado about nothing? Problematization of women same sex conflict at work', *Academy of Management Perspectives*, Vol.27, No.1, 2013, p.59

85 To see the clip, look up: https://www.youtube.com/watch?v=RS3iB47nQ6E

86 Suri et al., op. cit.

87 This phrase has been used many times by Warren Buffett in his talks. The origins of this quote can be attributed to Samuel Johnson who in 1748 published an allegorical fable about the path to the Temple of Happiness titled 'The Vision of Theodore'. The story

warned readers using a symbolic figure named 'Habit' who would bind the unwary in chains.

88   Kay, J., 'Why Sony did not invent the iPod', *Financial Times*, available from: http://www.ft.com/cms/s/0/7558a99e-f5ed-11e1-a6c2-00144feabdc0.html#axzz3TzAQXble

89   Staw, B.M., 'Knee-deep in the Big Muddy: A Study of Escalating Commitment to a Chosen Course of Action', *Organisational Behaviour and Human Performance*, 16, 1976, pp.27–44

90   Staw, B.M., Barsade, S.G., and Koput, K.W., 'Escalation at the Credit Window: A Longitudinal Study of Bank Executives' Recognition and Write-Off of Problem Loans', *Journal of Applied Psychology*, Vol.82, No.1, American Psychological Association, pp.130–42

91   A very good summary of this relationship is provided in this *Guardian* article: http://www.theguardian.com/uk-news/2014/jun/24/andy-coulson-criminal-david-cameron-confidence-conspiracy-phone-hacking

92   Morck, R., 'Finance in Corporate Governance: Economics and Ethics of the Devil's Advocate', *Journal of Management and Governance*, Vol.12, No.2, 2008, pp.179–200

93   Bandle, A., in an IMD publication on the collapse of Swissair authored by Inna Francis and Stewart Hamilton (2003, p.15).

94   We are great fans of William Bridges and can highly recommend his work. His books *Transitions* (Perseus Books) and *Managing Transitions* (NB publishing) are excellent and easy reads.

95   Unlike the conventional change curve which is based on bereavement counselling, the Bridges model of transition has three stages: Endings, the Neutral Zone, Beginnings. We go through these stages whether a change is good (marriage, promotion, new baby etc.) or difficult/hard (bereavement, divorce, illness, unemployment etc.).

96   There are many studies point to this 55percent failure of change projects in organisations to deliver the anticipated benefits. A recent study is by Towers Watson – the *Change and Communication ROI Study*, 2013.

97   Fournier, S., 'Consumers and their Brands: Developing Relationship Theory in Consumer Research', *Journal of Consumer Research*, 1998, pp.343–72

98   Valkenburg, P.M., and Cantor, J., 'The development of a child into a consumer', *Journal of Applied Developmental Psychology*, 22.1, 2001, pp.61–72

99   To read all the lyrics of 'The Gambler', go to: http://www.lyricsfreak.com/k/kenny+rogers/the+gambler_20077886.html

100 Bernardo, A., and Welch, I., *On the Evolution of Overconfidence and Entrepreneurs* (June 2001) Yales Cowles Foundation Paper No. 1,307, (quoting Werner F.M. DeBondt and Richard H. Thaler, Financial Decision-Making in Markets and Firms: A Behavioral Perspective)

101 Taleb, N., *Fooled by Randomness: The Hidden Role of Chance in Life and in the Markets*, Penguin, 2007

102 Ross, L., Greene, D., and House, P., 'The "false consensus effect": An egocentric bias in social perception and attribution processes', *Journal of Experimental Social Psychology*, 13.3, 1977, pp.279–301, available from: http://web.mit.edu/curhan/www/docs/Articles/biases/13_J_Experimental_Social_Psychology_279_(Ross).pdf

103 Carlson, E., Furr, R.M., and Vazire, S., 'Do We Know the First Impressions We Make? Evidence for Idiographic Meta-Accuracy and Calibration of First Impressions', *Social Psychological and Personality Science*, 2010

104 Washington State University, 'For pundits, it's better to be confident than correct', *Science Daily*, May 2013

105 Loewenstein, G., 'Behavioural Decision Theory and Business Ethics: Skewed Tradeoffs between Self and Others' in Messick, D., and Tenbrunsel, A., (eds) *Codes of Conduct: Behavioural Research into Business Ethics*, New York: Russell Sage Foundation, 1996

106 Prentice, R.A., 'SEC and MDP: Implications for the Self-serving Bias for Independent Auditing', *Ohio State Law Journal*, Vol. 61, 2000, available from: http://moritzlaw.osu.edu/students/groups/oslj/files/2012/03/61.5.prentice.pdf

107 Babcock, L., and Olson, C., 'The causes and impasses in Labour Disputes', *Industrial Relations*, 31(2), 1992, pp.348–60

108 Babcock, L., and Loewsenstein, G., 'Explaining Bargaining Impasse: The role of the self-serving bias', *Journal of Economic Perspectives*, 1997, pp.107–26

109 *Daily Telegraph*, 'One in six patients misdiagnosed', 21st September 2009

110 Berner, E.S., and Graber, M.L., 'Overconfidence as a cause of diagnostic error in medicine', *American Journal of Medicine*, Vol. 121, 2008, pp.2–23, available from: http://www.isabelhealthcare.com/pdf/Diagnostic_Error-Is_Overconfidence_the_Problem_0408.pdf

111 Johnson, D.P., and Fowler, J.H., 'The Evolution of Overconfidence', *Nature*, 15th September 2011, pp.477, 317–20

112 Roberto, M.A., 'Lessons from Everest: the Interaction of cognitive bias, Psychological safety and systems complexity', *California Management Review*, 45(1), 2002, pp.136–58

113 http://www.samatters.com/welcome/

114 Kashdan, T.B., 'Clues to When CEOs and Politicans Are Lying to You', *Psychology Today*, October 2010

115 Larcker, D.F., and Zakolyukina, A.A., 'Detecting Deceptive Discussions in Conference Calls', *Journal of Accounting Research*, Vol. 50, Issue 2, 2012, pp.495–540

116 Malmendier, U., and Tate, G.A., 'Who makes Acquisitions? CEO Overconfidence and the Market's Reaction', *Journal of Financial Economics*, 89(1), 2008, pp.20–43

117 Laux, V., and Stocken, P., 'Managerial Reporting, Overoptimism and Litigation Risk', *Journal of Accounting and Economics*, 53, 2012, pp.577–91

118 Barros, Lucas Ayres B. de C., and da Silveira, Alexandre Di Miceli, 'Overconfidence, Managerial Optimism and the Determinants of Capital Structure', *Brazilian Review of Finance*, 25th February 2007, available at SSRN: http://ssrn.com/abstract=953273 or http://dx.doi.org/10.2139/ssrn.953273

119 Ben-David, I., Harvey, C.R., and Graham, J.R., 'Managerial Overconfidence and Corporate Policies', No. 13,711, NBER Working Papers from National Bureau of Economic Research, Inc., 2007 (This research goes on to suggest that "The pervasive effect of this mis-calibration suggests that the effect of overconfidence should be explicitly modelled when analysing corporate decision-making".)

120 Schrand, C.M., and Zechman, S.L.C., 'Executive Overconfidence and the Slippery Slope to Financial Misreporting', 1st May 2011, AAA 2009 Financial Accounting and Reporting Section (FARS) Paper, Chicago Booth Research Paper No. 08-25

121 The University of Aalborg has published numerous research papers on cost overruns in infrastructure projects. To access these, go to: http://vbn.aau.dk/en/publications/delusion-and-deception-in-large-infrastructure-projects(17cbfab0-2d6e-11de-bcf7-000ea68e967b).html

122 Bush, G., Vogt, B.A., Holmes, J., Dale, A.M., Greve, D., Jenike, M.A., and Rosen, B.R., 'Dorsal anterior cingulate cortex: A role in reward-based decision making', *Proceedings of the National Academy of Sciences*, USA 99(1), 2002, pp.523–8

123 Goleman, D., *Emotional Intelligence: Why it can matter more than IQ*, London: Bloomsbury Publishing, 1996

124 Goleman, D., et al., *Primal Leadership: The Hidden Driver of Great Performance*, Cambridge MA: Harvard Business School, 2001

125 Shore, B., 'Systematic biases and culture in project failures', *Project Management Journal*, Vol. 39, Issue 4, 16th December 2008, pp.5–16

126 Boot, A., Thakor, A., and Milbourn, T., 'Sunflower management and Capital Budgeting', *Journal of Business*, 78(2), March 2005, pp.501–27

127 Martin, I., *Making it Happen: Fred Goodwin, RBS and the Men Who Blew Up the British Economy*, Simon and Schuster: London, 2013

128 Cass business school on behalf of AIRMIC, *Roads to Ruin: A Study of Major Risk Events – Their Origins, Impact and Implications*, 2013, sponsored by Crawford and Lockton

129 Bienefeld, N., and Grote, G., 'Silence that may kill: When aircrew members don't speak up and why', *Aviation Psychology and Applied Human Factors,* 2.1, 2012 (The researchers interviewed 1,751 airline crew staff.)

130 The Francis Inquiry examined the causes of the failings in care at

Mid Staffordshire NHS Foundation Trust between 2005 and 2009. See more at: http://www.health.org.uk/about-francis-inquiry#sthash. MSYdIg9W.dpuf

131 *The Times*, 'Step up to the mark and stop bitching', Health Correspondent, Chris Smyth, 5th November 2013

132 The Michael Bar-Eli research was cited in Rolf Dobelli's book *The Art of Thinking Clearly* (London: Sceptre Press, 2013).

133 You can watch Susan Boyle's performance via this link: https://www. youtube.com/watch?v=RxPZh4AnWyk

134 Parr, B., *Captivology: The science of capturing people's attention*, HarperOne, 2015

135 Agrawal, J., and Kamakura, W.A., 'The economic worth of celebrity endorsers: An event study analysis', *Journal of Marketing*, 1995

136 Menon, K., Boone, L.E., and Rogers, H.P., 'Celebrity Advertising: An assessment of its relative effectiveness', SMA conference, 2001

137 Tversky, A., and Kahneman, D., 'Judgement under Uncertainty: Heuristics and Biases', *Science*, Vol.185, 1974, pp.1,124–31

138 See D'Argembeau, A., Comblain, C., and Van der Linden, M., 'Phenomenal characteristics of autobiographical memories for positive, negative, and neutral events', *Applied Cognitive Psychology*, 17(3), 2002, pp.281–94; Hamann, S., 'Cognitive and neural mechanisms of emotional memory', *Trends in Cognitive Sciences*, 5(9), 2001, pp.394–400; Richards, J.M., and Gross, J.J., 'Emotion Regulation and Memory: The Cognitive Costs of Keeping One's Cool', *Journal of Personality and Social Psychology*, 79(3), 2000, pp.410–24

139 ISAF statistics for the worldwide locations with the highest shark attack activity since 1990: http://www.flmnh.ufl.edu/fish/sharks/statistics/statsw.htm

140 *Guardian*, 'Doctor driven out of home by vigilantes', 30th August 2000, Rebecca Allison

141 Silver, R.C., Holman, E.A., McIntosh, D.N., Poulin, M., and Gil-Rivas, V., 'Nationwide longitudinal study of psychological responses to September 11', *Journal of the American Medical Association*, 288, 2002, pp.1,235–44

142 Kosloff, S., Greenberg, J., and Solomon, S., 'The effects of mortality salience on political preferences: The roles of charisma and political orientation', *Journal of Experimental Social Psychology*, 46(1), 2010, pp.139–45

143 Van Vugt, M., Hogan, R., and Kaiser, R.B., 'Leadership, followership, and evolution: some lessons from the past', *American Psychologist*, 63(3), 2008, p.182

144 http://nancyfriedman.typepad.com/away_with_words/2006/09/what_journalism.html

145 Khurana, R., *Searching for a Corporate Savior: The Irrational Quest for*

Charismatic CEOs, Princeton, NJ: Princeton University Press, 2002

146 Lefley, F., 'Can a project champion bias selection and if so how can we avoid it?', *Management Research News*, 29(4), 2006, pp.174–83

147 *McKinsey on Finance*, No. 41, Autumn 2011, p.20

148 Pinto, J.K., and Patanakul, P., 'When narcissism drives project champions: A review and research agenda', *International Journal of Project Management*, 33(5), 2015, pp.1,180–90

149 To read about Lucy Kellaway's views on management fads go to:
http://www.ft.com/cms/s/2/3c7f1e40-a03e-11e2-88b6-00144fe-abdc0.html#axzz3YJuCszv4
A similar list has been offered by CBS:
http://www.cbsnews.com/news/
the-8-stupidest-management-fads-of-all-time/6/

150 Ponzi, L., and Koenig, M., 'Knowledge Management: Another Management Fad?', *Information Research*, Vol. 8, No. 1, October 2002, paper no. 145.

151 For the full article, see: https://hbr.org/2002/10/
spotting-management-fads

152 See, for example: Northcraft, G.B., and Neale, M.A., 'Experts, amateurs and real estate: an anchoring-and-adjustment perspective on property pricing decision', *Organisational Behavior and Human Decision Processes*, 1987, pp.39, 84–97

153 Ariely, D., Loewenstein, G., and Prelec, D., 'Tom Sawyer and the Construction of Value', *Journal of Economic Behaviour and Organisation*, vol. 60, 2007, pp.1–10

154 Thorsteinson, T.J., 'Initiating salary discussions with an extreme request: Anchoring effects on initial salary offers', *Journal of Applied Social Psychology*, 2011, pp.41, 1,774–92

155 Plassmann, H., O'Doherty, J., Shiv, B., and Rangel, A., 'Marketing actions can modulate neural representations of experienced pleasantness', *Proceedings of the National Academy of Sciences*, 105(3), 2008, pp.1,050–4

156 Dror, I.E., and Charlton, D., 'Why experts make errors', *Journal of Forensic Identification*, 56(4), 2006, pp.600–16

157 Englich, B., and Mussweiler, T., 'Sentencing under uncertainty: Anchoring effects in the courtroom', *Journal of Applied Social Psychology*, 31, 2001, pp.1,535–51; Englich, B., Musseiler, T., and Strack, F., 'Playing dice with criminal sentences: The influence of irrelevant anchors on experts' judicial decision making', *Personality and Social Psychology Bulletin*, 32(2), 2006, pp.188–200

158 Hart, W., Albarracín, D., Eagly, A.H., Brechan, I., Lindberg, M.J., and Merrill, L., 'Feeling validated versus being correct: A meta-analysis of selective exposure to information', *Psychological Bulletin*, 135(4), July 2009, pp.555–88

159 Teasley, B., Leventhal, L.M., and Rohlman, S., 'Positive test bias in software engineering professionals: What is right and what's wrong', in *Proceedings of the 5th workshop on empirical studies of programmers*, 1993

160 For more information go to: http://www.improbable.com/ig/ The website states that "The Ig Nobel Prizes honor achievements that make people LAUGH, and then THINK. The prizes are intended to celebrate the unusual, honor the imaginative – and spur people's interest in science, medicine, and technology".

161 The Ig Nobel Prize winners' research: http://prefrontal.org/files/posters/Bennett-Salmon-2009.pdf

162 You can read more about this story here: http://www.wired.com/2014/09/fantastically-wrong-n-rays/

163 For further reading go to: http://www.nhm.ac.uk/nature-online/science-of-natural-history/the-scientific-process/piltdown-man-hoax/

164 http://www.cbsnews.com/news/a-spy-speaks-out-21-04-2006/

165 *Guardian*, 'Karl Rove chastises Fox News for calling Ohio for Obama', 7th November 2012, story by Richard Adams

166 *Fortune*, 'Mr Buffet on the stockmarket', 22nd November 1999

167 Fiske, S.T., 'Controlling other people: The impact of power on stereotyping', *American Psychologist*, 48(6), 1993, p.621; De Dreu, C.K., and Van Kleef, G.A., 'The influence of power on the information search, impression formation, and demands in negotiation', *Journal of Experimental Social Psychology*, 40(3), 2004, pp.303–19

168 Porter, M.E., Goold, M., and Luchs, K., *From competitive advantage to corporate strategy. Managing the multibusiness company: Strategic issues for diversified group*, New York, 1996, pp.285–314; Rahman, M., and Lambkin, M., 'Creating or destroying value through mergers and acquisitions: A marketing perspective', *Industrial Marketing Management*, 46, 2015, pp.24–35; Schneider, C., and Spalt, O., 'Acquisitions as Lotteries? The Selection of Target-Firm Risk and its Impact on Merger Outcomes', 2015, available from: http://www.cass.city.ac.uk/__data/assets/pdf_file/0007/126745/Schneider.pdf

169 Bogan, V., and Just, D., 'What drives merger decision-making behaviour? Don't seek, don't find and don't change your mind', *Journal of Economics Behaviour and Organisation*, 72(3), 2009, pp.930–43

170 Endsley, M., 'Theoretical underpinnings of situational awareness: a critical review', in Endsley, M., and Garland, D.J., (eds) *Situation awareness analysis and measurement*, London: Lawrence Erlbaum Associates, 2002

171 Reported in the *International Business Times*, 'Aviation Authority Warns of Overreliance on Autopilots', 29th November 2014

172 Gaba, D.M., Howard, S.K., and Small, S.D., 'Situation awareness in anaesthesiology', *Human Factors*, 37(1), March 1995, pp.20–31

173 Fioratou, E., Flin, R., Glavin, R., and Patey, R., 'Beyond monitoring:

distributed situation awareness in anaesthesia', *British Journal of Anaesthesia*, 2010, pp.83–90, 105

174 http://www.institute.nhs.uk/images//documents/SaferCare/Human-Factors-How-to-Guide-v1.2.pdf

175 Zook, C., *Beyond the Core: Expand your market without abandoning your roots*, Havard Business Press, 2004

176 Op. cit.

177 Tett, G., *Fool's Gold: How the bold dream of a small tribe at J.P. Morgan was corrupted by Wall Street greed and unleashed a catastrophe*, New York: Free Press, 2009

178 Tett, G., 'The unease bubbling in today's brave new financial world', *Financial Times*, 19ᵗʰ January 2007

179 Tett, G., 'Silos and silences. Why so few people spotted the problems in complex credit and what that implies for the future', Banque de France financial stability review No. 14, July 2010

180 Tett, G., op. cit.

181 De Jager, P., 'Doomsday 2000', *Computerworld*, 6ᵗʰ September 1993, p.105

182 Guenier, 2000

183 Yourdon, E., and Yourdon, J., *Time Bomb 2000! What the Year 2000 Computer Crisis Means to You!* New York: Prentice Hall, 1997

184 Knights, D., Vurdubakis, T., and Willmott, H., 'The Night of the Bug: Technology and (Dis)Organisation at the Fin de Siècle', *Management and Organisational History*, 3(3), January 2008, pp.289–309

185 For interview, see: http://www.theguardian.com/technology/blog/2009/oct/05/stephen-fry-y2k

186 Tett, G., 'The lessons: The dangers of silo thinking', *Financial Times*, 14ᵗʰ December 2009

187 Barrett, M.E., 'Time Marches On: The Worldwide Watch Industry', *Thunderbird International Business Review*, May–June 2000, pp.349–72

188 Robinson, A., and Stern, S., *Corporate Creativity: How Innovation and Improvement Actually Happen*, San Francisco: Berrett-Koehler, 1997, p.249

189 For interview, see: http://www.youtube.com/watch?v=eywi0h_Y5_U

190 See: http://www.digitimes.com/news/a20080514PD208.html

191 See: http://www.electronista.com/articles/11/08/20/microsoft.maintains.pc.not.middle.aged.yet

192 For interview, see: http://venturebeat.com/2013/02/18/bill-gates-microsoft-mobile-strategy-mistake/

193 Kaufman, P., *Poor Charlie's Almanack: The Wit and Wisdom of Charles T. Munger*, USA: Walsworth Publishing, second edition, 2006

194 Zygna, A., 'The Cognitive Bias Keeping Us from Innovating', *Harvard Business Review* Blog Network, June 2013

195 For a summary of the story of the successful campaign, see: http://

www.pepsico.co.uk/news-and-comment/walkers-do-us-a-flavour-campaign-goes-global-and-wins-overwhelming-industry-recognition

196 Huston, L., and Sakkab, N., 'Connect and Develop: Inside Procter and Gamble's New Model for Innovation', *Harvard Business Review*, March 2006, p.2

197 For pictures of Green Giant Crisps, see: http://greengiant.com/pages/ProductsSnacks.aspx

198 Graham, F., 'Crowdsourcing: Turning customers into creative Directors', BBC news, 29th September

199 Pfeffer, J., and Sutton, R.I., *The Knowing–Doing Gap: How Smart Companies Turn Knowledge into Action*, Boston, MA: Harvard Business School Press, 2000, p.59

200 Kline, N., *Time to Think: Listening to Ignite the Human Mind*, London: Octopus Publishing, 2013

201 Ibid., p.35
(The ten components are: attention; incisive questions; equality; appreciation; ease; encouragement; feelings; information; place; and diversity.)

202 Heath, D., and Heath, C., *Decisive: How to make better decisions*, London: Random House Books, 2014

203 To get to an estimate, you can use the formula Best Case + (4 x Best Guess) + Worst Case and then divide by 6. To understand your standard deviation, subtract Worst Case from Best Case and divide by 6.

204 A very good blog on the use and value of checklists can be found here: http://www.artofmanliness.com/2014/12/08/the-power-of-checklists/

205 Research conducted by Deborah Mitchell (Wharton School), Jay Russo (Cornell) and Nancy Pennington (University of Colorado) in 1989 found that prospective hindsight – imagining an event has already occurred – increases the ability correctly to identify reasons for future outcomes by 30 percent. An article by Gary Klein in the *Harvard Business Review* (September 2007) sets out the concept of the pre-mortem very well.

206 Schein, E., *Organisational Culture and Leadership*, 2nd edition, San Francisco, CA: Jossey Bass, 1999

207 Schein, E., 'Empowerment, Coercive Persuasion and Organisational Learning: Do they Connect?', Henley Management College, Henley Research Center, 1997

208 Edmondson, A.C., 'Psychological Safety and Learning Behavior in Work teams', *Administrative Science Quarterly*, June 1999, vol.44, no.2, pp.350–83

209 Gurwitz, J.H., Field, T.S., Avorn, J., McCormick, D., Jain, S., Eckler, M., Benser, M., Edmondson, M., and Bates, D.W., 'Incidence and Preventability of Adverse Drug Events in the Nursing Home Setting',

American Journal of Medicine, 109, 2000, pp.87–94; Tucker, A., and Edmundson, A.C., 'Why Hospitals Don't Learn from Failures: Organisational and Psychological Dynamics That Inhibit System Change', *California Management Review*, 45, no.2, winter 2003; Edmondson, A., 'Speaking up in the Operating Room: How Team Leaders Promote Learning in Interdisciplinary Action Teams', *Journal of Management Studies*, 40, no.6, September 2003, pp.1,419–52

210 Edmondson, A.C., *Teaming: How Organisations Learn, Innovate and Compete in the Knowledge Economy*, San Francisco, CA: Jossey Bass, 2012, p.125

211 Ibid., p.126

212 Amy Edmondson quotes research by neuroscientist Professor Gregory Burns (ibid.) whose "brain-imaging experiments demonstrate that when those parts of the brain that normally process pain become activated by fear, the brain has less neural processing power for exploratory activity. Low-intensity fear leads to changes in perception, cognition, and behavior that include the narrowing of attention to focus on potential threats. High-intensity fear triggers a fight-or-flight reaction in the brain which reduces effective cognition even further". See also: Burns, G., 'In Hard Times, Fear Can Impair Decision-Marking', *New York Times*, 6th December 2008, BU2

213 Amy Edmondson again cites a number of pieces of research showing the link between innovation and safe environments (see *Teaming*, op. cit., p.128). Research includes: West, M.A., and Anderson, N., 'The Team Climate Inventory: Development of the TCI and Its Applications in Teambuilding for Innovativeness', *European Journal of Organisational Psychology*, 5, no.1, 1996, pp.53–66; Edmondson, A.C., Bohmer, R., and Pisano, G.P., 'Disrupted Routines: Team Learning and New Technology Adaptation', *Administrative Science Quarterly*, 46, 2001, pp.685–716

214 Gino, F., and Staats, B., 'Why Organisations Don't Learn', *Harvard Business Review*, November 2015
(This is an excellent article and we resonated with the findings of their research and how their four key points linked back so well to our framework. We are grateful for the research and structure the authors have given and hope that in amplifying on this structure we have given them due recognition and added further value to the thinking.)

215 Dweck, C., *Mindset: How You Can Fulfil Your Potential*, London: Robinson, 2012

216 Goffee, R., and Jones, G., 'Creating the Best Workplace on Earth', *Harvard Business Review*, May 2013

217 Rath, T., *Strengthsfinder 2.0*, Gallup Press, 2007

218 Op. cit., p.118

Index